THE LYRICAL NOVEL

THE LYRICAL NOVEL

Studies in
Hermann Hesse, André Gide, and Virginia Woolf

BY RALPH FREEDMAN

PRINCETON UNIVERSITY PRESS

PRINCETON, NEW JERSEY

Publication of this book has
been aided by the Ford Foundation
program to support publication,
through university presses, of works
in the humanities and social sciences

Parts of Chapters 3 and 4 have appeared previously
as articles in *Proceedings of the Modern Language
Association*, June 1958; *Western Review*, Summer 1954;
and *Accent*, Autumn 1957

Printed in the United States of America
Third Printing, 1966

For Lila

PREFACE

"THE NOVEL as a disguised lyric," wrote Hermann Hesse in 1921, "a borrowed label for the experimentations of poetic spirits to express their feeling of self and world. . . ." Novels of this type have always existed as alternatives to the novel of adventure or the novel of manners, having arisen from equally time-honored prose forms like allegories, idylls, prose poems, or Biblical dithyrambs. Dante's *La Vita nuova* suggested features of lyrical narrative before there had been a novel in the current sense at all. Still, surprisingly few attempts have been made to evaluate this genre or to find a method through which its nature might be defined. Yet the concept of lyrical fiction—the paradoxical submersion of narrative in imagery and portraiture— poses critical questions through which we can explore the nature of fiction as a whole. By introducing lyrical elements into a genre based on causation and time, writers have revealed fresh possibilities for the novel. Their manner has led to a more effective rendering of the mind and has opened up ranges of metaphoric suggestiveness that could not have been achieved by purely narrative means.

My effort has been to define the element in the traditions of three important western literatures that can account for this hybrid, yet distinct genre, and to inquire into the reasons for its persistence. Why, on the one hand, would writers wish to recreate the novel's world as a metaphoric vision, a picture, or a musical evocation of feeling, or, on the other hand, having done so, why would they insist on the "borrowed label" of narrative rather than resolutely turning to poetry? Through an analysis of the concepts behind the genre and through close readings of major novels by Hermann Hesse, André Gide, and Virginia Woolf, I have tried to formulate an answer.

My first answer, which I developed in my dissertation at Yale University in 1954, was primarily a definition of the structure of lyrical novels, of their various ways of transforming the materials of fiction (such as characters, plots, or scenes) into patterns of imagery. As I continued, however, I came to see that as a genre the lyrical novel expresses more than a shift of taste in literary history or a predilection for imagistic design. Rather, it epitomizes a writer's special attitudes toward knowledge. The lyrical novelist is faced with the task of reconciling succession in time and sequences of cause and effect with the instantaneous action of the lyric. Not only is time experienced spatially, to borrow a phrase from Joseph Frank, but also the distance between self and world is telescoped; the engagements of men in the universe of action are reexperienced as instances of awareness. The lyrical novel, then, emerges as an "anti-novel" in the true sense of the term because by portraying the act of knowledge, it subverts the conventionally accepted qualities of the novel which are focused on the intercourse between men and worlds. But in this form it also expresses a peculiarly modern approach to experience that has ripened into our current obsession with the conditions of knowledge. In this strangely alienated, yet somehow essential genre, the direct portrayal of awareness becomes the outer frontier where novel and poem meet.

My recognition of this underlying theme in lyrical fiction has grown through several years, but it is built upon the foundation laid by my teachers René Wellek and Henri Peyre and upon their continued criticism and encouragement. I am deeply indebted to them both: to Professor Wellek, especially for his helpful insistence on the relevance of nineteenth-century intellectual history; to Professor Peyre, whose encouraging skepticism led me to consider dispassionately a literary fashion which I might otherwise have accepted less critically. I am also indebted to my colleague W. R. Irwin for his discerning analysis of the manuscript and to Geoffrey H. Hartman and Clark Griffith, who read the work as a whole and gave generously of their criticism. Thanks are also due the many colleagues and friends who helped graciously with their advice: Sven M. Armens, Alexandre Aspel, Mary E. Bostetter, Richard Popkin, Theodore Waldman, and Ray B. West, Jr. I would like to express my thanks to Yale University for granting a Sterling Fellowship in 1952–53 and to the Graduate College of the University of Iowa for a research grant in 1958–59. I am especially grateful to the late Dean Walter F. Loehwing and to Professor Baldwin Maxwell, then chairman of the Department of English, for making the grant possible. For further help in this project I wish to thank Dean John C. Weaver of the Graduate College of the University of Iowa and Professor John C. Gerber, chairman of the Department of English. I would also like to thank Mrs. Helen Sherk for her assistance in the preparation of the index and especially Mrs. Gail M. Filion of Princeton University Press, who has been as sensitive and understanding an editor as an author could wish.

My most personal debt, however, is to my wife. Without her devotion and her active help, the wisdom of her advice and her encouragement, this work would not have been possible.

Iowa City
March 1963

CONTENTS

THE LYRICAL NOVEL

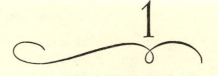

NATURE AND FORMS OF THE LYRICAL NOVEL

THE CONCEPT of the lyrical novel is a paradox. Novels are usually associated with storytelling: the reader looks for characters with whom he can identify, for action in which he may become engaged, or for ideas and moral choices he may see dramatized. Lyrical poetry, on the other hand, suggests the expression of feelings or themes in musical or pictorial patterns. Combining features of both, the lyrical novel shifts the reader's attention from men and events to a formal design. The usual scenery of fiction becomes a texture of imagery, and characters appear as *personae* for the self. Lyrical fiction, then, is not defined essentially by a poetic style or purple prose. Every novel may rise to such heights of language or contain passages that contract the world into imagery. Rather, a lyrical novel assumes a unique form which transcends the causal and temporal movement of narrative within the framework of fiction. It is a hybrid genre that uses the novel to approach the function of a poem. Not surprisingly, the expectations of a reader who has been brought up on more traditional standards for the novel are often frustrated, for the symbolic patterns he encounters seem to him antithetical to the very method on which narrative is built.

Essentially, what distinguishes lyrical from non-lyrical writing is a different concept of *objectivity*. It is a truism that the novel is not always realistic in the sense of being a "truthful" reproduction of external life. But its main tradition (the tradition we think of when "novel" comes to mind) separates the experiencing self from the world the experiences are about. Moll Flanders, David Copperfield, Ivan Karamazov, Hans Castorp—all these figures exist in and by virtue of a world, a milieu to which they react.

Man confronts other men in love and hostility; he gropes his way through the labyrinth of his own and other societies or measures his wit against the dangers of nature; he pits his moral or amoral sense against the values of others, rebels against historical currents in which he is caught or exemplifies their norms. Objectivity is achieved through the dramatic and narrative form which develops these actions. An artist will naturally remold them for aesthetic or ideological reasons, but the plot—i.e., the display of interaction between man and world in time—is usually also a measure of the novel's design. *Tom Jones* is the *locus classicus* of this form, for Fielding sought precisely such differentiating criteria which would be distinctive of the novel.[1] But novels as different from one another as Jane Austen's *Emma,* Flaubert's *Madame Bovary,* Thackeray's *Vanity Fair,* or Zola's *Germinal,* all seek to abstract an objective quality from the encounter between self and other, man and the universe beyond him.

The lyrical novel, by contrast, seeks to combine man and world in a strangely inward, yet aesthetically objective, form. This is not to say that lyrical writers are uninterested in the questions of human conduct that concern all fiction, but they view these questions in a different light. Their stages are not those on which men usually perform in the novel, but independent designs in which the awareness of men's experiences is merged with its objects. Rather than finding its *Gestalt* in the imitation of an action, the lyrical novel absorbs action altogether and refashions it as a pattern of imagery. Its tradition is neither didactic nor dramatic, although features of both may be used, but poetic in the narrow sense of "lyrical." A lyrical poem's form objectifies not men and times but an experience and a theme for which men and their lives, or places and events, have been used.

---

[1] See R. S. Crane, "The Concept of Plot and the Plot of *Tom Jones,*" *Critics and Criticism* (Chicago: University of Chicago Press, 1952), pp. 616–647. See also Wayne C. Booth, *The Rhetoric of Fiction* (Chicago: University of Chicago Press, 1961), pp. 215–219.

Similarly, lyrical novels such as Goethe's *Werther,* Hölderlin's *Hyperion,* or Djuna Barnes' *Nightwood* reflect the pleasure and pain or the dying of men as extended lyrics. Their objectivity lies in a form uniting self and other, a picture that detaches the writer from his *persona* in a separate, formal world.

We have so far discussed the lyrical novel as if it were an impermeable genre whose well-defined function leaves no room for ambiguity. But it should be obvious that the range and variety of lyrical fiction, from Hölderlin's dithyrambs to the later Gide's formal severity, preclude so rigid a definition of its form. The most obvious types may be easily identified, but others blur with normal narrative structures, and limits cannot be simply drawn. Most works of fiction, as Northrop Frye has shown, are composed of various elements, drawing on what we usually designate as novel, romance, confession, and satire.[2] Similarly, lyrical fiction crosses boundaries between types and methods of narrative, now showing itself in the romance, now in the confession, and often even in the conventional novel. Lyrical novels are determined not by any preordained form but by poetic manipulation of narrative types which writers have found ready-made or have constructed within an existing tradition of the novel.

Since the features of individual novels vary with their ingredients, an analysis must artificially separate their narrative and lyrical components. Some novels are more lyrical than others, and the unique organization of each work depends on its composition. But it is not merely a sliding scale of different elements that distinguishes these novels, nor a mere combination or compound, but also an internal conflict, a precarious balance of different, sometimes antithetical, techniques which creates a poetic effect. It is our purpose to show how a particular genre has emerged from an aggregate of such complex techniques, defining a mood, a type of literary sensibility, a way of approaching

[2] *Anatomy of Criticism* (Princeton: Princeton University Press, 1957), pp. 315–325 *passim.*

knowledge. For this reason, we shall first isolate purely lyrical qualities before turning to their more involved juxtapositions with other narrative forms.

————2

A passage from a novel almost purely lyrical may distill some of the crucial characteristics of the genre. Rainer Maria Rilke's lengthy prose fragment, *Die Aufzeichnungen des Malte Laurids Brigge* (1910), draws a picture of outer squalor and inner despair by filtering it through the mind of the poet's double, Malte, a sensitive young Dane in Paris. Conceived as a journal, the book imposes its images upon the prose discourse of narrative fiction, but at the same time it marshals them in a "formal" progression whose inevitability and depth betray the hand of a great lyrical poet. In the following scene, Malte, pursued by anxiety, fastens his fear on a person, an object:

> I knew at once that my idea was worthless. The dedication of his misery, unlimited by any caution or dissimulation, surpassed my means of understanding. I had grasped neither the angle of his posture's decline nor the horror with which the underside of his eye-lids constantly seemed to fill him. I had never thought of his mouth, which was indrawn like the opening of a sewer. . . . I had stopped walking, and while I saw everything almost at once, I felt that he was wearing a different hat and a Sunday necktie; it was patterned obliquely in yellow and violet squares, and as for the hat, it was a cheap straw hat with a green band. There is, of course, no significance in these colors, and it is petty that I have remembered them. I only want to say that they clung to him like the utmost softness of a bird's underside. He himself took no pleasure in it, and who of all people (I looked around) was allowed to think this get-up was for him?
> My God, it occurred to me with violence, thus *art* thou. There are proofs for thy existence. . . . And . . . now they

are shown to me. This is thy taste; herein thou takest thy pleasure. . . .

A description moving toward great intensity in the first paragraph is elucidated by a statement in the second. Two images introduce this development. The first of these expresses inner horror plastically: dread wells up within the underside of the eyelids, which express the entire character of the person before him. This graphic picture is underscored by the second image: the comparison of the man's mouth to an *Ablauf* (translated as "sewer"), a combination of toilet and gutter used in this book to suggest a hideous identity of filth and elimination, degradation and sexuality. The second part of the passage intensifies these images with an unexpected shift. Bright, tasteless colors liken the man to a strutting peacock. The two sets are combined both by an explicit statement and by implicit imagery. Asking himself why he remembers all these details, the poet answers himself by making a further comparison: the colors are like "the utmost softness of a bird's underside." The image denotes softness of shade as well as of texture; it links the impression of the man as a whole with the underside of his eyelids and bears out the suggestion that the horror "constantly seems to fill him." Transforming the localized eyelids into the bird representing the whole man, the passage reaches a point of concentration. But the horror evoked by soft, pliant sensuality is at once turned into its opposite. The gay colors are only for God's pleasure, and yet what dubious pleasure it is. In the contrapuntal exclamation, *My God . . .* , the poet draws the difficult conclusion. The man's very hideousness serves to celebrate his creator. Hence, he proves the existence of God. Rilke concludes Malte's soliloquy with the reflection:

That we would only learn to hold out before all things and not to judge. Which are the hard things? Which are the gracious ones? Thou alone knowest.

Breaking off abruptly, Rilke then turns to Malte's condition as a poor young man in Paris by referring to a new overcoat. The initial point of view is reestablished.[3]

The surprising thing about this passage is that it "works" both as a narrative and as a poem. Rilke shows himself a master of description, exposing the minutest details relevant to his hero's psyche. We see the strutting, sensuous man before us with his declining posture, gelatinous eyelids, and the toothless hollow of his mouth, the garish hat and necktie, and we know he has become the epitome of Malte's sexual dread. But at the same time the power of imagery acts through a peculiar medium of its own. Malte comprehends the man ahead of him as an image of human existence and of the knowledge of God. Clarifying statements and a movement of images have distilled this recognition from an otherwise commonplace occurrence. Pictorially, the images are not as intricately ordered as in Rilke's descriptive poems such as "Der Panther." The absence of verbal structuring sets it off from self-portraits in verse such as "Der Dichter" or from the tight, metaphorical rhetoric of the *Sonette an Orpheus*. Nor is there an inexorable progression as we find it, for example, in the movement from Angel to lovers in the second of the *Duineser Elegien*. Yet the lyrical prose we have considered uses similar methods to intensify feeling and theme, ordering all parts retroactively in a total image.

Conventionally, the lyric, as distinct from epic and drama, is seen either as an instantaneous expression of a feeling or as a spatial form. The reader approaches a lyric the way an onlooker regards a picture: he sees complex details in juxtaposition and experiences them as a whole. In Pound's famous phrase, the very notion of the image is defined as the rendering of "an emotional and intellectual complex in an instant of time."[4] Yet as a lyrical

---

[3] *Die Aufzeichnungen des Malte Laurids Brigge, Gesammelte Werke* (Leipzig: Insel-Verlag, 1930), v, 246–247.

[4] "A Few Don'ts," *Poetry*, I, 6 (March 1913), cited from *The Literary Essays of Ezra Pound*, ed. T. S. Eliot (New York: New Directions, 1955), p. 4. Note the use made of this concept by Joseph Frank in defining

poem moves from image to image, it also follows its own inimitable progression, acting through variations and expansions of themes, changes in rhythm, and elaborations of images to reach a point of greatest intensity at which the poet's vision is realized. Kenneth Burke has called such a movement a *qualitative* progression; Wolfgang Kayser aptly named it a *lyrical process*.[5] Time and action may be simulated, but the point of the poem's language is to reach a specific intensity by modulations of images.

In lyrical poetry, the process we have described is decisive. It exemplifies "lyrical" objectivity. But we have already seen that in lyrical novels such a progression exists in conjunction with narrative. Indeed, the tension peculiar to lyrical novels rests on this deliberate ambiguity. We follow in Malte's footsteps as if he were an ordinary character of fiction. We enter into his scene, expect time to pass, events to occur. But at the same time we know that this movement is a blind for a more decisive lyrical progression. The mere use of prose and the skillful handling of narrative have directed our attention to succession in time only to discover that we have actually entered into the rather different rhetoric of images. Lyrical novels (*Malte Laurids* included) exploit the expectation of narrative by turning it into its opposite: a lyrical process.

These distinctions assume that narrative progression is determined entirely by consecutive time. This is obviously an oversimplification: such rudimentary narrative hardly exists even in the simplest forms of detective fiction. Most novels buttress their characters' actions with meaningful schemes of encounters and images. But the distinction makes sense as a way of isolating narrative progression, just as the "lyrical process" is a way of isolating qualitative progression. As Jacques Rivière recognized in the "Roman d'aventure," narrative is the surge toward that

"spatiality" in modern literature. "Spatial Form in Modern Literature," *Sewanee Review,* LIII (1945), 221–246, 433–456, 643–653.

[5] See *Das sprachliche Kunstwerk. Eine Einführung in die Literaturwissenschaft* (Bern: A. Francke, 1951), pp. 160–162ff.

which does not yet exist. In lyrical poetry, by contrast, events are contained in one another. Consecutiveness is simulated by lyrical language: its surge toward greater intensity reveals not new events but the significance of existing events. Actions are turned into scenes which embody recognitions.[6] There exists, then, a qualitative difference between novels such as *Madame Bovary*, which use imagery to develop a character's progressive "conversation with life," and novels such as *Malte Laurids Brigge*, which utilize modes of narrative movement to function as lyrical poetry.

Within its purpose of weaving a fabric of images, the lyrical novel, unlike lyrical poetry, depends on the base of the novel. It shares with the form it exploits the common purpose of narrative, i.e., to enact what Wellek and Warren have called the writer's "fictional world" in order to communicate it to an audience.[7] A decisive difference between the two forms, however, is the *locus* of that world. In conventional narratives, the outer world is the thing. It is placed beyond both writer and reader, interposing between them and the theme. In the lyrical mode, such a world is conceived, not as a universe in which men display their actions, but as a poet's vision fashioned as a design. The world is reduced to a *lyrical point of view,* the equivalent of the poet's "I": the lyrical self. In the masquerade of the novel, this point of view is the poet's *mask* as well as the source of his consciousness, whether it appears as one or more disguised *personae* or in the more direct function of the diarist, the confessor, or first-person narrator.

The hero of *Malte Laurids Brigge* acts from such a lyrical point of view. Countless perceptions impose themselves upon him. At one point, buttons on a tray of notions offered for sale by an old woman writhe toward him. Remembering a delirium

---

[6] "Le Roman d'aventure," *La Nouvelle Revue française* (July–December, 1913). Cf. Henri Bonnet, *Roman et poésie. L'Esthétique des genres* (Paris: Librairie Nizet, 1951), pp. 67–69. Bonnet defines the poem by its plasticity, harmony, tonality; the novel by its temporal progression.

[7] *Theory of Literature* (New York: Harcourt Brace, 1949), pp. 222–225.

of his childhood, Malte recalls buttons on his bedclothes threatening to crush him. In Paris, an electric streetcar, ringing wildly, races over his prostrate body. A sewage pipe on the remaining wall of an old building creeps toward him like a hideous snake. His dying grandfather in Denmark is symbolically transformed into the bell that tolls his time as he becomes an image of death itself. Malte's passive awareness absorbs all these objects and transforms them into images. He *mirrors* the world as he sees it and so lends it a specific color or shape, distorting or even displacing it. His function in the novel, to cite Joseph Frank, is *self-reflexive*. Depicting experience and enacting it through a progression of images, the hero renders himself as a symbolic vision.

The passive protagonist's point of view draws the contours of the lyrical novel. The individual encounters absorbed by the *persona* of *Malte Laurids* only seem to be scattered at random. Actually they cohere as a texture, intermingling past and present, occult and real events, mythical and historical figures with persons in the hero's life. The cruelly realistic Parisian hospital is treated on the same level as the mysterious Abelone of Malte's childhood. Images, then, include not only objects and scenes but also characters, who exist as image-figures within the protagonist's lyrical point of view. Made credible by the form of the notebook, which does not need to distinguish between levels of time and reality, the figures of persons and things become part of an exquisitely woven pattern of tapestry, an artificial "world." The writer aims for the effect of lyrical poetry: to use whatever scene, characterization, action in time, and corresponding techniques are the *donnés* of the novel within which he works, not in the development of a fictional world, but in the rendering of objects, sensations, even ideas, with immediacy.

Lyrical immediacy is different from the immediacy of narrative action as we find it, for example, in the battle scenes of *War and Peace*. It is an immediacy of portraiture, an availability of themes and motifs to the reader's glance without the interposition of a narrative world. The form, the world, the sensibility of the poet evolve in the qualitative progression of the lyric, counterpointing, distorting, but always present in other forms of narrative.

⟶ 3

We have so far endeavored to isolate peculiarly lyrical qualities and have chosen for this purpose an unusually pure example of the genre. There have, of course, been other novels equally lyrical: De Quincey's *Dream Fugue,* for example, or Gide's *Nourritures terrestres.* But wherever lyricism is pervasive in a work of narrative prose, critics have doubted that such works are actually novels rather than extended prose poems. Our discussion of *Malte Laurids* has provided, I believe, some criteria by which its status as a novel can be measured. It is a work trading on the expectations of narrative: on description and even action in particular scenes and, in the book as a whole, on the novel of personal confession. Indeed, even this purest form of the lyrical novel could not be considered entirely outside its narrative context. The narrative directly affects the lyrical techniques and lends them the weight of their complexity. Similarly, as we shall see, *Les Nourritures terrestres* becomes an exciting experiment precisely because the loose array of disjointed images is fused with an underlying plot of the novel of education.

Narrative, then, is by no means irrelevant to the lyrical novel. It is used by the perverse poet as the object of his deformations. The hallmark of lyrical fiction is not the form of the narrative but the manner in which it is used. Actually, as we noted, lyrical novels appear in a variety of traditional forms, and it is the critic's task to investigate precisely how the lyrical qualities we have isolated function within their context. For example, diaries and letters were originally a means of promoting verisimilitude. Defoe so assures us in his introduction to *Moll Flanders.* Richardson's *Pamela,* Laclos' *Liaisons dangéreuses,* or Tieck's *Geschichte des Herrn William Lovell* uses letters to depict feelings and actions, but their attention is focused on an external world of events into which their protagonists' discoveries are projected.

But the same form can also become an effective way of presenting a hero's sensibility directly and of allowing him to act as a lyrical point of view. The author is identical with the hero, who portrays himself in his missives or journals. Rousseau pointed the way for such a lyrical usage of these forms without himself writing a complete lyrical novel. St. Preux's fervent exchange of letters in the opening phases of *La Nouvelle Héloïse* holds out the promise of a lyrical novel which is not fulfilled in the remainder of the book. The *Confessions* actually come closer to poetic fiction (as Friedrich Schlegel aptly perceived), but, of course, this book was not intended as a novel. Beyond Rousseau, however, a distinct type of lyrical novel extends from *Werther,* Sénancour's *Obermann,* and *Hyperion* to Gide's *Cahiers d'André Walter* and Rilke's *Malte Laurids*. In all these novels, a hero mirrors himself in significant figures and scenes through which his life is expressed.

A similar situation occurs in a narrative form which, far more intensely than letters and diaries, exploits the hero's inner life. Although both the interior monologue and the stream of consciousness have often been identified with poetic fiction, they share with the confession and the epistolary form an original narrative intention. By itself the direct depiction of the mind's content does not entail a lyrical form. The very notion of Dos Passos' "camera eye," for example, indicates that it can also be used to illuminate precisely all figures within the hero's perception. Indeed, the stream of consciousness can be an intensified device of naturalism, supporting the effort to get at the heart of the external conditions of man by sifting all details that pass through the protagonist.

In a lyrical use of the stream of consciousness, by contrast, a design of images and motifs emerges from associations of the mind. The most obvious early example is Sterne's *Tristram Shandy,* which seems to turn a semblance of the stream of consciousness in a "poetic" direction. To be sure, it is richly bedecked with vivid characters, full of satiric jibes at men and affairs. Its unity as a design is open to question and, in fact, rather resembles a haphazardly patched quilt. But Tristram's compound of comic scenes, memories, and tales told by others, seems to produce a loose and disjointed web displacing the external world and revealing the narrator's mind as he struggles to compose his book. Although it was most influential for the lyrical novel, especially in Germany, *Tristram Shandy* itself is ambivalent, lacking many of the characteristics of lyrical technique. But it is part of its comic effect that it plays on the possibilities of association and memory, on the one hand to divert the reader from its avowed intention of presenting Tristram's "life and opinions" and, on the other, to draw that identity of narrator and subject which was to become a hallmark of lyrical design. In his *Sentimental Journey,* Sterne actually wrote a lyrical novel, a "picture album," as Virginia Woolf once described it, "of the human soul." Without using the stream of consciousness, this small book describing a "journey of the mind" abstracts the mental impression from the concrete world and renders it in a coherent form.

In our time, the stream of consciousness has been used far more self-consciously as a means of psychological exploration and as an aesthetic device. Joyce's *Ulysses* comes to mind, but, like *Tristram Shandy,* it points the way to lyrical fiction rather than being a lyrical novel itself. The novel is built on an obvious counterpoint. On the one hand, we encounter the epic quest through the concrete world of Dublin, but, on the other, we observe the filtering of that quest through the conscious and unconscious stream. This contrast implies a semblance of lyricism. A narrator exposes himself while ostensibly reflecting the world of his perception. Instead of one narrator (including in himself the monologues of others), we encounter three equally important interior monologues which together create a web of motifs. Bloom, Stephen, and Mollie function as a triple lyrical self, a divided point of view. Their monologues transform the streets of the city, its tower, library, and bawdy-house, into a significant design which uses the way stations of the epic quest to lend it symbolic weight. A "lyrical process" based on the quest seems to move toward a moment of recognition in each of the characters, to be unified in the end by the novel's resolution as a whole. In many ways, then, *Ulysses* seems to use both the quest and the stream of consciousness for a lyrical purpose. But the Homeric scheme and the thesis novel underlying the work pull it also in different directions. The juggling of lyrical technique is only one aspect among many of this complex work, which extends from a parody of literature and language to a concise dramatization of men and events.

Proust's *À la recherche du temps perdu* likewise opens the interior monologue to a poetic version of the novel. In many ways, these novels seem even more pertinently lyrical than *Ulysses*. No epic structure establishes a consecutive order to which levels of time must conform. The plot bends with the modulations of memory. The opening pages of the overture state clearly that Marcel has absorbed the worlds of present and past and renders them as a design. Self and world appear undivided, and Marcel suggests a lyrical point of view. Yet Proust breaks out of the lyrical mode. Scene upon scene turns to an enactment of life and manners, thicknesses of history, psychological terror observed and externalized until the world being created is not tapestry like *Malte Laurids* or quilt like *Tristram Shandy,* but society itself in which men move, succeed, and die. Even more than *Ulysses,* Proust's novels become narrative explorations of personal and social lives as they are viewed from an over-all perspective.

An accomplished juxtaposition of the lyrical form with the stream of consciousness occurs in many novels by Virginia Woolf. As we shall see, the ruminations of her individual characters are part of a "public" monologue in which they share, a monologue spoken in the language and couched in the imagery of the omniscient author. This method is especially useful in her purely lyrical novel, *The Waves,* in which an artful design is composed of the soliloquies of several characters. Leon Edel's interesting observation that psychological novelists usually set out seeking verisimilitude and conclude as symbolists cannot be applied to the form itself. "What begins as an attempt to click the mind's shutter and catch the images of outer reality impinging upon it, ends up as an impressionist painting." [8] This is quite true of Virginia Woolf, but it does not necessarily apply to all stream of consciousness novelists. Dos Passos, Proust, or Joyce take different attitudes toward the stream of consciousness. The desire to enhance truthful observation may be one purpose; the refashioning of mental imagery into a texture of lyrical poetry may be another. Often they are intermingled, but whether one form or the other is used depends on the author's purposes and sometimes even on the limits of his talent.

Lyrical fiction, however, is not confined to such narrative forms as the journal, confession, interior monologue or stream of consciousness, which reflect the contents of men's minds. Perhaps the most influential form of the lyrical novel has been suggested by the picaresque, the episodic romance, and the allegorical quest. Although these forms are not inherently poetic, they were so conceived by German romantic critics, and in this guise they have influenced various types of the lyrical novel. Both the Spanish picaresque and *Don Quixote* were seen as romantic forms in which a portrait of life is created by the adventures of a wandering protagonist. In *Tom Jones* and *Humphry Clinker,* the method retains its narrative purpose, but in Novalis' *Heinrich von Ofterdingen* it is lyrically conceived. The hero's time-bound adventures are transformed into a sequence of image-scenes that mirror the nature of the protagonist's quest and represent it symbolically. The progression required by the narrative genre is converted into a lyrical progression produced by the elaboration of pictures and scenes. This adaptation of the episodic structure to poetry has produced incisive types of lyrical novels, variously intermingled with ingredients of the novel of adventure, from the German symbolic novel of the romantic age to *Moby Dick* and *The Heart of Darkness.* Especially in the German literary tradition, the episodic romance is one of the most widespread types of lyrical fiction. The hero,

[8] *The Psychological Novel, 1900–1950* (New York: Lippincott, 1955), p. 185.

as the poet's mask, wanders through worlds of symbolic encounters.

The emphasis on the protagonist as the poet's mask is inevitable in a genre which depends on the analogy between the
lyrical "I" of verse poetry and the hero of fiction. Since the formal
presentation of a self is a "self-reflexive" method, most lyrical
novels indeed seem to require a single point of view. But actually the tradition of lyrical fiction is considerably more generous;
it is capable of including many novels which feature several
important characters or suggest a panoramic form. *Wuthering
Heights,* for example, is intensely lyrical in its imagery and
language, yet its design conforms to that of an objective novel
which is not confined to a single figure. The narrator, Nellie
Dean, is no replica of the author; her consciousness does not
contain the two lovers as if they were images. Rather, Heathcliff and Catherine create between them an aura of passion upon
which Nellie Dean comments. Their intense feelings, which
counterpoint her narrow perspective, are reflected in the images
of nature, uniting inner and outer worlds. The lyrical perspective
is created by the concealed author, who manipulates both the
narrator's limited vision and the lovers' poetic scenery.

A more usual variation is the pattern of soliloquists. In a
straightforward narrative, as, for example, in Joyce Cary's trilo-
gies, different aspects of a drama may be viewed by several
first-person narrators whose versions of identical circumstances
enhance the complexity of the novel. By analogy, in lyrical
novels several monologues may be contrasted or paired in patterns of interlocking images. A lyrical novel like *The Waves*
draws its aesthetic rearrangement of time and life from such a
pattern of formal soliloquies, each of which reshapes an individual world. In *Les Faux-Monnayeurs,* Gide created a design
of image-scenes viewed by various figures, including the author.
The novel's form is made up of a pattern of these sequences
which acts both through the cumulative motion of the "lyrical
process" and through several juxtaposed levels of awareness.
These forms use narrative means to project modes perfectly

familiar in lyrical poetry. In verse, too, different "voices" can be reflected against each other, as Yeats has done effectively, or different *personae* can enact a stylized lyrical drama, as they do occasionally in Eliot or Auden. Lyrical novels, then, possess widely ranging possibilities of objectification. Their repertoire of possible techniques includes many variations of narrative form which they use in the manner of lyrical poetry, extending from a pure stream of consciousness to a controlled pattern of figures and scenes manipulated by an omniscient author. Epistolary novels and confessions, picaresques and novels of education have contributed to corresponding forms of lyricism. The novel of manners may furnish a base for the lyrical novel as much as the novel of adventure. But the precise nature of the poetic world it substitutes for time, cause, and place cannot always be described. It may include subconscious imagery and monologues, but it may also consist of patterns of symbolic encounters or a canvas of complementing figures. Its defining characteristics vary with the author's traditions, his country and time, with his personal sensibility and genius. But whatever form is used, his point of view is crystallized in his protagonists, who transform their perceptions into a network of images.

———4

A final question concerns the motive of lyrical novelists. Why should writers use storytelling, figures and scenes, the movement of time, however distorted or grotesque, to create a poetic world? Very likely, this way of manipulating the narrative genre is a peculiar dodge of *romanciers manqués*. And indeed, poetic spirits from Novalis to Gérard de Nerval and André Gide seem to have suffered from a lack of sturdiness with which to meet external life. But such an explanation is too simple, for it does not illuminate the importance of the genre or its persistence. Prose allegories, poetic idylls and picaresques, the use of fairy tale, dream, distortion and fantasy, of mental association and dithyrambs in prose—all these have subverted the novel since its beginnings, supplanting narrative with lyrical objectivity.

It would not, then, be enough to say that Sterne's *Sentimental Journey* or Nerval's *Aurélia,* the lyrical novels of Hermann Broch and Hermann Hesse, of André Gide and Virginia Woolf represent failures of personal sensibility, constructs of pathetic minds unable to create concrete worlds. As compensations for failure they may indeed bear witness to the personal tragedies of writers. But the very ambivalence of novelist and poet which requires these compensations has often converted "failure" into magnificent achievement. At the same time, the lyrical version of the novel has also been ideologically conditioned. To the extent that the empirical idealism of the eighteenth century and the transcendental idealism of the nineteenth have offered an appropriate climate for the fusion of self and world, writers have followed in the footsteps of thinkers. Whether as poets, as philosophers, or as bystanders baffled at the intellectual display of their times, they have sought to eliminate the disjunction of self and world in the very genre that seems most to require their separation.

These reflections about the form of lyrical novels, and the motives of their authors, give rise to the conclusion that a critical method for their scrutiny must be historically conditioned. Distinguishing characteristics are rooted in different ways of thinking about the novel, which in turn are deeply embedded in the literary tradition of each country. Although our main purpose is to investigate three distinct kinds of the contemporary lyrical novel, we would do well to relate each of these types to its corresponding literary milieu, which may define not only the nature of the form but also the impulse behind it. From the ambiguous relationship between narration and lyricism we can distill a general significance for the novel: the challenge of reconciling the "inner" and the "outer" with each other and with the exigencies of art.

THE LYRICAL TRADITION

1

THE ASSAULT of the twentieth century on inner experience has brought with it a profound reappraisal of the novel. Traditional techniques such as point of view and narrative plot have been utilized, not to produce a lively world of action, but to find formal analogues for a private world. Characteristically, many contemporary novelists have dissected a self—their own or that of their protagonists—and have turned it into a stage on which plot and themes are enacted with distance and often with formality. A poetic design rather than an external world describes the limits of that stage in *La Symphonie pastorale* and *Les Faux-Monnayeurs,* in *Ulysses* and *The Waves*. Progressively, the hero in the modern novel has abandoned his traditional role, substituting perception for action and, for external reality, a formal portrait of himself.

Concentration on the inner life of a passive hero and the consequent creation of a detached "poetic" form distinguish lyrical from non-lyrical narrative. Precisely this method of "subjective objectivity" is the manifestation of a genre which received its firmest outlines early in the nineteenth century. Modern lyrical novels are creatures of romanticism. Although in the eighteenth century poetic prose language and the novel of sensibility had opened a wide range of expression for lyrical enthusiasm, authors and heroes were still faced with a choice between an outer world of opinions and events and an inner world of sensibility and feeling. Characters had to assert themselves against conflicting pressures. Like Clarissa, Werther, or St. Preux, they were oppressed by a world external and hostile to themselves. Otherwise, they had to control their worlds, as Tom Jones learned to do, or else, as the title of Sterne's *Senti-*

mental Journey suggests, they had to accept and utilize the dominance of the inner sensibility. But the early nineteenth century had learned from Kant that the "inner" and the "outer" can be reconciled in a comprehensive philosophical system. The external world was conceived as an addition to the self's inner world, which might be ultimately unified with the subjective sensibility in a higher or spiritual self. The very idea of transcendentalism allowed its adherents to have it both ways: to achieve supreme objectivity and yet to remain intensely subjective by positing an ultimate unity of self and world in an absolute *self*.

This projection of a higher self is of great importance for a theory of the novel. A *symbolic hero*, absorbing the world of sense and mirroring it in an ideal form, enacts in fictional terms the main procedures of the early romantic dialectic. In Fichte's system, for example, the self is opposed by the external non-self. In a process of mutual interaction, self and non-self ultimately obliterate one another and, as the outcome of an infinite process, are transformed into the absolute self. Similarly, the hero in a novel, apprehending the world, absorbs the images reflected by the objects and scenes he encounters and achieves a union which may otherwise be obtained only in infinity. Protagonists in novels such as Goethe's *Wilhelm Meister* or Novalis' *Heinrich von Ofterdingen* exhibit through their search, their education, their romantic *Wanderschaft,* a total self in which inner and outer experiences are joined.

This romantic *Steigerung* of the hero-in-life to the hero-in-art is peculiarly apposite to a lyrical conception of the novel. The hero becomes the receptacle of experience at the same time that he is its symbolizing agent. He embodies objects and other minds and spiritualizes them through the intercession of art. But unlike the active heroes of realistic novels and portraits of manners, these symbolic heroes seek a spiritual image through their modes of awareness. Novalis' theory and practice illuminate such a lyrical vision. In the fragments on his own lyrical novel, *Heinrich von Ofterdingen,* he notes that the hero is a passive self in whom the encounters of life are symbolically reflected. "[The protagonist] is the poet's organ in the novel. . . . Poetic elaboration and contemplation of all of life's encounters." [1] Receiving experiences and remolding them as art, the poet, or his hero, proceeds to draw his own self-portrait.

This process of telescoping self and world is based in the main on the idealistic epistemology of the time. The artist represents himself in an object. He portrays his inner experience and by this act transmutes the object that expresses him into a manifestation of his "infinite self"—the visible work of art. The perceived object becomes part of the poet's experience while rendering his private sensibility public, but, in mirroring the poet's inner state, it loses its separate, independent character. In this way, perceived objects become manifestations of the poet's spirit—features of his self-portrait—as they are portrayed symbolically in the form of art. The "object" is the catalyst through which a finite, individual self is transmuted into an infinite, aesthetic self. [2]

Seen in this way, the relationship between the self and its world becomes that of a perceiver and his image in a mirror, in which the reflection is the transcendental representation of the actual features. In *Die Lehrlinge zu Saïs,* Novalis' wise men suggest that man's finite perception is analogous to God's creation and contemplation of nature. As the created universe is God's self-portrait, so the signs of nature are parts of the true decipherer's composite picture of himself. [3] And in his theory of "magical idealism," Novalis suggests that the imagination transforms nature from a mechanism into a poetic whole. [4] The artist

---

[1] "Paralipomena zum 'Heinrich von Ofterdingen,'" *Schriften,* ed. Paul Kluckhohn (Leipzig: Bibliographisches Institut, 1929), i, 239.

[2] "Philosophische Studien" (1795–1796), *Schriften,* ii, 193–194.

[3] *Schriften,* i, 28–34.

[4] "Das allgemeine Brouillon" (1798–1799), *Schriften,* iii, 227–228; "Neue Fragmentensammlungen" (1798), *Schriften,* ii, 335–339. Cf. Albert Béguin on Novalis' "transformation" of the physical world into dream. *L'Âme romantique et le rêve* (Paris: Librairie Jose Corti, 1946), pp. 194–195 *et passim.*

thus renders an image of infinite nature and his own infinite self; the symbolic hero is the passive instrument of this process. The result of such a doctrine is a tremendous overemphasis on imagination and dream, a dissolution of the universe into signs akin to the signs of human language, and a fundamentally anthropocentric view of the world.

The hero as an aesthetic image of nature leads to the technique of *mirroring*. Since the self is the point at which inner and outer worlds are joined, the hero's mental picture reflects the universe of sensible encounters as an image. The "world" is part of the hero's inner world; the hero, in turn, mirrors the external world and all its multitudinous manifestations. He *distorts* the universe or dissolves it into hallucination or dream in which its "true" (infinite and organic) nature is revealed. Thus, the magic of spiritual awareness unfolds a picture of infinite reality which is hidden to the ordinary glance. At the same time, the distortion of the world is also reflected on the mask worn by the hero as the author's self-in-art. He is a *mimic* portraying the poet's image of the world in aesthetic poses.[5]

Various romantic critics and poets have specified methods by which the self-encounters of passive heroes may be mirrored in ideal forms. For Friedrich Schlegel, for example, the successful poet reflects the world aesthetically; the subject is liberated from its dependence on the object and can express itself in art. In the novel, small portraits or *arabesques* ideally set limits to each experience and reflect it through playful and humorous illusion. "Romantic irony," achieved by author intrusions and frame-story devices, suggests in such writers as Ludwig Tieck and E. T. A. Hoffmann the attempt to break the aesthetic illusion and to produce the portrait of a hero simultaneously in life and art. Even playful wit, as Jean Paul Richter points out, must provide the bridge whereby we can pass from the real (that is, external) to the inner experience that fashions life in a transcendental

---

[5] "Neue Fragmentensammlungen" (1798), *Schriften*, II, 326–327, 356–357.

form.[6] But for Novalis, irony is also a state of mind, an awareness transcended by the "true presence of the spirit." [7] The world of objects is transformed and dissolved into a world of "magic"—a freedom gained in fairy tale and myth—which mirrors a passive hero's finite awareness in a spiritual state.

If mirroring and irony establish the relationship between the hero and the transcendental image, Novalis' theory of person and personality provides a clue for the understanding of the hero in relation to others. Each person, it appears from his overly brief account in the fragments collected in "Das Allgemeine Brouillon" (1798–1799), is a concrete instance of an undetermined general person. Thus, a person is a harmony of many contradictory elements which relate to the universal person in the same way that different manifestations of the universe relate to the harmony of nature.[8] This view, however, adds to the notion of the hero a distinct psychology, derived though it is from a conception of man and nature as imagination and fantasy. It suggests, as Novalis phrased it, that a person is capable of remaining one even though he is divided into many. "The genuine analysis of person as such produces only persons—person can only individuate, divide, and analyze itself into persons." [9] In fiction, poet and hero must adopt alien masks as they gather within themselves contradictory points of view.[10] As they

[6] *Werke* (Weimar: Hermann Böhlaus Nachfolger, 1935), Part I, XI, 111–112.

[7] "Neue Fragmentensammlungen" (1798), *Schriften,* II, 396; "Blütenstaub," *ibid.,* p. 20. See René Wellek, *A History of Literary Criticism* (New Haven: Yale University Press, 1955), II, 86.

[8] *Schriften,* III, 70–71. For the relationship between "person" and "universe," see "Fragmente der letzten Jahre," (1799–1800), *ibid.,* p. 337. In "Philosophische Studien" (1795–1796), Novalis writes of the relationship between "person" and "nature": "Die Person ist als Objekt *besonders,* als Subjekt ein Allgemeines. Die Natur ist als Subjekt besonders, als Objekt Allgemeines." *Schriften,* II, 254.

[9] *Schriften,* III, 70.

[10] *Schriften,* II, 326–327. Novalis notes specifically: "Die Poesie löst fremdes Dasein im eignen auf." P. 327.

approach the ideal self, they reconcile these points of view with one another. They become supreme mimics. Personality, Novalis said in another fragment, is the romantic element of the self.[11] The transcendental hero, like the poet who adopts the alien mask, must absorb others, as he must absorb the external world, to reflect an ideal image.

The transcendental or symbolic hero, as Novalis conceives him, is the aesthetic abstraction of the universal from the "real" person. He is the romanticized hero: the lower self, as Novalis put it, is identified with the higher self.[12] This process of abstraction, dubbed "romanticizing," is the act of lending to the known and finite the atmosphere of the higher and infinite in the realm of illusion and art, of transforming the individual moment into the universal absolute. For Friedrich Schlegel, the tautological statement that the *Roman* is a romantic book meant that it includes and transcends all genres in the symbolic depiction of finite man. For Novalis, the identification of the novel with "transcendental poetry" meant that it is a total representation of infinite man and nature. Defined as the proper mixture of poetry and philosophy, transcendental poetry is expected to yield a system which would embody the symbolic construction of the transcendental world.[13] The novel, as an infinite geometrical progression, meets this objective by rendering a total image of man for immediate apprehension.[14] For the transcendental or romanticized hero reflects a spiritual image of man's relation to his universe, rising from subjective sensibility and moving to a formal presentation.

[11] *Ibid.*, p. 398.

[12] *Ibid.*, p. 335.

[13] *Ibid.*, p. 327.

[14] "Der Roman als solcher enthält kein bestimmtes Resultat—er ist nicht Bild und Faktum eines *Satzes*. Er ist anschauliche Ausführung—Realisierung einer *Idee*. Aber eine Idee lässt sich nicht in einen Satz fassen. Eine Idee ist eine *unendliche* Reihe von Sätzen—eine irrationale Grösse—uneinsetzbar—inkommensurabel." *Ibid.*, pp. 356–357. For a description of the novel as a geometrical progression, see *ibid.*, p. 326.

From such notions of heroes and novels, it must follow that works of fiction written by the romantic generation in Germany often exhibited a peculiar, eccentric bent. Indeed, German novels and tales in the early part of the nineteenth century, where they did not imitate realistic English novels of the past, re-developed the novel of sensibility and the picaresque form in allegorical or fantastic directions. They sought a coincidence of content, vision and form, ironic juxtapositions of the actual and aesthetic, or a heightened expression of feeling.

This state of the novel is painstakingly described by Friedrich Schlegel, both in his crucial "Brief über den Roman" (1800) and in his *Geschichte der alten und neuen Poesie* (1812). The English novel is emphatically rejected because of the middle-class, mercantilistic spirit which lurks behind the techniques and attitudes of traditional realism.[15] Fielding, Goldsmith, Burney, and Smollett for the most part are consigned to oblivion because they "steal" their details from life, while Richardson and Sterne are acknowledged as masters. The novel—confessional or humorous or fantastic—is expected to transcend life through patterns of witty portraits conceived in play ("arabesques"), marvelous encounters or adventures, through a higher poetic spirit. Indeed, Schlegel offers a transcendental concept of the novel as part of his search for forms adequate to the new century. In the intellectually more precise *Geschichte der alten und neuen Poesie* especially, he concludes a discussion of Cervantes and the Spanish romance with an analysis of the actual and poetic elements of a work as they present the contrast between time and eternity. The poetic romance unites the treasures of the past with the wealth of the present in a painting, a *magic mirror* of life which also reflects the dawn of the future. Unifying all time, it becomes a "sense representation of the eternal." Essentially, this unity of time and eternity—the sensible render-

---

[15] *Sämmtliche Werke* (2nd. ed.; Wien, 1846), v, 223–224 *et passim*.

ing of the infinite—is the novel's function as a form of poetic art. It rises above the time-bound and parochial to a poetic rendering of life as a whole.[16]

The hero in a transcendental novel, then, is a passive purveyor of visions. Friedrich Schlegel had identified this hero even with Wilhelm Meister, noting in one of his fragments that a novel is actually the personification of an entire life, an encyclopedia of a man of genius.[17] But, in the hands of Novalis and others, the romantic hero became allegorical or symbolic and finally lyrical *par excellence*. In Novalis' *Heinrich von Ofterdingen*, the symbolic hero dreams of the Blue Flower of poetry, for which he then sets out to search. But this "flower"—representing the unattainable ideal—exists only in infinity. Heinrich's pilgrimage toward infinity is conceived in terms of the novel of education charted by *Wilhelm Meister*, but the encounters are allegorized. A Chorus of Merchants, an Oriental Lady, a Hermit, among others, appear in various episodes, illustrating stages of his progress. Later, Heinrich is taught by the Poet, Klingsohr; his imagination is stirred by the latter's daughter Mathilde (Inspiration). Each of these figures leads him closer to the Blue Flower, but each represents yet another aspect of himself and defines his progress and search.

The center of the novel is a revealing scene in which Heinrich views an image of himself. It not only clarifies the work in which it takes a prominent place but also elucidates the very concept of the lyrical novel. The scene occurs in the hermit's cave, where Heinrich is handed a Book of Life presenting an image of himself. Left alone while his host, the hermit, takes his companions on a tour, he browses through some old books until his glance is arrested by a volume written in a foreign language sufficiently familiar to give him a vague sense of its content, but alien enough to leave definite meanings obscure. Fortunately, however, there are pictures:

[16] *Sämmtliche Werke*, II, 79.

[17] Lyzeums-Fragment #78. *Friedrich Schlegel. Seine prosaischen Jugendschriften*, ed. J. Minor (Wien, 1882), p. 194.

They [the pictures] seemed to him quite wondrously familiar, and as he looked closer he discovered his own image quite clearly among the figures. For a moment he was fearful and believed he was dreaming, but when he looked again and again he could no longer doubt the complete resemblance. He hardly trusted his senses when on one of the pictures he soon discovered the cave and, next to himself, the old man and the hermit. Gradually he also found in the other pictures the Lady from the Orient, his parents, the Count and Countess of Thuringia, his friend the Court Chaplain, and many other acquaintances; yet their clothes were changed and appeared to stem from a different era. A large number of figures he could not name, although they seemed familiar to him. He saw his own image in many situations. Towards the end, he appeared to himself as greater and nobler. The guitar rested in his arms and the Countess handed him a wreath.

After enumerating various scenes which occur later in the novel, the passage concludes: "The last pictures were dark and incomprehensible; yet some of the dream figures surprised him with the tenderest delight. The conclusion seemed to be missing. Heinrich was very sad and desired nothing more than to be able to read this book and own it entirely." After the return of the party, Heinrich asks the hermit about the book. But his host does not remember it too well, except that it is "a *novel* about the marvelous fate of a poet in which the art of poetry is portrayed and praised in its manifold qualities and forms." [18]

The world thus presented is a wholly indrawn, vaguely symbolic world. In the slow progression of enumeration, each picture marches before Heinrich's eye. He is the center and the receptacle. Mirroring the novel as a whole, he is caught in miniature in an equally slow-moving picture. The images of life appear in a picture album which is also a novel, its true meaning disguised but evident to a closer glance. The irony in this pas-

---

[18] *Heinrich von Ofterdingen, Schriften*, I, 168–170. See also Friedrich Hiebel, *Novalis: Der Dichter der blauen Blume* (Bern: A. G. Franche, 1951), pp. 280–281, *et passim*.

sage is of a metaphysical kind; it depicts the discrepancy between the self and its experiences on the one hand, and, on the other, their combination in the work of art. Reflecting the self's world and ideas, this "infinite" work is made sensibly accessible to our experience.

The hero is a *wanderer* through space and time, his quest caught in an allegory which must in the end be fragmentary. But Heinrich's chief distinction lies in the fact that he is also the *creator* of his world, a passive creator on whom the existence of the world entirely depends. In him sensations and impressions are received, symbolic figures emerge and fall behind as trees pass by a traveler moving along in a very slow cart. In this way, episodes are turned into encounters and encounters into images. They determine the movement of the novel, which resembles the endless corridor of a picture gallery in which the images depicting the hero's encounters are ultimately gathered into his symbolic self-portrait.

Mirrorings of the poet and author in the theme, of the theme in the hero, and of author, hero, and theme in the form of the novel as a whole—these qualities define lyrical fiction at the turn of the eighteenth century. As we have seen, the *Bildungs-roman* furnished an important structure through which this mir-roring could take place. The hero wandering through space and time, gathering up both within his perception, experiences his visions reflexively as internalized self-portraits. Despite the bour-geois content, ultimately distasteful to Friedrich Schlegel and Novalis, the hero and structure of *Wilhelm Meister* lent them-selves to modifications not only in *Heinrich von Ofterdingen* but also in many different novels and tales, including Wacken-roder and Tieck's *Franz Sternbalds Wanderungen* or Eichen-dorff's *Ahnung und Gegenwart* and *Taugenichts*. Wilhelm Meister learns through his pilgrimage in space and his develop-ment in time. His experiences shape his consciousness, reflecting it in the magic mirror of art. In the same way, each of the roman-tic heroes searches for knowledge, for signs of nature to be transformed, through the intercession of art, into symbols of the ideal. Franz Sternbald learns about paintings, Heinrich von

Ofterdingen about poetry. Yet although they use the outward form of the Goethean model, and even echo its attempts at symbolization, both intent and form have become very different. Despite its picaresque form, its inserted parables and tales, its discussions of literature and art, *Wilhelm Meister* is a realistic novel which the romantic generation had to translate into its own terms. The German romantic vision of the novel was actually a narrow view that excluded the novel in its most definitive form as it had been evolved since the eighteenth century. Their rejection of bourgeois values was epitomized by their poetic concept of the novel, which excluded the depiction of life and manners as a dull preoccupation of philistines. The novel had to be bucolic or witty, allegorical or fantastic, indeed, self-consciously symbolic. As Novalis proclaimed, it must be "poetry through and through." [19] The hero must be the passive recipient of a phantasmagoria which passes for the external world; he must be the mimic representing his "ideal" in the world of sense.

━━3

The notion of the passive hero as a symbolic mask of the author left its mark on the very concept of the novel as poetry. But although it expressed a condition shared by many writers, its appearance in full-length novels did not achieve everywhere the same degree of popularity or even acceptance. If the lyrical novel was a crucial concept in German romanticism, in France and England it was confined to marginal efforts. To be sure, the novel of feeling continued to be used by French writers in the early nineteenth century. Chateaubriand's *Atala, René,* or *Natchez* render a hero's sensibility in heightened poetic language. Later, the magic of German romanticism touched different forms of poetic fiction. For example, Gérard de Nerval's *Aurélia* combined the passive hero and a fluidly poetic style, its loose and dissolving form anticipating lyrical novels in the symbolist vein later in the century. Even Flaubert concluded late

[19] "Fragmente der letzten Jahre" (1799–1800), *Schriften,* iii, 286.

in his life a lyrical novel he had begun early in his career. *La Tentation de St. Antoine* is dominated by the sensibility of a passive hero whose suffering creates both the form and the *raison d'être* of the work. Both *Aurélia* and *La Tentation* are poems as well as novels, but they form exceptions to the major trend of the romantic and the realistic novel in France.

In England, examples of lyrical fiction are even more isolated than in France because the very idea of the romantic imagination had been defined almost exclusively in terms of verse. In the eighteenth century, conditions for an English lyrical novel seem to have been extremely favorable. The novel of feeling had influenced German romantic thinking about the poetic novel, and both Richardson and Sterne had contributed to its definition. The vogue of primitive prose poetry in England, such as Macpherson's "Ossian," turned men's interest toward a poetic spirit unhampered by genres and forms. But such impulses were opposed to a climate of taste which conceived the novel as a realistic form. At a time when the romantic revolt in Germany found an important outlet in the lyrical novel, English romantic poets wrote almost exclusively in verse. Indeed, narrative poetry represents English romantic literature in the same way as Novalis' *Heinrich von Ofterdingen* signifies what is essential in German romanticism. Coleridge's *Rime of the Ancient Mariner* stands out as an English parallel in verse to German lyrical prose: the symbolic voyage *par excellence*. Some exceptions naturally exist in English romantic prose, especially De Quincey's *Confessions of an English Opium Eater* and, more pertinently, his *Dream Fugue*. Here we indeed find that fluidity of form and dream-like progression of internal encounters associated with lyrical narrative, but De Quincey was more important for the later development of the prose poem and *fin de siècle* lyrical fiction than for the novel of his time.

Even the English romantic novel, while necessarily reflecting current views of the imagination, remained largely a narrative expansion of discrete moments in time. To be sure, the landscapes of *The Bride of Lammermoor* differ considerably from those of *Tom Jones*. Instead of being confronted by two-dimensional descriptions efficiently delivered to get on with the plot, the reader is involved in palpable and grotesque experiences of a nature which emerges as a character of the novel. The Gothic novel of the romantic age, while exploiting the license of the romance to recount improbable events, distorted reality not only to achieve sensationalistic effects but also to provide pictures of brooding imaginations. But in the romantic novels of the time, such uses of language, scene, and adventure are not in themselves poetic, since they are conceived as external to both author and hero. Forms are controlled, not by images and their relationships, but by temporal and causal succession. The many different forms of the English novel in the early nineteenth century—the novel of sensibility and manners, the thesis novel, the Gothic novel, and the historical romance—did not express that climate of intense symbolic experience which was fully apparent only in verse. Despite exceptions like *Wuthering Heights,* the English tradition of the novel remained distinctly aloof from poetry in its method and approach.

The flowering of the romance toward the middle of the nineteenth century, which took place particularly in France under the aegis of Poe and Gautier, assured the continued existence of the romantic hero and furnished a significant variation of the genre. The intervening development of an organic and transcendental concept of the imagination (the influence, too, of German romantic prose) created a notion of the romance, epitomized by Poe, which differed considerably from that of the eighteenth and early nineteenth centuries. But, on the whole, the rise of realism in France, the prominence in England of the masterpieces of Victorian fiction, and the pressure toward objectivity in the German realistic *Bildungsroman* reduced the lyrical novel to minor importance. During this time, however, it underwent a process of revision parallel to the process of change from romantic to symbolist poetry. This development did not really take place in full-length novels. Chiefly it is in the evolution of the tale and the prose poem and in the refine-

ment of poetic theory that the ground for this change was prepared.

⌐4

In the lyrical novel, narrator and protagonist combine to
create a self in which experience is fashioned as imagery. For
Schelling or Novalis, the ideal was symbolized by the language
of sense; the organic unity of self and world was centered in
the poet, or his hero. Within him, the ideal was approached by
a magical transformation of encounters into symbolic forms.
But Edgar Allen Poe turned to the art object, the sounds of
poems and the furniture of the fictional stage, in which, through
the infusion of the marvelous, higher truths were to be implied.[20]
Thus, the elaborate machinery in "The Fall of the House of
Usher"—with its heavy screeching doors, its shrouded half-
living corpse, its inserted poem, its parallel story of Ethelred—
neither satisfactorily resolves the story in a plausibly realistic
fashion nor reflects directly the author's inner life. Rather, all
of these elements establish an *aesthetic situation* which engulfs
narrator and subject in the final apotheosis. The protagonist
now directs attention toward a hidden psychological terror or
guilt which, in complex relationships between the narrator's
consciousness and that of the figure on the story's stage, absorbs
the external world in a climactic passion and represents it as art.
A hero's allegorical quest depicted by means of symbolic encounters is replaced by an enactment of his inner condition
caught in a specific object or situation through which the
higher truth is portrayed.

Poe's tales show, then, that figures representing a divided self
can be brought together in a situation which objectifies their
union in an aesthetic and psychological form. In Baudelaire's *Petits
Poèmes en prose,* this limited form is cast in a uniquely poetic
mold. Baudelaire transmuted into poetry Poe's projection of the

---

[20] "Fancy and Imagination," *The Complete Works of E. A. Poe* (New
York, 1902), VII, 126–127.

divided self with an increasingly sharp emphasis on the symbolic vision and its dissolution into objects. His prose poems exploit the split between narrator and hero as a lyrical device to portray simultaneously the poet-hero's inner drama and his consequent detachment. This method is based on a "dramatic" juxtaposition of self and world which had been already implicit in Baudelaire's verse. But his *Petits Poèmes* are far from being a belated pendant to *Les Fleurs du Mal*. Rather, they translate the conflict within a self's divided point of view, evident in the verse poems, into the explicit drama of prose. The poet detaches himself from the scene; one part of himself enacts the moral point in symbolic gestures, while the other part of himself functions as an observer who is detached at the very time that he is drawn into the scene.[21]

As a whole, the prose poems are a varied collection, ironic and passionate, cruelly realistic and loftily symbolic, prose renderings of verse and narrative parables. But most of them create poetic images by utilizing tools of narrative and description, including the divided point of view. The poet and his mask—the narrator and the figure on the prose-poem's stage—dramatize an internal conflict and symbolize it objectively through a situation or object. In "Le Fou et la Vénus," for example, the poet projects onto the poem's stage the mask of a clown and pits him against the distant image of beauty, luring and rejecting him with its impassive unconcern. In "Le Mauvais Vître" the interaction between narrator and mask is that of poet and glazier, assailant and victim.

The relationship of the double to its symbolic form is particularly vivid in those prose poems whose narrative movement draws attention to character and situation. For example, a story like "Mlle. Bistouri" creates an opposition of poet and mask which

---

[21] For the distinction between the prose poem and lyrical fiction, see Suzanne Bernard, *Le Poème en prose de Baudelaire jusqu'à nos jours* (Paris: Nizet, 1959) pp. 438f. et passim. For a seminal study of the French prose poem, see Franz Rauhut, *Das französische Prosagedicht,* Hamburger Studien zu Volkstum und Kultur der Romanen, No. 2 (Hamburg: Friedrichsen, de Gruyter and Company, 1929).

is resolved in a dramatic climax. The poet uncovers a woman's fixation on blood underlying her pathological insistence that he is a doctor. The resolution enacts an obsession reminding us of Poe's "Ligeia." As in Poe's tales, such an obsession is revealed, and the story resolved, through a dramatic turn which objectifies the relationship between narrator and subject. And, as in Poe, the drama is internal, contained within a consciousness that symbolically displaces the external world. But, for Baudelaire, the relationship between the detached narrator and the subject as his *pendant* and opposite is not left as a resolved narrative climax. Through the interaction of the two selves we are made aware of their essential unity in the author. We also see them brought together in an artificial object, the symbol of art. Moreover, this symbolic object acts as an *image* to portray the inversion, or dramatic counterpoint, of the "plot." It contracts the hero's encounter with his "double" into a metaphoric situation and thus constitutes an image quite different from the reflexive visions of Heinrich von Ofterdingen.

Baudelaire's prose poems usually present a symbolic drama that contracts and intensifies the progression of images by which lyrical fiction is defined. The point of view of prose narrative is reformulated as the self's relationship with its double; aesthetic objectivity is achieved by concentrating inner drama in metaphoric objects. In the prose poems of Arthur Rimbaud, and in the aesthetic which supports them, this conception of lyrical prose reached a point of crisis. *Je suis* is transformed into *Je est* in an act of heightened intensity in which the poet reaches the unknown without the employment of the conscious will. Baudelaire's prose poems had projected the coherent, if divided, self through an internal drama caught in the aesthetic situation or object, but Rimbaud's prose poems exploded it into a pandemonium of objects. In the place of the poet and his double, we confront a continuous interchange between a composite self and its dispersal. Individual things are expelled by a formal point of view. A vision through the arc of a spider web becomes slaughter houses, laden barges, a piano on an Alpine glacier,

a mythical witch; a weather-vane cock turns into the vast skirts
of a woman. These objects are not only emanations of the subconscious they are also symbols of the infinite unknown penetrated by the poet's magic.

At the other end of the scale, the evasive formality of Mallarmé's prose poems is achieved by juxtapositions of sounds and
motifs. Aesthetic relations and associations are instrumental in
shaping the forms of the prose poems to reveal, as in "Le Démon
de l'Analogie," the "undeniable presence of the supernatural."
Or else, as in "Le Nénuphar Blanc," each sensual image is
negated until only the white void of the symbolic water-lily is
left to define purity. Aesthetic purity, identified with nothingness or absence, bears, however, some very practical implications for prose poetry and for the related form of the lyrical
novel. It replaces the passive hero with a percipient who withdraws from encounters and objects that assume an independent
existence of their own. Through evocation, implication, and
dream, Poe's "aesthetic situation" becomes the lyrical arena in
which theme and content are displayed in constellations of symbols.

Whether in psychological drama, in a dissolution of the self
into detached things, or its transformation into patterns of images, the poet, and his hero, created a detached form of himself
through which he might include and transcend the external
world. French prose poetry in the nineteenth century thus produced a pattern to which later lyrical novels responded and con-
formed. For these novels introduced a new romantic hero—an
extension of Stendhal's Julien and Novalis' Heinrich—who developed relations among artificial objects as equivalents of the
external world.

———5

Since the prevailing modes of prose fiction in the nineteenth
century were largely based on realism, it is not surprising that any
reaction should gather its strength from the development in
prose poetry and poetic theory which had continued the ro-

mantic heritage in a more radical form. One of the chief characteristics of early symbolist fiction was the renewed emphasis on the hero as the passive purveyor of visions. In his *Manifeste* of 1886, Symbolism's vehement theoretician, Jean Moréas, sought to demonstrate that the evolution of prose fiction and fantasy must be analogous to that of poetry: the poet had to appear as a fictional protagonist. "In the 'symbolic' conception of the novel," Moréas wrote in the *Manifeste,* "a unique personage moves in worlds transformed by his own hallucinations, his temperament: in this deformation lies the unique reality. Beings with mechanical gestures, with vague outlines, act around the unique hero: they are for him but pretexts for sensations and conjectures. His is the tragic mask, or that of the clown, of a perfect as well as a rational humanity." [22] For Novalis, poet and heroes were mimics, because they included alien personalities and represented the ideal. But for Moréas, the passive hero uses the world as a pretext for his own sensations. The idealistic emphasis remains, but "unique" reality now lies in the hero's deformation of his world. The symbolic hero becomes a clown whose mask mirrors a deformed world as artifice.

Although Moréas claimed for himself many of the important French writers of the nineteenth century, Stendhal and the Goncourts among them, his theory actually drew upon a novel which had appeared two years earlier—J. K. Huysmans' *A rebours.* Huysmans wrote later that he had conceived his novel with no particular plan in mind, that it had occurred to him because all theories, particularly naturalism, had come to a dead end. All naturalism could do, he argued, was to repeat the same empty formula.[23] But in ostensibly not conforming to a formula, Huysmans produced a new one. His form echoes the romantic pilgrimage toward a transcendence of the world of sense at the same time that it represents its denial. On the one hand, *A rebours* is

---

[22] Reprinted in Léon Vanier, *Les Premiers Armes du symbolisme* (Paris, 1889), pp. 40ff.

[23] Preface to *A rebours* (1903), *Oeuvres Complètes de J. K. Huysmans* (Paris: Les Editions de G. Crès, 1928–1934), VII, x–xi.

loose and episodic, resembling the corridor images in *Heinrich von Ofterdingen;* on the other hand, its design evokes the tapestry of Mallarmé's prose poems.

In view of Huysmans' profound conflict between the Christian ethic and Schopenhauer's negative alternative—a conflict which had reached a climax just before *A rebours*—the novel emerges both as an elaboration and as a *reductio ad absurdum* of the moral and aesthetic implications of Schopenhauer's philosophy. A release from Schopenhauer's overwhelming and destructive Will can occur only through a negation of life and its conversion into detached art, free of any concepts. Accordingly, Huysmans created a hero whose salvation, indeed, whose very existence, is in the balance as he searches for such an artificial denial of life to achieve a release from the tyranny of the Will.[24]

In *A rebours,* then, the hero's passivity no longer depends on his capacity as an experiencer, or on his ability to absorb or mirror the external world, as it had in early transcendentalism. Rather it depends on his search for a key outside nature through which, in negation, the needed release from causality can be found. The romantic pilgrimage through a world of images is replaced by the inner wanderings of an essentially sedentary self. For Novalis, the hero became part of the universal forms of nature, but, for Huysmans' hero, nature had become defunct; the cricket is in its gilded cage. Des Esseintes is plunged from indulgence into asceticism, into the indulgence of art and, finally, into reflections of himself in literature and painting. The psychological horror of his disintegration is caught in objects which do not raise it to an ideal level but rather detach it in the impersonality of artifice. Deforming experience and bending it into art, Huysmans' hero becomes Moréas' "unique personage," who wears a mask on which the image of the deformed world is imprinted. This negation of life makes itself felt in Huysmans'

[24] For the relationship between Schopenhauer and the concept of the self in symbolist fiction in general, see the recent interesting study by Karl D. Uitti, *The Concept of Self in the Symbolist Novel* (Gravenhage: Mouton and Company, 1961).

satanism through which he sought to recapture Baudelaire's internal drama. Even the attempt to corrupt others cannot have its desired effect.

In its illumination of a degree of passivity which mounts to a negation of life, Huysmans' novel nevertheless availed itself of the pertinent conventions of romantic fiction. We wander through a sequence of internal and symbolic episodes; we find inserted verse and miniature pastiches as well as deliberations about language and literature. But Huysmans employs all these techniques with a negative edge. Partly a fantasy, partly a realistic portrait, *A rebours* is an extended prose poem in which the hero reduces all other persons to objects and transforms even his visions into things, life into form. If toward the end of the novel this solution is called into question, its very structure paradoxically portrays the absurdity of the attempt.

This expansion and negation of the romantic premise establish *A rebours* as an illustration of the symbolist hero and of the method of the *fin de siècle* prose poem. One of Des Esseintes' theoretical statements includes the claim that the prose poem is the ideal novel because it can contract the novel's substance into one or two pages; "it manages . . . to contain in its small volume, in a state of 'meat,' the power of the novel which suppresses all the analytical passages and descriptive involvements." Huysmans continues that Des Esseintes had often wished to write a *concentrated* novel whose words imply vast perspectives through which the reader can expand his dreams, but which contract experience into single moments portraying time and space simultaneously through their magic power.[25] But although *A rebours,* a loose and extended novel, does not fulfill this prescription, many of its individual passages and scenes reveal its affinity with prose poetry, which is praised as the highest form.

It is easy to see how such a conception of the hero would introduce that "era of passivity" of which Claude-Edmonde Magny

[25] *Oeuvres complètes,* VII, 301–302.

speaks in her history of the French novel.[26] The symbolist hero, like the symbolist poet, externalizes his visions and renders them as art. The major and minor works of prose fiction which appeared in the eighteen-eighties and nineties in Belgium and France share a similar distortion and destruction of the external world. In Edouard Dujardin's *Les Lauriers sont coupés,* this end was sought through an interior monologue, a *tour de force* in which a narrative is developed without the aid of concepts or causality. Others transcend actuality by refashioning allegories, sentimental journeys, even Gothic romances; others still dissolve the known world into vague constellations of feelings. In novels as varied as Villiers de l'Isle Adam's *L'Eve future* and Moréas' *Le Thé chez Miranda,* grotesque scenes and sequences of *tableaux* suggest and deform the outer world, converting the contents of the mind into the contents of art. André Gide's only extended work of narrative prose deliberately written in the symbolist manner, *Le Voyage d'Urien,* is a voyage to nowhere in which symbolic figures appear to passive heroes who sail haphazardly on a vaguely defined ocean of life. To Mallarmé's great relief, these voyagers fail to reach any final port. As they move on continuously in endless successions of way-stations, it becomes clear that the romantic hero and form have been significantly changed. If *Heinrich von Ofterdingen* remained a fragment, we surmise it did so because the ideal was unattainable even in allegory. But if *Le Voyage d'Urien* (which refers us to Novalis) ends nowhere, even though the small book is concluded, we gather that the unattainable has become the ideal.

———6

As romantic aestheticism has radiated from Germany, so symbolist aestheticism has radiated from France to influence the writing of poetry and prose in most western countries. In Germany, for instance, a naturalistic vogue and an equally vigorous revival of lyricism were accompanied at the turn of the century

[26] *Histoire du roman français* (Paris: Edition du Seuil, 1950), pp. 7–40 *passim.*

by a rash of imitations of aestheticist prose poems and tales on the model of Maurice Maeterlinck. But in England the growing effect of symbolism was felt most strongly in poetry. The native tradition of the middle-class novel of manners stood out as a genre almost as inviolate as classical tragedy had been in France.

Toward the end of the century, however, a variety of books appeared in England which seemed at least to modify this impermeable structure. The prose poem, especially in the form of Oscar Wilde's artificial fairy tale, though never an indigenous English form, became a relatively accepted genre. Works of poetic prose such as Wilde's *Picture of Dorian Gray* or Walter Pater's *Child in the House* suggest some of the poetic implications of symbolism. Moreover, poetic interludes, scenes, and lyrical conceptions of heroes intruded upon various English novels. For example, George Meredith's early novels, through their language and imagery, transform outer experience into states of mind by infusing nature with emotion. Preoccupations with symbolic experience, emphasizing essentially passive heroes, are suggested in some of Thomas Hardy's novels, most strikingly, perhaps, in *Jude the Obscure*. But it is no coincidence that the symbolic hero made his most vivid appearance in the fiction of Joseph Conrad, in which narrator and subject are often juxtaposed in a single protagonist who explores the occult meaning of the world of fact.

In contemporary fiction, a poetic form has been often associated with the work of D. H. Lawrence. Compelled to encompass all external life, Lawrence infused characters and scenes with lyrical intensity and often abbreviated his figures into types which his vision illuminated. Especially in such early novels as *The Rainbow,* but also in his later work, Lawrence described life from a perspective in which man fuses with the external world therein to find his soul. Novalis, or even Conrad, placed physical life within a realm of the intellectual or spiritual imagination. But, for Lawrence, physical nature itself was the spirit in which man's intellectual and moral being was to be absorbed.

At the same time, a compulsion for statement more and more obscured the poetic manner of his language and forms; Lawrence's language chants and denotes rather than symbolizes and acts. His poetry, at its best, is a Whitmanesque incantation of facts—of the social environment exorcised with sharp derision and of physical nature celebrated and especially created for his figures. Imagination is rendered as "fact."

A change was produced by the refinement of the stream of consciousness, which in the hands of James Joyce and Virginia Woolf became a formidable tool for poetic fiction. At a time when the "great tradition" of the English novel seemed bankrupt, the symbolic form and the stream of consciousness were welcome innovations. As an outsider, Joyce especially remained close to a poetic tradition. His *Portrait of the Artist as a Young Man* can be read as a lyrical novel par excellence, evoking formally the awareness of a self. But, as our earlier discussion of *Ulysses* has shown, Joyce did not wholly align himself with an idealistic or symbolist position. Stephen's aesthetic theory, insofar as it reflects Joyce's own, modifies symbolism through an Aristotelian distinction between self and thing, while it qualifies Aristotelian realism with an emphasis on the self. In the final analysis, Stephen's famous definition of the drama typifies the omniscient yet poetic point of view which served both Joyce and Virginia Woolf as a means of reconciling a poetic form with the narrative requirements of their genre. The poet's apprehending self first identifies himself with his creation, then withdraws, leaving behind a panorama of figures suffused by an effaced consciousness. To be sure, such a poet enacts the role of the symbolist poet who absorbs a world deformed by his vision and then separates it from himself. But he also becomes a version of the conventional omniscient author who includes an independent world in his poetic perspective. Especially in the work of Virginia Woolf, this delicate balance between a poetry of imagination and a narrative of fact is scrupulously observed.

—7

Lyricism in prose narrative remains, of course, an arbitrary concept which can be discerned in varied forms, but its general outline is recognizable as an image of a modern consciousness which has shaped our thought about the novel. In the nineteenth and twentieth centuries, pressures toward a formal conception of private visions have mounted in proportion to the growing tension of the age between inner and outer experience. Henry James evoked manners and places through particular points of view as well-defined perspectives of the external world. Marcel Proust, as we have seen, converted the memory of his *persona* into a rich tapestry of external life. But others have been more narrowly lyrical. Hermann Hesse fell back on romantic allegory, André Gide on the methods suggested by the symbolist prose poem. Virginia Woolf sought to portray the components of consciousness in a poetic perspective. In any event, symbolic heroes, and their appropriate forms, have lent defining characteristics to a novel which acts as an equivalent of lyrical poetry.

3

ROMANTIC IMAGINATION
Hermann Hesse as a Lyrical Novelist

THE NOVEL AS A DISGUISED LYRIC

— 1

T HE ADORATION of young German readers for Hermann
Hesse during the nineteen-twenties and early thirties was
rooted in a shrewd recognition of a common language. They
shared a peculiar rebellion against the industrial civilization they
held responsible for the past, which expressed itself in an occasionally strained, often sentimental return to nature and spirit:
a revival of romantic values. With the phenomenal success of
Demian (1919), Hesse had made himself the spokesman of this
generation of youth as Thomas Mann had been the spokesman
for the immediately preceding one. In a preface to his selected
works (whose publication he later prevented), Hesse stated his
own sense of his place in the tradition of German letters: "Narrative as a disguised lyric, the novel as a borrowed label for the
experimentations of poetic spirits to express their feeling of self
and world; this was a specifically German and romantic matter,
here I felt immediately a common heritage and guilt." This
guilt, Hesse continues, is shared by many of his contemporaries
and predecessors, for German prose is an enticing instrument
for making music to whose lure many poets have succumbed
without realizing that lyricism must be accompanied by a gift for
storytelling.[1]

---

[1] "Vorrede eines Dichters zu seinen ausgewählten Werken" (1921).
Betrachtungen, Gesammelte Dichtungen (Berlin-Zürich: Suhrkamp Verlag, 1957), VII, 252 (hereafter cited as *Dichtungen;* parentheses in the text
refer to this edition). Hesse's lyricism is stressed by Ernst Robert Curtius,
who points out that Hesse desired neither aesthetic nor social ties but
rather sought immediate self-expression. Hence, Curtius concludes, Hesse's

Although Hesse's awareness of his lyrical conception of narrative was often accompanied by anguish, he felt that in a time of mechanization there is a great need for a survival of romantic values, of which he saw himself as the last standard-bearer. He admired Thomas Mann's ability, in *Doktor Faustus,* to equip his showcases lavishly with characters and scenes, to create a world of profusion against which Leverkühn's organized and transparent inner world stands out in sharp relief.[2] But Hesse's work as a whole seems to invoke Novalis and Hölderlin—or Indian and Chinese thinkers who, it seemed to him, expressed similar ideas—to show that the lively world of experience finds its most subtle reflection in a heightened vision of the self caught by the magic of art. In a preface to an American edition of *Demian,* Mann himself distinguished between his own intellectual and Hesse's lyrical bent: "Very likely in my own country I was nothing but a gray sparrow of the intellect among a flock of emotional Hartz songsters. . . . But Hesse? What ignorance, what lack of culture, to banish this nightingale . . . from its German grove, this lyric poet whom Moerike would have embraced with emotion, who has produced from our language images of purest and most delicate form."[3] It is quite true, as Ernst Robert Curtius has suggested, that this amazingly faithful

works are lyrical rather than epic, for the world implied by the latter is absent in them. "Hermann Hesse," *Kritische Essays zur europäischen Literatur* (Bern: A. Francke, 1950), pp. 212–213. In *Die Nürnberger Reise* (1928), Hesse identifies the romantic spirit with an anti-modern spirit and readily allies himself with it; *Dichtungen,* IV, 128–129. Hesse's authoritative biographer, Hugo Ball, speaks of his subject as the "letzte Ritter aus dem glanzvollen Zuge der Romantik"; *Hermann Hesse: Sein Leben und Werk* (Berlin: S. Fischer, 1927), pp. 26–27. For a fuller study of Hesse's relationship to German romanticism, see the Bern dissertation by Kurt Weibel, *Hermann Hesse und die deutsche Romantik* (Winterthur: P. G. Keller, 1954).

[2] Letter to Thomas Mann, 12 Dec. 1947 in *Briefe, Dichtungen,* VII, 668–670.

[3] "Foreword," *Demian* (New York: Henry Holt and Company, 1948), p. vi; "Einleitung zu einer amerikanischen Demianausgabe," *Die Neue Rundschau* (1947), p. 246.

reproduction of the romantic tradition has placed Hesse outside the main stream of the European novel from Flaubert to Joyce, Gide, and Mann.[4] But Hesse used romanticism as a tool for the development of a unique approach, leading to a sharp analysis of the self, the meaning of personal identity and the conditions of self-consciousness, which he explores in contemporary terms.

— 2

Hesse's new kind of romanticism is perhaps best expressed in two famous titles: *Blick ins Chaos* (1920) and *Weg nach Innen* (1931).[5] The fashionable romantic form that had been his stock in trade for some time moved in an oddly analytic direction. Hesse's postwar novels are concerned with the inner world turned inside out, yielding not only dreams, memories, or hallucinations *per se* but also the world underlying perception, which is dissolved and recomposed in the self's inner landscape. If Hölderlin's Hyperion and Novalis' Heinrich reflect their encounters directly in expressions of feeling and symbolic images, Hesse's protagonists penetrate further to the conditions of awareness, exhibiting society and nature in an internal perspective.

As it confronts the world, the self seeks to absorb its opponent. In a frightening scene in "Eine Traumfolge," included in *Märchen* (1919), the protagonist seizes society's most offensive exemplar and hammers him to his liking. (III, 329–330) Characters opposing an alien social reality, whether in "Klein und Wagner" or *Der Steppenwolf,* are dissolved either through death or schizophrenia. This alien reality or "world" is variously identified with anything seemingly external to the self, including

[4] Curtius, "Hermann Hesse," pp. 215ff.

[5] Kurt Weibel identifies the *Weg nach Innen* with Hesse's affinity for German romanticism which finds its apex in *Siddhartha.* Beyond *Siddhartha,* he suggests a new direction, moving toward an affirmation of man's place as a skilled practitioner of his craft within the universal harmony—an attainment suggesting a Goethean "classicism" of (masculine) *Geist.* See *Hermann Hesse und die deutsche Romantik,* pp. 7f., 24–28, 76–77, *et passim.*

objects of perception, non-intuitive reasoning, social pressures, or mercantilism; in short, it is a very wide concept and includes the very world of perception as well as contemporary reality. If, then, the self attempts to come to terms with the world by uniting it with its psyche, it can be successful only if the experiences absorbed by the self are not inimical to "nature," that is, to sensuous reality. In *Narziss und Goldmund,* the natural world of *Bilder* within the self (of Goldmund) is easily linked with experiences of nature; only then can the intellect (Narziss) intervene and impose form upon the sensuous-natural material. But if the "world" is immediately identified with a non-intuitive, anti-sensuous, or even dehumanized world, the kind of failure must result which Hesse describes in his *Nürnberger Reise* (1928). As in perception both form and sensuous content are joined in the self, so the tension between a sensuous self and a hostile, desensualized world must also be joined in the self. Hesse is forced to deal with the conflict of self and world, sense and intellect, quite as much in psychological as in social or intellectual terms.[6]

The perennial split between the individual and the world beyond him is portrayed, not in dramatic action, but in symbolic or allegorical self-representation. Echoing Novalis' idea of the artist as a supreme mimic dissolving alien existence in himself, Hesse renders his conflicts as symbolic "self-portraits." In his novels, representative characters mirror their divided selves in drawings, statues, and fictional biographies. As might be expected, these figures also depict their divided condition with sharply psychological implications, evolving schizophrenic dis-

---

[6] Poetry (an intuitive, sensual apprehension of the world) must lead to "Streit und Zerfall mit der Wirklichkeit"; *Dichtungen,* IV, 149.

This explains the dual conflict which is so often seen in Hesse, that is, the conflict of the self with the external world and the conflict within the self. As the self seeks to absorb the world, the two oppositions coincide. Cf. Peter Heller, "The Creative Unconscious and the Spirit: A Study of Polarities in Hesse's Image of the Writer," *Modern Language Forum,* XXXVIII (March–June, 1953), 28–40.

tortions far more intense than those envisaged by Novalis. These
psychological self-portraits include particularly Hesse's versions
of the "eternal self" regulating the "I" of poet and hero. Besides
functioning as a Freudian superego, or, more pertinently, as a
Jungian collective unconscious, this higher aspect of the self acts
as a *daemon* who guards its activities and comments upon them
ironically.[7] Hidden faculties of control, as well as possible resolutions of inner conflict between self and world, are revealed externally by teachers and guides like Demian or Leo of *Die Morgenlandfahrt*. Internally, they might appear as the hero's double
vision—images of the inner man in which both the ideal and the
mortal self are juxtaposed.

Hesse's various interpretations of the artist's relationship with
his experience turn primarily on the opposition of sense and intellect, which is associated with that of dark and light, mother
and father, sensuality and ascetic control. An analysis of Hesse's
use of these categories shows them to be elusive. *Geist,* both
spirit and intellect, includes diverse connotations, ranging from
the regulating, paternal force of control to the destructive
power of a rationalistic culture, although often it also includes
the clarity of a divinely rational spirit. Its counterpoint, *Seele,*
on the other hand, is both sensuality and soul, associated with
sexuality, debauch, sense experience, and the recognition of the
mother image or the collective unconscious.[8] There is no doubt

[7] "[Ich] kenne besser als irgendeiner den Zustand, in welchem das ewige
Selbst in uns dem sterblichen Ich zuschaut und seine Sprünge und
Grimassen begutachtet, voll Mitleid, voll Spott, voll Neutralität." *Die
Nürnberger Reise, Dichtungen,* IV, 158–159. In "Kindheit des Zauberers,"
the universalizing, controlling force of the self, referred to as the "demon,"
is *der kleine Mann* who compels the child Hesse to follow him and who
directs even the activities of Hesse, the older magician and grown artist
(IV, 458ff.).

See also Oskar Seidlin, "Hermann Hesse: the Exorcism of the Demon,"
Symposium, IV (Nov. 1950), 327–328, 337, *et passim.*

[8] See Seidlin, "Exorcism of the Demon," p. 333. For specific discussions
of *Geist,* see Max Schmid, *Hermann Hesse: Weg und Wandlung* (Zürich:
Fretz und Wasmuth, 1947), pp. 108, 123–125, 210–217. See also "The

about Hesse's primary impulses: in *Narziss und Goldmund* integration was to have taken place chiefly through *Seele,* in *Das Glasperlenspiel* through *Geist.* But intuitively he weighs his evidence on the side of *Seele.* Sexuality, the world of the senses, must be experienced in its wholeness; it must be reflected in the magic vision of the imagination—the lesson of *Der Steppenwolf.* Sensuality makes possible artistic integration, but it must be wedded to the ordering intellect or else chaos will result—the lesson of *Narziss und Goldmund.* Even in *Das Glasperlenspiel,* its hero, Josef Knecht, turns his back on the paradise of *Geist* and reenters sensual nature, there to find his death. Indeed, although Hesse greatly admired *Geist* and thought it indispensable to artistic creation, he nowhere allowed it to triumph in the end: neither in the intuitive vision of harmony in *Siddhartha* nor in the ethereal clarity of *Das Glasperlenspiel.*[9]

A reciprocal tension of *Geist* and *Seele,* then, is woven into the fabric of Hesse's narratives. Continuously requiring and counteracting one another, these opposing poles act like antinomies which recall Fichte's *Wechselwirkung,* the thought underlying Novalis' and Hölderlin's *Fragmente,* and even Schiller's opposition of *Form* and *Stoff* to be reconciled in the *Spiel* of art. In consonance with this analogy, Hesse views the artist's *Stoff,*

Creative Unconscious," pp. 35–36. Heller cautiously suggests that integration through *Geist* does not take place even in *Das Glasperlenspiel* (pp. 39–40).

Max Schmid develops the opposition of *Geist* and *Seele* in his attempt to show Hesse's relationship to Ludwig Klages' *Kosmogenischer Eros* and *Der Geist als Widersacher der Seele; Weg und Wandlung,* pp. 12–14, 94–96, 100–102, 210ff. *et passim.*

[9] Intuitive vision or *Schau* need not be that of *Geist.* For a comparison of the "romantic" vision of harmony in *Siddhartha* and the "classical" vision of harmony in *Das Glasperlenspiel,* see Max Schmid, *Weg und Wandlung,* pp. 210–211. Yet the end of *Das Glasperlenspiel* suggests that the absolute dominion of *Geist* is called into question by Knecht's rejection of Castalia and by his "legendary" death in the mountain lake. See also Hilde Cohn, "The Symbolic End of Herman Hesse's *Glasperlenspiel,*" *Modern Language Quarterly,* xi (Sept. 1950), 347–357.

the material of *Seele,* as the sensual component which entails
sexuality. Indeed, Hesse's concept of *Seele* in the double sense
of non-intellectual, intuitive vision (*Schau*) and sensuality enables him to move from the opposition of creative sensuality
(feminine) and controlling intellectuality (masculine) to their
integration, literally, in an over-soul, a transcendental soul. On
the way to this union of *Seele* and *Geist* in a heightened self,
Hesse's characters often reenact Christian salvation from and
through the immersion in sensuality. The search for fulfillment,
which for Hesse seems to involve both the Augustinian notion
and Nietzschean transcendence, is shown in many different
ways: in Klein's and Knecht's deaths by water, or, in *Demian,*
in Sinclair's final vision at the moment of his death. On these
occasions, *Seele* is raised from a psychological to a metaphysical
level of existence as resolution approaches; it is transferred from
a sensual to a transcendental plane. But this transcendental *Seele*
is not unrelated to the *Seelenwelt* of the artist's material. In her
double function of mistress and mother, woman embodies for
Hesse the libidinal force which represents the artist's material
(the world of nature he must incorporate and merge with his
own) and the maternal goal, the *Urgrund,* in which salvation
and aesthetic reconciliation are found.[10] "We all," Hesse says
in his introduction to *Demian,* "come out of the same abyss."
(III, 100) In the womb, the original matrix of experience, what-

---

[10] In "Eine Traumfolge," the symbol for art is a woman, mysterious
but decidedly sexual, who dissolves into a child as the artist carries her
into a different realm; *Dichtungen,* III, 330–331. In "Märchen," the artist's
song is made possible by a kiss which from then on inspires his art;
Dichtungen, III, 296. Indeed, the artist's search is intrinsically sexual; sequences of debauch, in "Augustus" or "Klingsors letzter Sommer," in
Knulp and "Klein und Wagner," and in *Siddhartha, Demian, Der Steppenwolf* and *Narziss und Goldmund* act as moments of essential experience, as the matter that goes into the making of art.

Max Schmid views Klein's death as a dissolution of the self in the
stream of experience, Knecht's death as self-discovery through which the
master can pass on his mission to his pupil; *Weg und Wandlung,* pp. 49–
50, 189–191.

ever its possibilities of chaos may be, integration is reached. By acquiring a vision of this ground, the poet can attain to *Seele* in its transcendental function. He can, with Novalis, become the "transcendental physician." [11]

Hesse appears to use a variety of related concepts to express the relationship between the personal self which absorbs the contradictory flow of experience and some higher or symbolic self in which its oppositions are resolved. These include the unities of Yoga mysticism and Jung's collective unconscious. The obvious indebtedness of this notion to the romantic reconciliation of opposites reminiscent of Schiller and Novalis, however, does not obscure Hesse's peculiarly analytic twist. It is of no small moment that the self and ideal self mirrored in one another correspond to the libidinal self and its universal archetype. The absolute has been derived from psychological experience which is raised to its higher level through the mystic's insight or the artist's imagination.

—3

For a contemporary romantic like Hermann Hesse, the novelist projects inner schisms into a hero who ultimately raises his inadequate sensual self to the state of a harmonious or symbolic self. As we have seen, the conflict between self and world is projected into an ego that can unify them only in mystical revelation or in the illusion induced by art. For Hesse, these two realms are interdependent—the mystic's vision encompassing more fully any unity achieved by art, the poet's apprehension sustaining in time the harmonies briefly envisioned in the mystic's trance. Both function through an act of will, which is efficacious in a realm of creative illusion. In *Siddhartha,* Hesse suggests that the soul is ready to achieve unity by being able to

Miss Cohn views Knecht's death in water as a symbolic act through which the spirit can be passed from teacher to pupil. In her judgment, the maternal archetype of water, a Jungian notion, is combined with the Christian idea of baptism and rebirth. "The Symbolic End," pp. 355–356.

[11] "Neue Fragmentensammlungen," 1798, *Schriften,* II, 326.

think the idea of unity at any given time within the manifold
stream of experience. (III, 716, 720) The artist, however, reenacts this vision or *Schau* through his imagination.

Two principles are involved in this concept of the imagination,
both of which are reminiscent of Novalis. The relationship between the self in the world of sense and its higher projection
suggests Novalis' notion of "romanticising." The dual nature
of the aesthetic act as mystical integration and as psychological
dissolution and resolution parallels Novalis' use of the term
"magic" as a merging of dissonances which may manifest itself
as madness in individual experience but which, publicly exhibited
and consciously applied according to rules, becomes analogous
to art.[12] Hesse's concept of "magic" is quite similar, although it
has been enriched by Jungian, Buddhist, and Taoist thought,
and is directed more fully toward a penetration of the individual
consciousness.

For Hesse, the poet, or his *persona,* apprehends the manifold
and refashions it into a form of the imagination. Magic, then,
corresponds to the creative will of the imagination. In the slight
fantasy "Kindheit des Zauberers" the poet himself is a magician,
who, as Hesse puts it elsewhere, "forces reality, through magic,
to suit his meaning." (IV, 487) A mature version is the "magic
theater" of *Der Steppenwolf,* in which an imaginary stage represents spiritual unity comprising the dissonances of the inner and
outer life. The schizophrenic hero, who is projected onto this
stage, is shown how to discover such a unity, and to accept with
detachment its illusory character.

Magic, so conceived, supersedes temporal sequence and even
verbal expression. Jean Paul Richter had demanded that poetry
should speak through the objects of nature, transcending the
analytic world of philistines and pedants.[13] Hesse's narratives
may express the hope for a language which can "say the un-

[12] See Novalis' definitions of "magical idealism," "Das allgemeine Brouillon," *Schriften,* III, 227–228; "Neue Fragmentensammlungen," *Schriften,*
II, 335–339.
[13] *Werke,* Part I, 233.

sayable" as in *Der Steppenwolf* or show a preference for those characters who communicate through images rather than words as in *Narziss und Goldmund*. They include innumerable examples in which visionary belief or the myth of poetry are held more effective than discourse or reasoning—the tools of *Geist*. A similar prejudice against temporal progression is suggested in the amusing climax of Hesse's whimsical autobiography, "Kurzgefasster Lebenslauf." The author (a modern Socrates waiting for his hemlock in the nightmare of a Kafkaesque bureaucracy) climbs on the train of his own painting and disappears in a cloud of smoke.[14] The "dull consecutiveness" of time has been canceled out in a world of appearance and play. Hesse's narrative and descriptive techniques implement this view of "magic" in peculiarly modern terms.

— 4

The moment of reconciliation must be frozen in time. To elicit "magic" from the materials of crude experience, Hesse must represent unity within the flow of time. The artist must capture the mystic's vision through his medium of words. This relationship between "dull consecutiveness" and the vision of integrating magic, particularly evident in the novel, had been thoroughly explored in romantic aesthetics.

In practice, Hesse borrows a good deal from romantic sources, notably from Novalis, to portray the relation between the time-bound experiences which his protagonists encounter and their reflections in timeless art. Two motifs or methods, suggestive of *Heinrich von Ofterdingen,* have been used with particular frequency. The first of these is the poetic symbol, the Blue Flower of poetry, through which the ideal above time can be portrayed simultaneously with a movement through time (the quest). The fairy tale "Iris," for example, borrows from Novalis the description of Anselmus' search for a flower which represents mystical vision and, ultimately, art. In Hesse's postwar novels, specific

[14] *Dichtungen,* IV, 487–489. "Kurzgefasster Lebenslauf" was written with Jean Paul's "Konjekturalbiographie" in mind. (IV, 469)

symbols such as the sparrow hawk and "Abraxas" in *Demian* or the flower symbolism of *Der Steppenwolf* portray reconciliations of opposites like light and dark, intellect and soul, unity and manifold beyond the time-bound order of the characters' lives. But for Hesse the object of the quest often represents not only poetry but also a hoped-for or achieved resolution of schizophrenic states through which a torn self is raised to a condition of illusory magic. Even in periods in which Hesse suppressed psychological meanings, he chose aesthetic symbols, such as statues in *Narziss und Goldmund* and *Die Morgenlandfahrt* or the Game of Glass Beads in *Das Glasperlenspiel,* to represent a unification of dissonances frozen in time through sensibly or intuitively accessible representation.

The second method posits a wanderer through space and time who acts as a perceiving eye, that is, as the passive romantic hero, in whom encounters and dreams are mirrored as art. Hesse poignantly utilizes the theme of wandering in *Der Novalis* (1907, published 1940), in which the structure and symbolism of *Heinrich von Ofterdingen* are suggested by a description of the transformations suffered by an old copy of Novalis' works. This story epitomizes the characteristic tension in Hesse's narratives between the world of images experienced in consecutive time and the sensibility of the experiencer which they ultimately portray. Moreover, as Hesse uses this method, perception is turned inward. Like Wilhelm Meister and Heinrich von Ofterdingen, Goldmund and Haller wander through the world of sense and symbolic dream, their sensibilities modified by events and encounters. But Hesse, the twentieth-century novelist, dissects them more sharply. Unlike Wilhelm and Heinrich, Goldmund and Haller move through worlds which mirror, directly and allegorically, their internal states of mind, that is, disintegrations and resolutions occurring beneath the ordinary level of conscious and even unconscious experience.

Music and painting are likewise effectively employed to portray a union of opposites beyond time. Music functions as a combination of contradictory elements in self and world, either pro-

ducing the dissonance of their continuous conflict, which it is
the artist's hopeless task to resolve, or harmonizing opposites
in the "appearance" of art. In the famous passage from *Der
Kurgast,* Hesse dramatizes this point in terms of a significant
personal longing:

> If I were a musician I could write without difficulty a melody
> in two voices, a melody which consists of two notes and se-
> quences which correspond to each other, which complement
> each other, which condition each other, which in any event
> stand to one another in the closest and liveliest reciprocity
> and mutual relationship. And anyone who can read music,
> could read my double melody, could see and hear in each tone
> its counterpoint, the brother, the enemy, the antipode. Well,
> and just this double-voiced melody and eternally moving an-
> tithesis, this double line I want to express with my own mate-
> rial, with words, and I work myself sore at it, and it doesn't
> work. (IV, 113)

As a writer, Hesse longs to be a musician, not because he might
feel more at home in a non-literary métier,[15] but because music
embodies the very concept of harmony within dissonance which
is his prevailing theme. The clash of opposites and their reconciliation is not only heard and made visually apparent to the
reader of musical notations; it is also dramatized. As each note
is accompanied by its antipode, it catches moments of unity in
a world where contrasts shift, unite, and separate. In one sense,
this view of music takes on a psychological dimension, as an
expression of schizophrenia caught by the musical interplay of
contrasting motifs. But in another sense, the *Wechselwirkung* of
the antipodes is reminiscent of Fichte's *Wissenschaftslehre* and
especially of Schiller's dialectic of form and matter and their
reconciliation in the *Schein* of art.

In its function of presenting simultaneously the harmony and
dissonance of opposing motifs, music seems to solve the conflicts

---

[15] Cf. Curtius, "Hermann Hesse," pp. 213–214.

in self and world. It is, in the phrase of Wackenroder and Tieck's *Phantasien über die Kunst,* the only art form which "reduces the most manifold and most contradictory movements of our soul to the *same* beautiful harmonies." [16] As we shall see, music functions as precisely such a symbol in *Das Glasperlenspiel.* It resolves dissonance by organizing experience and directing it toward a total vision rather than toward its consecutive or analytic explication. In this way, music can be seen, with Bettina von Arnim, as the quintessence of imagination. It is "the infinite within the finite, the element of genius present in all forms of art." [17] Its language, composed of magic formulae, is apt to frighten away philistines as new, indefinable worlds are opened up. An example of this view of music is Hesse's famous distinction in *Der Steppenwolf* between *rauschende* and *heitere Musik.* The former is chaotic music, likened to that of Wagner. A deceptive vision of unity is achieved by the massive sound which blurs boundaries between contradictory elements and themes. Its chaos, apparently triumphant, merely reflects diversity in an indistinguishable mass. The latter is clear, detached music likened to that of Mozart. Its ordered harmonies show the interplay of contrasting motifs with precision; its detachment prevents the blurring of boundaries between self and world and so reflects an independent unity.[18]

If music deepens the melody of life and catches it in art, the effect of painting works precisely in the opposite direction: it freezes the fluid manifold of experience in timeless portraiture. Hesse himself was a diligent water colorist and occasionally he even dreamed of turning to painting altogether as one of his

[16] *Phantasien über die Kunst, für Freunde der Kunst* (1799). Cited in *Kunstanschauung der Frühromantik,* ed. Andreas Müller (Leipzig: Philipp Reclam, 1931), p. 114.

[17] *Goethes Briefwechsel mit einem Kinde,* I, 181f.; II, 283f. Cited in *Kunstanschauung der jüngeren Romantik,* ed. Andreas Müller (Leipzig: Philipp Reclam, 1934), pp. 226–227.

[18] See *Der Steppenwolf, Dichtungen,* IV, 402–403; *Das Glasperlenspiel, Dichtungen,* VI, 99–100.

major forms of expression. His small landscapes are reminiscent of romantic idylls: a church by a lake, a cluster of trees and houses, a cottage amid mountains with dusk drawing over the darkening water. His pictures are distinguished by an obvious desire to be precise both in the literal rendering of his subject and in the feelings he wished to convey. In his fiction, however, he viewed painting more analytically and metaphorically as a means of enhancing the idea of unity in illusion: the magic painting on the prison wall in "Kurzgefasster Lebenslauf." Diverse experiences, entire inner worlds are gathered in pictures: the statues carved by Goldmund and the peepshow sequences viewed by Haller. In each case, the inner world in which time is not necessarily a factor and the outer world which exists in time are rendered together to lend themselves to instantaneous apprehension.

In Hesse's narratives, pictorial presentation occurs in two important ways. One significant usage is that of the idyll as suggested in Jean Paul Richter's novels and in Friedrich Schlegel's notion of the arabesque. In "Kurzgefasster Lebenslauf," the idyllic picture is humorously treated; in *Nürnberger Reise,* changing landscapes are often portrayed through the author's changing attitudes in the act of painting. Throughout Hesse's novels, stories, and fairy tales, idyllic moments and scenes occur as essential structural elements through which the hero's quest is accentuated and ultimately defined. But in another usage, that of the self-portrait, painting has a further symbolic function. Like Heinrich von Ofterdingen, who reads his own life as a book of pictures in the Hermit's cave, Hesse's protagonists, and occasionally the author himself, depict their experiences so as to unify past, present, and future in a single moment of apprehension. Perhaps the most striking example of this method, extending Novalis' view of the interrelation of the arts, is the self-portrait drawn by the hero in "Klingsors letzter Sommer," which combines the effects of painting and music through a poetic description.[19]

[19] "Neue Fragmentensammlungen" (1798), *Schriften,* ii, 359.

In the context of the narrative, Klingsor draws his self-portrait against a background of the "music of doom," which he hears as an accompaniment to his painting. This music frees Klingsor from a need to represent himself and his inner world naturalistically, because its harmonies and dissonances dissolve spatial forms. It liberates his vision so that the painting he creates is a self-portrait embodying less its object, his own image, than his inner dissolution within the context of a larger world. It leads him to modify the world as he perceives it and to absorb it into his imagination. At the same time that music releases the limitations of his painting, his painting acts to control the chaotic implications of the experience of music, setting spatial limits and distributions into which the musically inspired vision of intoxicated harmony can be placed. As a result, the painting is a double exposure of a limited self and an unlimited universe. It emerges as a work of imagination which expresses Hesse's view of the function of art as the heightened image of the self, in which self and world are imposed upon one another in creative illusion.

> And not only his own features or his own thousand faces did he paint upon this picture, not merely his eyes and lips, the suffering gorge of his mouth, the split rock of his forehead, the root-like hands, the twitching fingers, the contempt of reason, death in his eye. He also painted, in his self-willed, crowded, compressed and twitching signature, his belief, his despair. (III, 611–612)

This painting is not composed of the orderly sequence of pictures that Heinrich von Ofterdingen views in the hermit's cave. It is rather a condensed image of world and man, produced by a kind of "magic," in which seemingly disparate elements, landscapes and features, coalesce. This rationale of Klingsor's self-portrait also applies to other works. In *Narziss und Goldmund,* different images are marshaled in the orderly sequence of allegorical progression, yet they are gathered up in the statue carved by Goldmund. In the Game of *Das Glasperlenspiel,* which can be seen simultaneously as musical harmony and abstract representation, distinct elements are condensed into a "picture" denuded of any visualizable aspects. Elsewhere, portraitures abound in Hesse's work, depicting the inner man as he absorbs an alien world and resolving his conflict in timeless images.

In this way, all of Hesse's techniques—from picaresque structures to music and painting—suggest a concept of the imagination which combines the nineteenth-century reconciliation of opposites with a twentieth-century meaning of psychological conflict. His solution in the novel, based on the passive hero of the romantic tradition, is a *lyrical* solution. Three of his postwar works which have determined his reputation—*Demian, Der Steppenwolf,* and *Das Glasperlenspiel*—serve to measure the extent and limitation of Hesse's success in a romantic version of the lyrical novel.

THE SYMBOLIC HERO

—1

In most lyrical fiction, the concept of the hero presupposes the notion of the romantic protagonist and his symbolic identification with the author. Rejecting dramatic objectivity, Hesse believed that the writer's detachment does not necessarily consist in his effacement by a fictional world but in aesthetic self-portraits achieved through representative heroes. In his introduction to *Demian,* he clarifies this point: "Poets, when they write novels, usually act as if they were God and could survey any human story and grasp and depict it as if God were telling it himself. . . . This I cannot do, as little as these poets can do it." (III, 101) Instead, the poet should step into his hero's shoes to reflect his personal experience. Ironic play on the close identification of author and hero abounds in Hesse's work. For example, the name of Emil Sinclair, the hero of *Demian,* coincides with the pseudonym Hesse had used in the early editions of the book. Elsewhere he endows his heroes with his own initials, as in *Die Morgenlandfahrt,* or gives them versions of his own name, as in *Der Steppenwolf*. The reason behind this whimsical method is the same as Tieck's: to ensure a direct relationship as well as distance between the living self and its artistic creation.

Demian (1919), Hesse's first postwar novel, marks a radical departure from his previous work. Books like *Unterm Rad* (1905) and *Rosshalde* (1914) were important as mirrors of their time; the vagabond picaresque *Knulp* (1915) had etched out the contours of a new romanticism. But *Demian* is remarkable for its unique presentation of a symbolic hero in a poetic form without disturbing the main outlines of the conventional novel. Both the story and the structure are concentrated in the only palpable figure, Emil Sinclair. In his hour of death (he has been mortally wounded in battle), he tells how he had found maturity after a life of anxiety and doubt and how this self-discovery had issued in a comprehensive vision of a new world rising from death and chaos. His story, clearly symbolic of German youth engulfed by the First World War, contains two elements: a consecutive movement based on the *Bildungsroman* and a gathering of this action in a pattern of images rendering the hero's vision as a portrait. On the one hand, Hesse recaptures with great precision the talk and manners of schoolboys and students. But on the other hand, by interlacing consecutive action with patterns of imagery, he succeeds masterfully in blending the actual and the occult so that the reader lives in both worlds simultaneously.

The *Bildungsroman* describes Emil Sinclair's growth from childhood to maturity. It is developed in three stages. The first is the child's sudden awareness of anxiety and guilt at the threshold of puberty, as he realizes that the universe is divided into the respectable world of "light," inhabited by his parents and sisters, and the sinister, yet always subconsciously attractive world of "dark," which looms at the fringes of middle-class existence. At this crucial juncture Max Demian, his boyhood friend and lifetime guide, emerges to teach him the gospel of the Elect: the need to realize oneself at all cost and to transcend all the conventional dichotomies of good and evil. The former is expressed by the idea of the Sign of Cain signifying the initiates who do not shrink even from fratricide to fulfill their destiny; the latter is caught in the emblem of the two-headed Persian god Abraxas, who combines within him the male and the female, God and Satan.

The second stage is an intermediate phase during which Demian is mostly absent and Sinclair, now a student in high school, becomes more and more the victim of his fascination for the world of "dark." Away from home in the provincial city, the perennial outsider delights in being for once accepted in the company of those who set themselves above the common crowd through their wild living and drinking. But the accompanying dissatisfaction and guilt also lead Sinclair to new aspirations. His recognition of pure love at this stage of sexual awakening comes to him through a vision of feminine beauty—a girl whom he identifies with a picture and then seeks to paint, i.e., to recreate as an internal image. Abruptly, this experience leads him to sever his connections with the world of "dark" and to turn toward guides and teachers who might show him the way to higher stages of self-realization. This phase is also marked by his important relationship with an unconventional organist and ex-theologian, Pistorius, who, knowing "Abraxas," shows Sinclair the importance of the inner vision and of the efficacy of the human will in transcending the external world.

In the third phase, the contrived formula of the *Bildungsroman* is altogether dissolved in a mystical vision. When Sinclair meets Demian again as a young adult, he had come to accept self-transcendence, achieved by a lengthy and arduous effort, as the true meaning of Demian's teaching. The reunion with his friend is equivalent to the union of the self with its ideal image, which is now broadened to include not only Demian but also the figure of the universal Mother. Significantly named Frau Eva, Demian's mother leads Sinclair to apprehend the entire world in a single vision. But his love for Frau Eva is not consummated until, on his death-bed, he receives from Demian her saving kiss. At this point Sinclair realizes that all the figures and visions that had appeared to him on the road to salvation had really been images within his own soul.

———2

As a symbolic hero, Emil Sinclair is obsessed by a need to render himself completely. Both the manner of his confession and the theme of the novel are expressed in the sentence Hesse also used as a motto: "I only wanted to try to live completely what sought to break out of me. Why was that so hard?" (III, 189–190, 101). Underlying this tortured question are concepts of the self, and of the unconscious, which define not only Sinclair as a character, and the physiognomies of the other figures, but also the form of the novel.

Aspiring to complete self-revelation as the first step toward salvation, Hesse's hero values the latent powers of the subconscious as more significant than either mental abstraction or the natural universe. (See III, 102.) In the early stages, the hero withdraws from external reality into an exclusively inner world, which is the subject of his confession. "Images, pictures or wishes rose within me and drew me away from the external world so that I had livelier and more real intercourse with these dreams or shadows than with my actual environment." (III, 188) [20] In viewing bizarre forms, Sinclair realizes how boundaries between impression and fantasy, the external and the internal, can be blurred, how the self can create forms which reflect the universal act of creation. (III, 198) In the final stages these visions of the universal power are identified with the hero's self-portrait, concentrated image, or symbol, of the self.

The allegorical quest is also a tour de force in self-revelation, involving special concepts of the unconscious and of the self as a symbol. In the introduction, obviously intended as an integral part of the novel, Hesse writes: "Every man . . . is not only

[20] "Darum leben die meisten Menschen so unwirklich [Pistorius also tells Sinclair], weil sie die Bilder ausserhalb für das Wirkliche halten und ihre eigene Welt in sich gar nicht zu Worte kommen lassen." *Dichtungen,* III, 206.

himself; he is also the unique, very special point at which the world's appearances intersect, only once in this way and never again." (III, 101) Sinclair's growing realization of this uniqueness and universality of the self is rendered in the novel both psychologically and philosophically. His concealed wishes and guilt feelings have recognizable, if delicately presented, psychoanalytic implications. Most classic of all is the entire conception of the theme: the Jungian projection of the individual toward the universal unconscious. At the same time, these directly accessible psychoanalytic meanings are supplemented by mysticism. The inner life of Hesse's protagonist is informed by ideas which vaguely intermingle Zoroasterism, the Nietzschean "transvaluation" of good and evil, and Schopenhauer's demonic Will. Like the psychological allusions, these ideas, however imprecise, point toward the hero as the crucial vessel of the novel's theme and form.[21]

[21] For the combination of psychoanalytic motifs with mystical, and theological symbols, see Edmund Gnefkow, *Hermann Hesse. Biographie 1952* (Freiburg in Br.: Gerhard Kirchoff Verlag, 1952), pp. 20–21, 48, 70ff.; Richard B. Matzig, *Hermann Hesse in Montagnola. Studien zu Werk und Innenwelt des Dichters* (Basel: Amberbach Verlag, 1947), pp. 15–16. Hugo Ball calls *Demian* "an infernal journey through the self" and clearly relates it to an "acting out" of a psychological experience. *Hermann Hesse,* p. 159. Rudolf Schmid points out that all effects in the novel are bound to the individual; action upon others is really action against the self; *Hermann Hesse,* p. 149. Max Schmid speaks of the work as representing the symbolism of Hesse's *Weg nach Innen,* embodying the conflict of consciousness and experience, as a simultaneous surrender and challenge of the outside world; *Weg und Wandlung,* p. 39. The strongest statement is that of Foran, who declares that the only value in *Demian* is its therapeutic value for Hesse; *Queens Quarterly,* LV (1948), 185–186.

The exclusive emphasis on the psychoanalytic meaning of the novel is disputed by both Gnefkow and Max Schmid, who stress Hesse's use of Indian and Persian myths and his general religious preoccupations in *Demian.* The most vigorous opposition to the psychoanalytic interpretation comes from Oskar Seidlin, who sees in Sinclair's quest the universal human myth of the exorcism of the demon, which portrays the search for self-liberation from "awakening" to a religious *Urerlebnis.* "Exorcism,"

In his introduction, Hesse proclaims that *Demian* is neither smoothly fashioned nor easy to read "like conventional stories"; it is tincted by madness and dream "like the lives of all men who refuse to lie." (III, 102) The complete expression of the self is identified with the vision of the world as an internal image. Developed from the inner man, who includes all dichotomies within himself, this "true reality" creates the self in its symbolic function.

⟶3

Within the allegorical structure, the stages of the hero's progress are marked by three characters. But they are not only guides leading him to his ascending visions; they are also pictures of his own changing condition. An ultimate unity, this triad of figures embodies Hesse's thesis of the "manifold within unity." Demian is the most inclusive figure, supplemented by the other two members of the triad, the intercessor, Pistorius, and the "mother," Frau Eva. Signifying the elect, Demian is Sinclair's transcendental ideal; as part of the latter's vision, he is also an aspect of the hero's self.

Although on the surface Demian is described realistically—first as a schoolboy, later as a student, and finally as a mature intellectual and soldier—supernatural traits are not far beneath the surface. Passages showing him as a person of insight and character are soon matched by accounts of his truly supernatural wisdom. He instantly perceives Sinclair's dread of moral degradation, when, beset by a blackmailing classmate, the latter steals money at home to satisfy his oppressor. Possessed of supernatural intuitions, only he can recognize the Sign of Cain on Sinclair, discover the emblem of the sparrow-hawk, or communicate with the hero in an occult correspondence. Occasionally, Demian suggests that supernatural affinities are explained by the will in a state of hypnosis, but Hesse usually broadens

pp. 335ff. See also Matzig's explication of the Abraxas figure, which he views as a symbol for "transvaluation"; *Hermann Hesse in Montagnola*, pp. 21-33.

the examples until such explanations alone are insufficient. (See III, 150ff.) Demian is man, animal, and god. Watching him from afar, Sinclair marvels how his friend "wanders among them [his fellow students] like a star, surrounded by his own atmosphere, following laws of his own." (III, 145) When Sinclair catches him unaware during a class in school, he finds him petrified, unworldly, an image above all conflict. (III, 161) This withdrawal is that of a timeless self: ". . . for I saw in his [Demian's] glance . . . this odd, animal-like timelessness, this unthinkable age." (III, 157) In this way, Demian is transformed from a natural state to that of an inanimate *symbol,* representing the higher vision.

As a figure both timeless and acting in time, Demian's function is also an internal one. He appears and disappears, but even in his physical absences he is a typical symbol in Sinclair's mind, ready to be called upon whenever he is needed. Sporadically dropping out of sight after the events of early boyhood, he returns briefly when Sinclair is about to destroy himself by drinking and debauch. His final reappearance, as we noted, coincides with the hero's deepest understanding, and he is eventually joined with Sinclair at the moment of a death. Even Sinclair asks himself whether Demian's voice was not one "which could come only from within myself." (III, 135)

An inner voice, Demian is a controlling conscience. As Oskar Seidlin has shown, he is a *daemon* or "eternal self," directing Sinclair from awakening to maturity and liberating him from himself through his final religious vision.[22] His presences and absences mark stages in a process of deepening awareness as the concluding moment is prepared for: merging with the image of his mother, Demian is revealed in the dark subconscious mirror in which Sinclair finds the knowledge he sought. He is Sinclair's symbolic or transcendental self. Like the ideal of many romantic heroes, he can be joined with him only after death.

If Demian is a pervasive symbol in the hero's consciousness, the former clergyman and organist Pistorius, whom Sinclair dis-

[22] "Exorcism," *passim.*

covers playing "amoral music" in a deserted church, marks an important transitional phase. Pistorius clearly reflects an aspect of Sinclair himself, but rather than being continuously meaningful he acts as Demian's incarnation at a particular time and place. A visionary and "priest" of occult religions, he seeks to create new symbols leading to a transcendence of the abyss opening between good and evil. Sinclair is attracted by his self-willed, unconventional music, breaking the boundaries of tradition; their mystical bond is established by their common knowledge of Abraxas which connects the organist with Demian's teaching. But despite these affinities with Demian, Pistorius makes mistakes: he cannot fully realize his own visions. He mirrors Demian's universal image in the inadequate world of men. At the same time, he appears more palpably human than Demian. The mystical guide is crystalized as the psychotherapist who as a person shares in the frailties of humanity which he teaches his disciple to avoid.[23] On this level, which is continuously interlaced with the mystical and theological, the "eternal self" appears more directly as an external figure with whom "transference" is established and destroyed. The inevitable break occurs after Sinclair had reached an advanced point of self-recognition and had himself played Pistorius' role toward a younger boy at school. (III, 207–215) The occasion for their separation is Sinclair's knowledge that his teacher is unable to tell "true dreams" and indulges instead in discursive lectures about "dead religions." (III, 217)

The final image of salvation, Frau Eva, is also the most shadowy figure of the triad. A symbol for the union of opposites, she includes the male and the female, light and dark. On a primary level, she is an allegorical figure representing salvation, the eternally feminine, the origin of all men. In another function, however, she is also a "figure," the intersection of all the images and symbolic motifs which have staked out Sinclair's ascent. She mirrors the hero's inner self in a wider perspective. At one point, Sinclair describes her as "the symbolic image of my life," seeking to lead him "more and more deeply into myself." In his love for her, he feels a juxtaposition of sensual and spiritual love, of reality and symbol. (III, 242) As an ultimate transcendental symbol, moreover, Frau Eva reconciles the "eternal self" and Sinclair's more limited self in the world of sense. Or, to translate this allegory into Christian terms, the divine guide and the maternal prototype join to achieve the hero's salvation. But actually the resolution takes place in notably un-Christian terms, for salvation coincides with complete self-projection. As Demian, and temporarily Pistorius, taught Sinclair "to live out completely what seeks to break out of me," so Frau Eva taught final self-discovery within the mirror of oneself. Through her influence on Sinclair as a person, as an image, and as a symbolic figure, she creates his unified awareness of self and world and renders it visible in the novel.

These three major figures portray through their contrived actions the conflicts and images within Sinclair himself and project the movement of the allegory toward its goal. Indeed, the allegory is shaped by the idea, which they express, that the self must render itself completely, reconcile the oppositions which divide inner and outer nature, and mirror itself and its visions in the novel. Their entrances and exits, and the events they precipitate, define the self as a unique intersection of appearances and as a universal vision. But this movement is also fashioned by a corresponding portrait of the self as a texture of individual images, perceptions, and motifs whose precise constellation completes the novel's lyrical design.

———4

Despite its fluid allegorical form, *Demian* is not yet complicated by an involved dialectic. For this reason, the poetic texture can be clearly discerned as a world of images created by the symbolic hero. Picturing and painting, associated with subconscious imagery, are among its determining characteristics.

For example, the opposition of light and dark is shown as concrete pictures. The two worlds into which Sinclair sees his universe divided as a child are described respectively as worlds of
"clarity and cleanliness," "washed hands, clean clothes, good
manners" as opposed to those of "servants," "ghost stories,"
"slaughter houses and prisons, drunks and screaming women,
cows giving birth and horses collapsing. . . ." (III, 103–104)
These worlds are continuously juxtaposed. The forbidden hide-
out of Sinclair's tempter contains bundles of rusty wires and
other garbage under the vaulting arc of a bridge at the bank of
a lazily flowing river (III, 107); the vestibule of his parents'
home, on the other hand, contains a glass door behind which
hung his father's hat, his mother's parasol: "Home and tenderness streamed towards me from all these things." (III, 113)
Moreover, in a manner reminiscent of Rilke's *Malte Laurids
Brigge,* Sinclair, as a passive hero, often experiences significant
objects as if they were acting toward him. Passively he looks
on as familiar objects in his home—clock, table, Bible and mirror, bookshelf and pictures—recede into the background, leaving
him only his "freezing heart." Active objects dramatize a break
with the past for a passive protagonist. (III, 116ff.)

This role of objects in the hero's consciousness is viewed by
Hesse as an act of symbolic self-encounter. During a crucial
conversation with Pistorius, Sinclair is asked to see himself in
the images cast by the fire. A symbolic figure—the yellow
sparrow-hawk—emerges from a single flame that shoots up in
the onlookers' perspective. All images converge in a single
moment that gathers up time in imaginative insight:

> In the dying glow of the fire, golden, glimmering threads
> were running together in nets; letters and pictures appeared,
> recollections of faces, of animals, of plants, of worms and
> snakes. (III, 197)

Here Hesse's method is more complex. The objects not only
picture themes and experiences but also act as motifs, as heraldic
symbols of the opposing worlds. And indeed Pistorius teaches

that evanescent outlines combine with an "inner music" to create images through which the self is defined. (III, 197)

In *Demian,* as also in the later *Steppenwolf,* Hesse relies chiefly on this picturing technique to render the progression of the novel. It is primarily described by the visions which Sinclair perceives in dreams and externalizes in drawings. The movement toward his ideal self-portrait depends on the development of several recurrent motifs: the yellow sparrow-hawk, the portrait of Beatrice, the two-headed god Abraxas, and, finally, the image of Frau Eva. Demian, the mentor and guide, intrudes upon each of these pictures. In Hesse's method, these motifs retain their original meaning, but, as in a piece of music, they also merge with one another, appear in constantly fresh combinations, and usher in a forward development. The sparrow-hawk, which Demian first discovers above Sinclair's door, is an emblematic answer to the conflict between the two worlds and expresses the idea of Cain. The picture of Beatrice—combining a girl casually seen in the street with a reproduction of a pre-Raphaelite painting—becomes the second emblem of salvation, that of pure love, at a time when Sinclair had almost given in to drink and debauch. His earlier attempts to draw the sparrow-hawk are now combined with efforts to draw Beatrice and end eventually as a painting of Demian—and himself. The third motif is Abraxas, who is shown as a bird breaking out of the world as if it were a gigantic egg. The motif of the bird (suggesting the sparrow-hawk) is the lyrical equivalent of the outward flow of the *Bildungsroman,* in which Abraxas connects Demian and Pistorius and functions as an occasion for an occult communication between Sinclair and his earlier mentor. Correspondingly, the juncture of Abraxas and the hawk enriches Sinclair's knowledge and allows him to return to his painting of Beatrice with fresh understanding. His maturer perception of the feminine painting directs him toward the fourth motif—his apprehension of Frau Eva. His final vision revealed in the flash of gunfire is her figure viewed as a universal image encompassing the entire world. It results in Sinclair's ultimate self-discovery and concludes the book. The narrative progression coincides with a lyrical movement.

The various transformations of the painting, and their eventual convergence with the sparrow-hawk emblem, furnish an excellent example of Hesse's technique. In the early phases, Sinclair makes an altar of the reproductions of the Beatrice painting: he prays to the picture, fashioning a world of "light" of his own creation. (III, 174–175) But he soon begins to draw and paint her features, and, after abandoning any pretense of copying the reproduction, he finds that each successive painting of her face resembles more and more an image of his dreams. With each fresh start it comes to mirror more closely a unity of the inner and the outer visions: "It looked more like the head of a youth than the features of a girl. . . . [The] chin was strong and firm, but the mouth blossoming with red, the whole a little stiff and mask-like, yet impressive and full of secret life." (III, 176) This description refers not only to the picture. The words "stiff," "mask-like" yet full of "secret life" are frequently repeated motifs which are associated with Demian. (III, 161) The "picture" moves outward from Beatrice to Demian, a progression soon stated: ". . . with a start I recognized the picture. . . . How could I have discovered it so late! It was Demian's face!" (III, 177, 181) Moreover, as his self-recognition deepens, he realizes that he had drawn not only Beatrice or Demian but also himself: "The picture was not like myself . . . , but it was that which made my life, it was my inner nature, my fate or my demon." (III, 178)

After the painting of Beatrice had been joined with the Abraxas motif new attitudes emerge: the enlarged picture is now also a challenge to its creator. As Sinclair prays to the final version, "cold with inner exertion," it *reacts* to his entreaties.

> I questioned the picture, I accused it, I caressed it, I prayed to it; I called it mother, I called it beloved, I called it whore and woman of the streets, I called it Abraxas.

He also envisions himself wrestling with its image as Jacob had wrestled with the Angel of the Lord and receiving from it a similar redemption. The picture responds:

> In the shine of the lamplight, the painted face transformed itself at each supplication. It became bright and luminous, black and sinister, closed pale lids over dead eyes, opened them again and shot out glowing glances like bolts of lightning; it was woman, was man, was girl, was a small child, an animal, was blotted into a stain, became again large and clear.

Such a conversion of a picture of one's own creation into an icon, finally into an antagonist, illustrates Hesse's technique. The girl's features merge with masculine and feminine qualities and with all ages and phases of life. "Animal" and "blotted into a stain" again suggest Demian. The picture becomes a transformed replica of Sinclair at the same time acting toward him like an external force. Finally, after intense inner concentration it becomes a higher vision of the self:

> I closed my eyes and now I saw the whole picture within myself, more violent and more powerful. I wanted to kneel before it, but it was so very internal that I could no longer separate myself from it; [it was] as if I had become pure I. (III, 211–212)

But the image of the "great beloved" had also been connected with Abraxas:

> . . . I lived with Demian, with the sparrow-hawk, with the picture of the great figure of my dreams who was my fate and my beloved. That was enough to live in, for everything looked outward to the great and wide expanse, and everything pointed toward Abraxas. (III, 190)

This is as far as Sinclair can take the revisions of the original portrait of the young girl Beatrice. Before her image can wholly merge with that of Frau Eva, woman must be introduced in her function as mother. An earlier dream image had suggested Hesse's deliberate involvement of the two feminine functions: Sinclair's mother welcomes her son at the front door of their childhood home under the emblem of the sparrow-hawk. Her maternal embrace soon becomes intensely sexual, intermingling bliss with horror induced not only by the association with Sinclair's mother but also by her resemblance to Demian. A "divine service as well as a crime" (III, 188), the dream symbolizes Abraxas. Subsequently, this dream recurs in various associations. In the end, the scene is repeated in the actual meeting with Frau Eva, in which all previous motifs are carefully intertwined. The confrontation concludes: "With moist eyes I stared at my picture [of the bird] and read in myself. Then I lowered my gaze: under the emblem of the bird in the open door stood a lady in a dark gown. It was she." (III, 231–232)

In the final phase, the painting or picture, which dominates the novel's center, is displaced by the inner vision. Frau Eva teaches Sinclair the value of dreams without the crutch of an external reproduction. This change enables him to achieve more and more successfully a concentrated vision of himself. As Demian explains, through concentrations of the self the saving figure can be made alive in moments of need. The meaningful sign becomes a symbol not by accident but by a conscious effort. In this way, Sinclair seeks his union with Frau Eva literally in an act of the imagination; he experiences her presence and finds himself. "At this moment I felt as if I bore a crystal in my heart and I knew it was my self. Coldness rose within me up to my chest." (III, 249–250)

At the same time that *Sammlung* or mystical concentration becomes the equivalent of the picture, fresh dreams join the earlier motifs. Sinclair's love for Frau Eva is compared to a young man's love for a star he cannot reach, because at the moment of his flight he doubts its possibility. (III, 240–241, 243) A storm-tossed landscape flown over by the heraldic bird anticipates the concluding scene. (III, 245) At last in the ultimate vision which occurs when Sinclair receives his final wound, all past pictures and images are contracted into one. Frau Eva had taught him that the inner evolution of the most sublime "dream" is equivalent to a final realization of the self both as a unique being (the pure self) and as a universal being (the transcendent vision). Such a vision, which in romantic terms is attainable only in infinity, can be achieved in extreme mystical concentration or at the point of death. Sinclair's vision, though entirely internal, acts like Klingsor's self-portrait, mirroring the world at large. Just before the shell explodes, Sinclair remembers the symbols which had led him toward self-realization: sparrow-hawk, Abraxas, Frau Eva. Then his feeling broadens into a vision which bursts asunder as the symbolic star, of which Frau Eva had told him, is transformed into the fateful shell:

> There was a great city in the clouds and millions of people streamed from it, swarming broadly over wide landscapes. Into their midst there stepped a powerful divinity, sparkling stars in her hair, high as a mountain range, with the features of Frau Eva. Into her, the long lines of men disappeared as into a gigantic cavern and were gone. The goddess cowered on the ground; brightly the Sign shimmered on her forehead. A dream seemed to wield great power over her; she closed her eyes, and her great features contracted in pain. Suddenly she screamed piercingly, and from her forehead sprang many thousand luminous stars, which swung in majestic arcs and semicircles across the black sky. (III, 255)

The vision is seen in the same way that Sinclair viewed the animation of Beatrice's picture. But now the experience is not resolved in a prayer or an act, but becomes the transcendent moment at which all symbols are exploded and combined anew in this final vision of self and world. The epilogue requires only the mother's kiss, conferred by the dying Demian, who miraculously appears on the bed next to Sinclair's, as a confirmation of this unified experience. In an image Sinclair recognizes that he and Demian are one: "But when sometime I rediscover the key and climb down wholly into my self, down where images of

fate slumber in dark mirrors, then I need only to bend over the
black mirror to see my own picture which is now wholly like
his. . . ." (III, 257)

At the point of death, at which all significant images unite,
a constellation of pictures is achieved which becomes the ultimate
self-portrait, the inner landscape of the self. Under the veneer
of a novel of development, the reader has followed the transformation of a hero into a symbolic hero. Progressing from childhood to maturity, he constantly redraws his own image, ascending from his awareness of the perceived object to its image in
his mind and finally to its symbol with which he wholly identifies himself. Hesse succeeds in drawing a spiritual self-portrait
while leading the reader through successive stages in time and
picturing the attainment of self-recognition as a symbolic vision
of a "new world" born of catastrophe. Using portraiture as a
lyrical form, he also exploits the movement of the conventional
novel. His hero—neurotic and vulnerable in the world of sense
—becomes a symbolic representative of himself, and his world,
on the "road to salvation."

THE ALLEGORICAL NOVEL

—1

The symbolic hero in the lyrical novel is analogous to the
lyrical "I" in verse poetry. He is the cause of the novel's world,
its landscapes and stylized textures of faces and events. In his
point of view, perceptions, illusory or real, are transmuted into
imagery. But he also plays the role of the protagonist: he unifies
not only symbolic images but also the novel's scenes. The relationship between these two roles played by an identical figure
constitutes an important dimension of lyrical fiction. In most
lyrical novels, this tension is reflected in an ambiguous world
composed simultaneously of a texture of images and of the
linear movement of narrative.

The symbolic protagonist is "self-reflexive," because his behavior in a world of simulated time and place actually mirrors

his own psyche and renders it in detached forms. His experiences are determined not so much by events in an external world as by events which symbolize that world. Therefore, a typical strand in the lyrical novel is, at least in its broadest sense, allegorical. But the type of allegory induced by the symbolic hero is not the same as that of *Pilgrim's Progress*. There is, as a rule, no consistent correspondence between the hero's encounters and representative ideas or concepts outside him. Rather, the hero acts in an arena in which events are related to himself. The figures and scenes he confronts signify ideas which, in turn, symbolize his own inner condition.

2

Der Steppenwolf (1927) skillfully adapts a narrative form to self-reflexive allegory. Like *Demian,* it portrays the world of a symbolic hero. The theme of the sensitive adolescent isolated from society is replaced by that of the middle-aged artist alienated from a perennially hostile modern world. In much of his postwar fiction prior to this novel, Hesse's rejection of contemporary civilization had been negative. His heroes were made to withdraw from its values either into the Orient or into an oddly anachronistic world compounded of the Middle Ages and the romantic nineteenth century prior to the industrial revolution. But *Der Steppenwolf* uses the theme of the artist's alienation directly by dwelling on the hero's encounters within the hostile world itself. It is Hesse's only major work to deal exclusively with a twentieth-century urban environment and to exploit its major symbols: jazz music, asphalt streets, electric lights, bars, motion pictures, and night clubs. Part of a canon of "Crisis" poems and short stories, *Der Steppenwolf* views urban life as symbolic of modern man's cultural and psychological disintegration. Signifying an important, if passing, phase in Hesse's work, it replaces withdrawal with revolt. It expresses the artist's rebellion against a humorless culture.

This cultural critique is channeled into the microcosm of the novel's hero, Harry Haller, who enacts the inner schisms of his society through his divided nature as a human Wolf of the Steppes. A modern replica of the romantic seer, Haller embodies the condition of his time, which is objectified in the novel. His fictional notes try "to overcome the great illness of [his] time not through circumventions and embellishments of the truth, but through the effort to make the illness itself the subject of the presentation." (IV, 205) A social and cultural disease is mirrored in the consciousness of a lyrical self.

Hesse's technique of describing from within a hero's mental and spiritual disintegration is determined by his use of the notebook. This method enables him to render a hero's inner life yet to remain, on the surface at least, within the conventions of the realistic novel. As in *Werther,* the fiction is maintained that these notes had been found after Haller's disappearance and had been edited by his landlady's nephew. Moorings in "reality" are established from which Hesse frees himself to pursue a man's rebellion, decline, and apparent failure in series of increasingly hallucinatory events. The action centers on a crisis in the life of a man approaching his fiftieth birthday whose life-long commitment to a respectable bourgeois existence has become an intolerable burden. Like Thomas Mann's Aschenbach in *Der Tod in Venedig,* Haller's crisis is one of despair, of doubt in the meaningfulness of his past achievement and the adequacy of his future intentions. He experiences his problem as the discrepancy between the ideal world, which he still finds in Goethe, Novalis, and Dostoyevsky, and the real world of his time. Hesse calls him an *outsider,* using the English word to emphasize the hero's position in a world dominated by the language of jazz. For the same reason Hesse chose for his character the Christian name "Harry"——a jazz-age version of his own name, Hermann, while retaining the latter as the name of a "youthful friend." Harry, the outsider, is the modern writer, uprooted from his middle-class past, unable to return to the eternal harmonies which only great art can reproduce.

Haller's dual allegiance shows itself in a double, and eventually in a multiple, personality. The outsider thinks of himself as part man, part wolf. As a man, he is sensitive, rational, well read, ascetic in his pleasures and sparse in his demands on life. As a wolf, he is thirsting for "living blood" and quick to offend the philistine. The bourgeois man had suppressed his wolf nature until middle age, but at the brink of failure he releases the wolf within him, who begins to dominate the controlled personality. Potential schizophrenia becomes a fact which the hero believes he can resolve only through violent death—murder or suicide. In this way, Hesse's perennial motif of compulsive dissolution becomes prominent.

The opposite aim, which Haller fails to achieve, is to find pure detachment in the impersonal magic of art, represented by the cold laughter of the immortals, Goethe and Mozart. An hallucinatory "magic theater" is the arena in which this resolution is attempted. It is introduced by a subterranean world of half-real, half-fantastic characters who also reflect accurately the pleasure world of the modern city. These figures—a saxophonist named Pablo and two prostitutes, Hermine and Maria—teach Haller to elicit from his repressed personality the "magic" of the senses until he is "ready" for the Magic Theater itself. Once in the inner sanctum, Haller is eventually led to witness a show in which parts of his divided personality are displayed in various pantomimes. After numerous metamorphoses of the characters, Haller enacts his complete collapse at the same time that he is shown a vision of imagination, humor, and play.

Hesse's way of setting down precisely a hero's disintegration as he experiences it implies the identity of Haller's inner life and the novel's world. But the hero's image is also reflected against a set of universal beliefs. In the preface to the 1942 edition of *Der Steppenwolf,* Hesse declared that he had not intended to present only an internal picture. Rather, he had wished to show a sufferer's state of mind measured against a positive and "cheerful world of beliefs above person and time." [24] Two elements of the story introduce this world of beliefs. The first is a mysterious Treatise, which analyzes the causes of

[24] Cited in Matzig, *Hermann Hesse in Montagnola,* p. 70.

Haller's condition and sets down positive principles. The other
is the Magic Theater, in which these same principles are enacted.
But it is part of the novel's paradoxical make-up that physically
these authorities appear in Haller's notes, i.e., in his consciousness. Hesse indeed sets universal values against a subjective
meaning of his book, but at the same time he has seen to it
that they are mirrored in his hero's psyche.

This telescoping of a private consciousness and a universal set
of values within the figure of the hero suggests the mirroring
of a personal in an impersonal, a transcendental self. Moreover,
the ironic reflection of a psychologically inadequate hero in an
objective ideal which he himself imagines creates aesthetic distance
without requiring the author to resort to an external, dramatic
presentation. Hesse's method is self-reflexive, i.e., romantic, irony.
It displaces, in terms suggested by Friedrich Schlegel, the stage
of life with self-representation, whose objectivity is vouchsafed
by the identity of producer and product, the self-in-life and the
self-in-art. The expressionistic nightmare of a man's descent
into schizophrenia becomes the well-organized picture of an
ascent toward sublime recognition. The symbolic hero faces
himself in an ultimate self-encounter.

~~~~~3

The allegorical form determines the structure in most of
Hesse's novels in a manner akin to Novalis' version of Goethe's
Bildungsroman. In *Der Steppenwolf,* however, its progression
does not lead the hero from his earthly state toward the ideal,
as it still does in *Demian.* Rather, the protagonist is reflected in
a multitude of mirrors which juxtapose the sense-self and the
transcendental self. Although there are many superficial resemblances between Haller's search for a resolution and Heinrich
von Ofterdingen's search for the Blue Flower, the great difference
between them is obvious. The encounters experienced by Hesse's
hero actually penetrate beneath the mind and reveal images
of the subconscious. In *Der Steppenwolf,* the symbolic mirror
replaces the Blue Flower as the center around which the novel

is built. It reveals more directly the implications of Novalis' allegory which are suggested by the scene in the hermit's cave.

Self-encounter as a form of mirroring is indicated by the reflections of lights on the wet pavement of city streets; by Hermine's significant glances in her pocket-mirror; by constant discussions of mirrors. The Magic Theater is Pablo's Cabinet of Mirrors, where the hero sees a universal image of himself. The small mirrors into which Haller is required to gaze become a full-length mirror that reveals first his dual personality, finally the multiple self. Moreover, this very action is prefigured in the Treatise, which teaches that self-encounter, the glance into the chaos of one's own soul, will strip the self of all its disguises and so prepare it for possible salvation or failure: "Possibly some day he [Harry] will learn to recognize himself, and will get a hold of one of our little mirrors. . . ." (IV, 241) In this way, the Treatise acts as a magic mirror, in which psychological dissolution and symbolic resolution can be joined. The mirror is an effective device, because it can be used both on a psychological and on an aesthetic level. Its reflection renders in timeless form the subject's features in life. It can trace the flow of subconscious imagery and can represent the ideal image of the self as it is represented in art. Through its action, the allegory is rendered in a lyrical or self-reflexive form, connecting the hero's experience with its image.

Der Steppenwolf is developed as a structure of various triads which mirror one another. The symbolic hero, Harry Haller, stands in the center of all these triads and connects the various levels. The first such triad is provided by the external form. Its most evident element is the editor's introduction, which supplies the point of view of the outside world. The second is the Treatise, which appears to be external but which actually forms part of Haller's imaginative record. The third part of the triad is provided by the notes which contain both the Treatise and the Magic Theater.

The introductory pages written by the editor form the realistic envelope familiar from many expressionistic plays. They describe the great puzzlement and awe with which a solid bachelor regards a set of notes his aunt's shy roomer had left behind. His astonishment, however, is not entirely unmixed. It includes an inkling of understanding as well as an ingredient of condescension not unlike the condescension Haller expresses for the editor's limited world. Generally, the editor poses as Haller's mirror. He corrects his hallucinations by regarding them in the perspective of "real" world.[25] At the same time, his fascination for the underside of life revealed in the notes, mirrors inversely Haller's nostalgic attachment for the editor's solid values. Motifs taken up in the notes are sometimes first described by the editor (e.g., IV, 186–189, 210ff.). In this way, Hesse uses the editor not only to supply a formal framework for the hero's inner confusions, as in *Werther,* but to illuminate Haller through the distorting mirror of an opposite, yet deeply related, personality.

The second device, the *Traktat vom Steppenwolf,* is one of those unique inventions we sometimes encounter in Hesse which transform a rather undistinguished, occasionally even modish, plan into a work of great originality. The Treatise handed to Haller by a mysterious man in the street is a grimy, impersonal booklet which turns out to be exclusively concerned with its reader. Indeed, its objective language appears to be a detached analysis of his own condition, directed peculiarly at him, while it foreshadows his adventures in the Magic Theater. On a psychological level, this coincidence causes no surprise, since it is an obvious symptom of Haller's hallucination. But on the level of Hesse's more profound intentions, it functions as a

[25] The editor suggests that the events described in the notebook are for the most part poetry, but not in the sense of arbitrary invention. Rather, they are to be taken as an attempt at self-expression, of representing deeply experienced events of the soul in the guise of visible events. He supposes that these occurrences, which are partly fantastic, took place during the last period of Haller's stay in the editor's home, and he does not doubt that even they have some basis in a "real, external experience"; *Dichtungen,* IV, 203.

symbolic mirror. The conversion of dream-like solipsism into an apparently actual reality is a familiar expressionistic technique. In *Der Steppenwolf,* the detached authority with which the artist's condition is analyzed reflects Harry Haller's particular condition as part of the more universal picture of the bourgeois writer. The higher authority issuing the document—ultimately the "'immortals" of the Magic Theater—appears to be Haller's "eternal self." He is placed in a universalizing mirror.

The Treatise is a contemporary restatement of the romantic position, enriching the old dichotomies with the social relevance of the nineteen-twenties. It also seeks to replace a purely psychological outlook on man's divided state with a mystical and ideological rationale. The stigma placed on the illness of schizophrenia is removed by making of this divided state a positive value for the spiritual rebel and a necessary transition to new self-discovery. The antagonistic elements within the self are man's sensual and spiritual nature—*Trieb* and *Geist*—which the extraordinary man must reconcile in a higher unity. (IV, 228) As in Thomas Mann's *Tod in Venedig,* the artist is plagued by the self-imposed restrictions of the ascetic intellect, which he seeks to revoke by an unconscious longing for sensual chaos. For Hesse such a dissolution of the personal self is an important step in the tortured *Steppenwolf's* cure. He extols the outsider willing to face courageously the abyss of individual disintegration. Haller's tragedy is not that he is initially drawn into its vortex but that he cannot accept, at the crucial moment, the solution proffered by the immortals.

As an artist of bourgeois origin, Harry Haller is plagued by an uncontrollable urge for order and conformity, a compulsion which is countermanded only by an equally strong revulsion against the mediocrity of middle-class values. The bourgeois clings to the fiction that the self is a single entity. The *Steppenwolf* knows the fiction for what it is, but he is heir to his ambiguous allegiances and so maintains, sentimentally, at least part of the bourgeois' love for the undivided self. In response to this conflict, he seeks to dissolve altogether, to destroy his identity by suicide. He can be saved only if he is made to accept unequivocally his dual identity as a *Steppenwolf* and to project it playfully into the detached magic of art. In the "sovereign realm of humor" the poles of saint and sensualist are "bent together," transcending and unifying "all areas of humanity through the beams of its prisms." (IV, 239–241)

In its concluding phase, the Treatise goes beyond the notion of a dual self and suggests, with the assistance of Novalis, that each person actually consists of innumerable persons.[26] The artist and the mystic are peculiarly conscious of this fragmentation. (IV, 244) For example, true drama should not assume an enduring form of the self, as the Greeks had believed, but should, like the Indian epic, present all of its characters as aspects of a single self. The human personality is "nothing but a narrow, dangerous bridge between nature and spirit." (IV, 247) By accepting and transcending the divisions in his own nature and in the world at large, the *Steppenwolf* reaches a higher identity: not that of a single self but of Man as a whole on his way to God. Thus the final appeal of the Treatise:

> The way to innocence, to the uncreated, to God does not lead back, but forward, not to wolf or child but always more and more into guilt, ever more deeply into the process of becoming Man. Nor will suicide seriously help you, poor Steppenwolf. You will have to go the longer, more arduous, harder way towards becoming Man; you will have to multiply your duality, to complicate further your complications. Instead of narrowing your world, of simplifying your soul, you will have to become always more world; finally, you will have to include the entire world in your painfully widened soul in order to reach, perhaps, the end, the state of peace. This is the way Buddha has gone, the way every great man has gone. . . . [Becom-

---

[26] Hesse's careful exposition of the nature of "I" or "person" in the Treatise bears distinct characteristics of Novalis' *Personenlehre*. Compare *Dichtungen*, IV, 244–245, and Novalis' notes on the subject in "Das Allgemeine Brouillon," *Schriften*, III, 70–71.

ing] God means: so to have widened one's soul that it may again comprise the entire universe. (IV, 249–250)

The third member of the triad is the manuscript of notes which actually depicts Haller's attempt to redeem himself. The editor's introduction is organized along narrative lines; the Treatise is ostensibly an exposition of ideas; the notes, which include several forms, provide a chronicle of a man's gradual departure from reality. It is Hesse's fine artistic achievement to juxtapose, in the notes, the hallucinatory and the real world without ever stating their discrepancy. Reality and illusion mirror one another in a single poetic constellation. The opening, for example, is quite credible as the description of a lost soul wandering in an inhospitable city. Haller is first moved toward an illusory world by an image: the mysterious electric lights flashing the message of the Magic Theater—"Entrance Not for Everyone"—"For Madmen Only"—on a deserted church wall. For some time Haller himself thinks of this message as a "hallucination" or "vision." (IV, 258) The final push toward illusion is given in a highly concrete narrative scene: a visit to a bourgeois acquaintance, a denizen of academia, during which Haller rebels against the vulgarity and absurd jingoism of accepted society. The tensions generated by this meeting are released in Haller's explosive reaction to a trite reproduction of Goethe's likeness. The wolf nature breaks out of the respectable exterior and an infuriated, suicidal Haller is literally propelled into the subterranean world. After some days of roaming in wet streets he steps across the threshold of the realm of illusion, the night club of the *Black Eagle*. Both incidents, then, catapult Haller into an interior universe. But if the "real" world gradually assumes hallucinatory qualities, the imaginary world maintains a foothold in actual life: jazz music, cafés, even the dancing lessons Hermine administers in Haller's room or the ballrooms and loges of the Magic Theater, all these reflect the definite contours of the cosmopolitan city into which Haller symbolically descends.

—— 4

The notes are part of Haller's inner world: that of the Magic Theater. They also draw the main outlines of the *Bildungs-roman*. To comprehend fully the dual nature of these notes, we must keep continuously in mind the paradox which pervades them. Haller is literally *taught* the way to transcend himself, but he always remains the center, the lyrical consciousness in which teachers and teachings are engaged. This double action is illustrated by the two different ways in which the Treatise can be regarded. As the exposition handed down by a higher authority, it forms part of the external structure we have discerned, joining the editor's reflections and the notes as a whole. But once we see the treatise as part of Haller's own record, we note a more significant internal structure. In this crucial triad, it is one of the three forms taken on by the symbolic hero, the other two being the *Steppenwolf* construct and the Magic Theater. The novel's paradox is enacted by this triadic form, because the various instruments of teaching are also manifestations of the self.

The impersonal blueprint for Haller's instruction (the Treatise) and his confrontation with the figures representing the immortals set the goals and measure the progress of his education. He is guided in particular by three characters who appear to be familiar allegorical personages, for Hermine, Maria, and Pablo resemble Demian, Pistorius, and Frau Eva in many important ways. Hermine awakens the hero and shows him the possibility of the ideal; in this way, she suggests Demian. Maria, like Pistorius, is an intermediary figure, necessary to the hero's development but ultimately inadequate. Pablo, like Frau Eva, is the most inclusive symbol leading the hero toward the transcendence of himself. But in *Der Steppenwolf,* these relationships are made more complex. Its triad of characters produces a contraction of the allegory into a picture in which experience and symbol, self and ideal are identified through intricate mirroring. They reflect the triadic structure of the whole, mirroring Treatise, Theater, and *Steppenwolf* in involved and occasionally strained juxtapositions. These figures portray not only different aspects of the hero, or particular stages in his growth or decline, but also different types of mirroring which are unified in the concluding scenes.

Hermine exemplifies a direct correspondence between self and ideal. The affinity between her name and Hermann Hesse's links her closely with Harry Haller. The mirroring suggested by the play on names is fully expressed in their relationship. Haller constantly reiterates that Hermine is his double, that she has qualities he himself lacks, yet that in most respects she seems to reflect significant parts of himself. She actually sees herself as Haller's mirror: "Don't you understand, my learned friend, that I please you and am important to you, because I am a kind of mirror for you?" (IV, 297) In the final dance of the Magic Theater she becomes momentarily identical with Haller: "We both stood still and gazed at each other. . . . Before her glance, from which my own soul seemed to look at me, all reality collapsed, even the reality of my desire for her. We glanced at each other, transformed by magic; thus gazed at me my poor little soul." (IV, 366–367) In her profession as a prostitute, an artist of the body, Hermine mirrors Haller's profession as a writer, an artist of the intellect. (IV, 278–280) Her naïve sensuality reflects inversely Haller's sophisticated taste. (IV, 289–290) They are similar as children of the same destructive, satanic spirit. (IV, 317) But Hermine is also an authority: initiating Haller into the rituals of her world, she teaches him to accept his sensual nature with humorous detachment. Their sexual consummation is held out as an ultimate goal, because in such a union the inadequate self would join its more complete image. But it is also necessary that Haller fail: the union is possible only if he can realize it in playful illusion.

Hermine projects not only the hero's precise image but also the personality he aspires to be. Obviously, as his reflection, she contains masculine qualities.[27] Combining the appearance of boy and girl, mother and masculine friend, her features are "like living breath, waves of boy-likeness, of hermaphroditic magic." (IV, 297) But, in contrast to Haller's intellectual rigidity, she accepts the nature of the multiple self which contains both sexes. She is a formed image of the self, a new creation of its being. Haller soon realizes that her teachings are not original but that she recreates his own world, lends it a new significance. His multiple nature is now gradually revealed to him. "These were, so it seemed to me," Haller mused at one point, "not her thoughts but mine which the prophetess had read and inhaled and returned to me so that they now assume form and stand newly created before me." (IV, 346) Like Demian, Hermine becomes the hero's "eternal self." Beginning with her request for absolute obedience, she distills from her subject a superior self-awareness that accepts its multiplicity. Moreover, in teaching Haller the way to sensuality, she also teaches him, in Hesse's inverse dialectic, the way to sainthood traveled by artists such as Mozart who provide ultimate detachment. (IV, 345–347) As Haller approaches Hermine, she comes to personify the resolution of his conflict in the world of *Seele*. She is his "magic mirror." (IV, 298)

Hermine directs Haller to the other figures of the triad, his physical mistress Maria and the saxophonist Pablo. Maria embodies pure, physical love; to her, everything is "plastic material of love and of magic." (IV, 335) Supple, non-boyish, all woman and lover, she counteracts analytic reflection. When Haller laboriously contemplates his divided nature, she appears in his bed like an answer produced by a conjurer's trick. (IV, 327) Her sensuality continues to attract Haller, even though she refuses, by definition, to present the slightest intellectual challenge. (IV, 334) Her mission is to infuse Haller's sensually impover-

[27] Note Harry's recollection of his "youthful friend Hermann" on various occasions; in the Magic Theater the same person is revealed as one of Hermine's disguises. She uses her bewitching feminine powers in the disguise of a man. *Dichtungen,* IV, 359–361.

ished personality with the awareness of nature and soul. The German word *Bild* means both *image* and *picture:* in Hesse's dialectic, Maria's function is to elicit such *Bilder* of the inner life as counterpoints of thought. During a night with her, Haller envisions many *Bilder* of his life rising within the consciousness of one who had "lived for so long empty and poor and without pictures. . . ." Moreover, they are "magically released by Eros," and amaze Haller with the wealth and variety of "the picture gallery of my life" which he had thought to be barren. (IV, 332–333) Images of the subconscious, concealed by the (paternal) intellectual self, are released by (feminine) sensuality to reintroduce the hero to his memories and dreams.

Interceding between Haller's nature and the ideal of salvation, replacing spiritual with physical love, Maria alludes to and inverts the idea of the Holy Virgin. But it is the crux of the allegory that she does not wholly succeed. Despite Haller's delight in her, he is also always drawn to a reflective state. His ambivalence is clarified in the concluding scenes of the masked ball. Although he enjoys Hermine's greater understanding, he must look for Maria (IV, 339–346); while dancing with Maria, he is "called" by Hermine. (IV, 358–359) On the one hand, Maria is a puppet, subservient to the higher teacher Hermine and even manipulated by her as Hermine, in turn, is a tool of Pablo and thus of the "immortals." But, on the other hand, she is also Hermine's physical self purged of all hermaphroditism. As a professional lover, she embodies all the feminine qualities reflected in the symbolic prisms of Theater and Treatise.

This larger function suggests that Maria is not only an intercessor but also a mirror. But the direct correspondence between subject and symbolic image, which is exemplified by Hermine, is replaced by a reflecting lens in which many different figures are brought together—an embodiment of the Magic Theater's mirror as explained by the Treatise. This function of unifying all disparate elements in a single organic whole is fulfilled by Maria's sexual nature; sexuality not only releases multitudinous images but also combines them in an ecstatic unity—an *unio mystica* of the senses. In the ballroom scene, Haller experiences this mysterious union in a dance—the public enactment of sexuality: ". . . the exultation of a festive communion, the secret of the person's submergence in the mass, the *unio mystica* of pleasure. . . . I was no longer I, my personality was dissolved in the intoxication of the festival as salt is dissolved in water . . . all [women] belonged to me and I belonged to them all. We all took part of each other. And also the men were part of it, in them, too, I existed . . . their smiles were mine, their wooing mine, my wooing theirs." (IV, 361–363) In Maria, such a union mirrors the interlocking levels of the novel as a whole. In teaching Haller the secrets of sexual technique, Maria reflects knowledge gained from more important unions. Her liaisons include Pablo, who is also Hermine's lover, and especially Hermine herself. All these relationships are combined in Maria as a symbolic reflection of the Treatise's unifying glass. When Haller learns of these intricate connections, he at once identifies himself with Hermine's "boy-likeness" and suggests a correspondence between sexual partners and parts of the human soul, between psychological fragmentation and the prismatic mirror of the ideal. "New indirect, complicated relationships and connections emerged before me, new possibilities of love and of life, and I thought of the thousand souls of the *Steppenwolftraktat*." (IV, 339) Maria is a mirror uniting dissonances in the harmony of the sexual act, a pure, sensual counterpart of the pure harmony of music.

The master magician and jazz artist Pablo, on the other hand, combines the functions of both Hermine and Maria. His calm yet sensuous demeanor indicates a final unity which is transcended only toward the end when sensuality is turned into the spirit of Mozart. Although on an immediate level Pablo is the masculine representative as Maria is the purely feminine, on a higher level he approaches complete transcendence. He is the supreme teacher, counseling both the surrender to life and total detachment, the acceptance of the body and the attainment of harmony. Taking neither life nor world seriously, he portrays harmony through the grace of an amoral existence. (IV, 311, 313–315, 321–322) He speaks all languages, but he speaks especially well with his body, his eyes, and the sound of his voice. Similarly, he plays all instruments, but the sensual, cacophonous magic of his saxophone is his most perfect means of expression.

Pablo is the magician-artist of *Kindheit des Zauberers*. When Haller first meets him as the leader of a small jazz band, he is as struck by his physical charm as he is repelled by his exotic, animal-like exterior. But Haller is soon captivated by Pablo's playful magic through which he subtly teaches the mystery of the subterranean life. With his music and his opium cigarettes, Pablo achieves the illusion of sensual harmony. In the early phase, for example, he creates the opium-induced vision in which both he and Haller join with Hermine and Maria in a sexual orgy. But when in the Magic Theater he exchanges roles with Mozart, he also projects a similar resolution in the realm of *Geist*. It is at this stage that Pablo assumes his "transcendental" function. As the director of the Theater, he leads Haller to the brink of self-recognition and emerges as the master figure behind both Hermine's and Maria's activities. Seen in this way, Pablo is also the master mirror—an embodiment of his own *Spiegelkabinett*—in which all other figures, and hence all of Haller's aspirations, are joined. Moreover, as both a magician and Mozart, he transcends the sensual and spiritual realms and projects their reconciliation in the illusory play of art. Pablo, then, is the final magic mirror. Personifying Treatise and Theater, he becomes the means by which the triad of characters is identified with the triadic structure.

—————5

In Hesse's novel, the mirror exhibits a double nature. Its primary function resembles that of a picture reproducing its subject in a symbolic design. On this level the mirror suggests a Platonic correspondence of subject and image, echoing the Narcissus figures of Valéry and Gide, Novalis' cave image, or

Hesse's own water images of *Eine Stunde Hinter Mitternacht*.
We observed in *Demian* how a novel can progress through successive expansions of such self-portraits until a picture is achieved
which coincides with the ultimate vision. But in *Der Steppenwolf*, the mirror assumes an additional function, exploiting the
capacity of glass to refract a single object in multiple parts. Its
manner of splitting an entity into its myriad components, yet
holding all its segments together on an illusory surface, coincides
with Hesse's conception of the Magic Theater. Haller's self-
contemplation in Pablo's mirror illustrates this dimension of
the mirroring technique, contrasting sharply with Sinclair's
analogous contemplation of the Beatrice icon:

> . . . and I saw, a little dissolved and cloudy, a ghostly, in-
> ternally moving picture, heavily working and yeasting within
> itself: my own self, Harry Haller. . . .

This inwardly fermenting picture is immediately animated:

> . . . and within this Harry [I saw] the *Steppenwolf,* a shy,
> beautiful wolf, though glancing about himself confused and
> anxious, his eyes glimmering now with evil now with sadness,
> and this figure of a wolf flowed through Harry in incessant
> movement, akin to a great river in which a tributary of differ-
> ent color churns and blends, fighting and full of unresolved
> longing for form. Sadly, sadly the flowing, half-formed wolf
> regarded me with his beautiful shy eyes. (IV, 369)

Movement, depicted as water, suggests the vague boundaries
between two contrasting images as they coalesce and define one
another in their striving for form. The fluid picture renders
Haller's inner worlds in a single reflection; it depicts them
formally and makes duality rationally accessible. Moreover, the
mirror is analyzed into individual pictures (the wolf in various
poses, the river and its tributary), which cohere as images rather
than as a temporal movement.

The mirror image can also be animated in depth. A unified
Haller gazes at a mirror to discover within it not only shifting

outlines of two figures displayed on a two-dimensional surface but a charade enacted by innumerable Hallers, who turn the surface of the glass into a three-dimensional stage. Haller's entrance into the Magic Theater is characterized by this conversion:

> With a laugh and a funny little caress he [Pablo] turned me round and I confronted a gigantic wall mirror. Therein I saw myself.
>
> I saw, for a tiny moment, a well-known Harry, only in an unusually pleasant mood, with gay, happy, laughing features. But hardly had I recognized him when he fell apart, and a second figure separated itself from him, then a third, a tenth, a twentieth, and the entire gigantic mirror was full of Harrys and Harry-fragments, innumerable Harrys, each of whom I saw and recognized for only a split second. (IV, 372–373)

As the mirror's surface becomes a stage, figures *act* as if they were performing a show of the imagination. In this way, the mirror motif expands into that of the theater, while retaining its function of reflecting in illusion the subject's appearance in life. "[And all these figures] were I . . . they ran off to all sides, left, right, into the depth of the mirror and out of the mirror." (IV, 373) An attractive sixteen-year-old version of Harry Haller leads the way into the corridor of the Magic Theater with its imaginative skits. The story progresses through a shift in the physical nature of image and picture: the mirror turns into a peep-show in which Haller's present, past, and future are dramatically portrayed.

The notion of *show* bears further scrutiny as a lyrical method, because it involves a broader conception of mirror and picture. The hero is installed as the witness of a performance which depicts his inner life split into its manifold components. He is both audience and participant, the actor on a stage of life and the puppet on the stage of illusion and play. This deceptive division of the hero into two distinct roles has its root in Hesse's

technique of objectifying the mirror by seeming to separate the
subject gazing at the glass from the more composite image he
reflects. In the realm of illusion, the personality must be dis-
regarded (it must be taken off like a coat); its "magical" image,
contracting into one the divided features in life and the possibility of their integration in play, must alone dominate the
hero's expectations. Before setting up Haller as both a participant and an audience of the show, Pablo serves him (as well
as his "double," Hermine) opium cigarettes and liqueur,
creating the atmosphere of magic. He then exhorts them:
"[We] are here in a magic theater. There are only pictures here,
no reality. Pick out pretty and gay pictures and show that you're
no longer in love with your questionable personality." (IV,
372) Hermine disappears through a wall mirror. After learning
to laugh at the *Steppenwolf* in a pocket mirror, Haller steps
through the magic mirror we have described. The looking-glass
is a magic entrance into a show of the inner self.

In the peep-show sequence, Haller's personality is manipulated
in a series of farcical maneuvers. These shows, with all their ironic
implications about automobiles, amusement galleries, and caba-
rets, are serially distinct images whose very sequence portrays
Haller's inner nature: his *Welt der Bilder*. He first enacts his
aggression against modern society in a *Great Hunt on Automobiles,* joining a friend of his boyhood in sniping happily at
cars. In the skit, *Introduction to Personality Building,* he reviews
the manifold figures of the full-length mirror as they are converted into chess-men by the magician Pablo, who briefly recreates a whole life from their fragments, then allows Haller to
put them in his pocket. In the next show, *Miracles of Step-
penwolf-Training,* Haller is led to another vision of his divided
self: a frightening inversion of his own "training" in which a
wolf trains a man until the man obediently turns into a beast,
devours living flesh, and lustfully laps warm blood. Conversely,
the final visions start with a peaceful promise of resolution: the
wish-dream *All Girls Are Yours,* into which Haller's youthful
self had disappeared earlier and which he now dares visit. But

after this rehearsal of his emotional life from youthful love to disturbing sexuality, the last sequence of the Theater introduces him to the act, *How to Kill Through Love,* in which his failure is portrayed.

The expansion of the mirror image into individual scenes or acts is an important mode of lyrical progression. In *Der Steppenwolf,* such a movement is often achieved through the fade-out techniques of the motion picture; its peep-show sequence also resembles vaudeville shows (as decelerated versions of the film) and picture galleries in which individual portraits successively observed are ultimately blended into a single impression. Taking the concluding phase of the Magic Theater as an example, however, we note that a movement based on the hero's ambivalence between involvement and detachment can be portrayed also through counterpoints. Haller's confrontation with a mirror, which recurs periodically, always depicts his divided self in which the "wolf" gradually predominates. But these meetings with mirrors alternate with the appearances of Mozart, who functions as an image denoting "detachment." Thoughts of death lugubriously contemplated before a wolf image in a mirror are followed by the immortal strains of *Don Giovanni.* Mozart's ice-cold laughter underscores the counterpoint, and his ironic visions put Haller's sentimentality to shame. After the "murder," which intervenes as a contrapuntal return to the "involved" self, Mozart scores his point again, annihilating Handel's "holy" music by spitting it out of a loudspeaker. This way of proceeding by expansions and counterpoints can be observed particularly clearly in the death sequence. When Haller is crushed to the ground after trying to fly off to eternity on Mozart's peruke, he faces his darkest self in a full-length mirror. He smashes the looking-glass which opens to the scene of Pablo and Hermine in the slumber of satisfied love. Destroying this picture with his mirrored knife is an instantaneous reaction; the magic stage is soiled with the blood of reality. But when Haller contemplates the cold beauty of Hermine's body, the image shifts toward its opposite. Her immortal beauty reflects the death-cold silence of the universe. The image extends further: the silence becomes a form of ethereal music, the music of Mozart and the immortals. Mozart's immortal spirit returns to the scene. In the final act, *Harry's Execution* (incidentally also the last act of the peep-show), this progression is gathered up in a double image that contracts *Seele* and *Geist* in an identical illusion. Mozart turns into Pablo. The "master mirror" functions as a supreme magician who puts the Hermine figurine into his pocket. The play of magic on which Pablo-Mozart finally rings down the curtain unites the *Steppenwolf*-Haller with his transcendental image. "Sometime I would learn my game of figures better. Sometime I would learn laughter. Pablo waited for me. Mozart waited for me." He is ready to traverse once more "the inferno of my inner self." (IV, 415)

This method of progression has its analogy in the expansion not only of pictures but especially of musical chords. Hesse himself has likened his design to that of a strictly fashioned sonata built around the "intermezzo" of the Treatise.[28] This observation makes clear that in the novel the parallelism between imagery and music is conscious. Its progression can be compared to musical *sequences* of repetitive and contrapuntal notes. Moreover, as point and counterpoint of a divided self are mutually sounded, chords reflect both harmony and dissonance, which, translated into Haller's psychology, suggest the vision of detachment and the multiple self. It is, then, no coincidence that Mozart dominates the concluding scenes. The conflict of man and wolf, peace and bestial anxiety, which pervaded most of the Magic Theater, is converted into a higher opposition by his sublime detachment. Mozart translates Haller's confusions

[28] This point has been analyzed in some detail by Theodore Ziolkowski, who cites the following interesting statement by Hesse: "Rein künstlerisch ist der Steppenwolf mindestens so gut wie der 'Goldmund,' er ist auch um das Intermezzo des Traktats herum so streng und straff gebaut wie eine Sonate und greift sein Thema reinlich an." *Briefe, Dichtungen,* VII, 495. Cited from "Hermann Hesse's *Steppenwolf.* A Sonata in Prose," *MLQ,* XIX (1958), 115–140.

into the universal categories of art. When he flashes Brahms and Wagner upon the scene amid rising clouds and gigantic mountains, he creates a counterpoint to himself. His detached *heitere Musik* contrasts delightfully with their involved *rauschende Musik* of heavy instrumentation; he walks about light-footed and ethereal, while his adversaries are black men burdened by their time and by superfluous notes. Mozart, then, is also the "involved" Haller's opposite as both image (*Gegenbild*) and note (*Gegenton*). But since he is actually one of Pablo's magical disguises (or Pablo one of his), he is himself a contrapuntal figure, including both *Seele* and *Geist*. Motifs and chords reflecting such inner oppositions can present paradoxes without making them seem less paradoxical. They animate the movement of contrasts and render it as playful art.

Within this musical and pictorial movement, the mirroring technique gives rise to a lyrical allegory in which the divided self is ultimately contracted with its ideal image. A book is composed in which all figures and events are reflections of the hero's soul, in which a magic disquisition and a Magic Theater are symbolic extensions of himself. The course of the novel obviously also reflects the progression of dreams. Its pattern uses the most violent anxieties, the most far-fetched wish-dreams as well as the most meaningful hallucinations, to present a moral scheme. There are, of course, parallels between an illusory and an actual murder, between the acceptance of multiplicity in play and actual schizophrenia. Hesse mounts his charades against the background of the reader's knowledge of these relevancies. But his aesthetic plan was to lead him also beyond psychology.

Ostensibly, Hesse wanted to show that psychic torment is not resolved through scientific analysis but through the recognition that man's inner schisms do no more than mirror the disease of a divided world. Similarly, the idea of harmony in humor, detachment, the "magical" imagination, reflects a conviction that integration can take place only outside the social arena of our time. As romantic writers had believed in the elevation of self-awareness to an ultimate form of knowledge, so Hermann Hesse believed in the transfiguration of the outsider, embodying all the contradictions of a schizophrenic civilization, to become a symbolic ideal. The pilgrimage through the "inferno of my inner self" is really a trek through a hall of mirrors in which progression is countered by self-portraiture. *Der Steppenwolf* is a lyrical novel in which the fragments of a psyche are caught, multiplied, and ultimately reflected in symbolic imagery.

PORTRAIT OF TIME

—1

Hesse's achievements in lyrical fiction had established him early as an important romantic writer. By the beginning of the twenties, his work had borne out this reputation, for *Knulp* (1915), *Demian* (1919), his stories and fairy-tales, and especially *Siddhartha* (1923) had enriched a fashionable form. *Der Steppenwolf*, with its urban scenery and expressionistic techniques, seemed to indicate a new direction for Hesse's art. But a closer reading of the novel made it clear that it was no more than a translation of romantic conceptions into a somewhat different terminology. Only in the work of the nineteen-thirties and early forties did Hesse achieve anything approaching a reorientation of his basic romantic impulse within the framework of poetic narrative. Returning to settings in which he was more at home—medieval worlds variously modified—he evolved a new type of lyrical novel. *Narziss und Goldmund* (1930) began this phase with a rich, imagistic texture; but gradually, from *Die Morgenlandfahrt* (1932) to *Das Glasperlenspiel* (1943), Hesse's lyrical novel came to parallel more and more the novel of ideas without actually dissolving the structure of expansions and counterpoints or without abandoning the symbolic hero.

Before turning to the intricate philosophical mirroring of Hesse's *chef d'œuvre*, *Das Glasperlenspiel*, it might be useful to glance at the two important books which follow *Der Steppenwolf* in rather quick succession. *Narziss und Goldmund,*

which has been translated as *Death and the Lover,* appeared
only three years after *Der Steppenwolf,* as if Hesse had felt the
need to recover promptly from his immersion in the symbolic
city. The contrast is sharp enough, if we consider the medieval
setting of the new novel, its lush imagery (both tender and
cruel), its sensitive depiction of nature and rural landscapes.
The style, too, is as finely wrought and sustained a poetic prose
as Hesse had written since *Siddhartha.* But *Narziss und Goldmund* retains the psychological exploration of the self. Like *Der
Steppenwolf,* it is based on the divided hero, who now appears
in the form of two figures—a sensuous artist and an intellectual
priest. Goldmund is the man of sense; he is the artist-lover who
must escape from the monastery in which he had been taught
by the novice Narziss; a romantic *picaro,* rejecting ascetic *Geist,*
he must gather images from innumerable encounters with
women, knights, and rogues so that he may carve his *summa,*
the statue of woman as beloved, mother, and saint. Narziss is
the ascetic, the man of the Church and of verbal knowledge
who rises to become a Bishop and a power in his world. Their
mutual need brings them together in the end when the artist
returns to create his masterpiece and then to die. Goldmund's
art requires his friend's controlling intellect; Narziss' word needs
the "golden mouth" to preserve reasoning from narcissistic circularity and to complete God's work. Hesse's new direction
shows itself in an explicit concern for the "word," in his loving
treatment not only of Goldmund but of Narziss as well. This
fresh emphasis appears in a highly imagistic novel, for *Narziss
und Goldmund,* more successfully even than *Der Steppenwolf,*
recreates a symbolic analysis of self-consciousness in a delicately
lyrical form.

In the more rigorous allegory, *Die Morgenlandfahrt,* translated
as *Journey to the East,* a juxtaposition of actuality and illusion
becomes the main issue and the subject of dramatic tensions.
Projected into a future following the "next" war, it describes, in
its first phase, a medieval setting of the past, which, in its final
phase, becomes that of a contemporary town. It creates a utopian

Order of the Elect, who sought a vision of harmony in a common Orient of the imagination. Past, present, actuality, fantasy,
all belong in a single realm, where Percival and Sancho Panza,
Clement Brentano, Klingsor, Goldmund, Heinrich von Ofterdingen, and Puss 'n Boots ride and celebrate together. The novella
also features the divided hero composed of Hesse's fictional
persona, the "musician" H. H. and of his "eternal self," the
servant Leo. Up to a point the progress of images follows that of
the romantic picaresque, but when H. H. loses Leo in the
gorge of *morbio inferiore,* a sudden shift in decor switches not
only the content of the novella but its form as well. As the hero
searches first for the "lost" servant, then for the exact nature of
his own guilt, he undergoes a series of trials at which Leo eventually emerges as the highest judge. The story turns into a
Kafkaesque charade opening into the climactic image. When
H. H. rediscovers his "complete" self in dusty archives, it has
assumed the form of a statue in which he and Leo are joined back
to back. *Die Morgenlandfahrt* still employs the method of dissolving images and scenes, but it presents them in the fresh
context of a utopian vision and a philosophical idea.

────2

In *Das Glasperlenspiel* (*Magister Ludi*), Hesse sought to
break through to conventional narrative, to integrate the "play
of art" with a concrete picture of life. Choosing the outward
form of the chronicle, he approximated Thomas Mann's rich
Guckkasten world in elaborate, even Byzantine descriptions
narrated by a pedantic historian. In a rather peculiar way, this
novel contributes to a growing number of modern utopias. The
"historian" writes around the year 2400, relating events which
are history for him, yet which are considerably in the future
from our point of view. But the world he projects is wholly unlike similar visions to which we have become accustomed. It is
not like Huxley's *Brave New World,* which, even satirically,
assumes the Victorian idea of progress. Nor is it like Orwell's
1984, presupposing the essential depravity of man. Rather, it

presents the ideal almost as a *fait accompli,* intermingling all the ideal settings and worlds of Hesse's previous novels: the pious and well-ordered Middle Ages, the rational discipline of the eighteenth century, the poetic inspiration of nature of the romantic age, the timeless domain of the Indian Yogi. This book, which ripened during the late nineteen-thirties and the Second World War, establishes the author's rural vantage point in the Swiss Alps as the surviving oasis of a chaotic world. But it is a part of the novel's intricate construction that the idea is called into question. *Das Glasperlenspiel* is a carefully balanced picture of opposing motifs. Time and timelessness, reason and feeling, *Geist* and *Seele* confront one another in various juxtapositions.

The crucial construct in this novel is the Educational Province of Castalia. It is a secular Order of the Elect which came into being when the "feuilletonistic epoch" of the twentieth century had been destroyed by wars, when civilization had returned to that of the Middle Ages and knowledge tended to revert once more to the religious orders. Conceived as a citadel of learning to prevent the degradation of all secular culture, this Province devoted itself to the propagation of thought as an end in itself. Although messengers would go out into the world, although it would supply teachers, curricula, and books, Castalia remained essentially aloof. (VI, 176) Unlike the religious orders, which were directly involved in transient human affairs, it maintained an intellectual aristocracy, dedicated to the purity of *Geist*. Representing the paternal intellect, the Province excluded women and procreation, frowned upon all sensual involvements, and divorced itself as much as possible from sensibility and *Seele*. (VI, 162, 168, 174, 181, 188, et al.)

The most original invention in the novel is the Game of Glass Beads. As the Game is described by the chronicler, we discover much of its genesis and its function. The nearest analogy is the game of chess, but figures and moves are given various complex meanings related to all aspects of knowledge. It is also a mathematical analogue of the Yogi's concentration, whose individual vision orders flux into harmony. But the Game is objectified; it constitutes, to use Hegelian terminology, an "intellectual representation" of the spirit.[29] Antecedents of the Game include Pythagorean and scholastic systems as well as eighteenth- and nineteenth-century concepts of a universal language. Mathematics and harmonics unify disparate motifs: "Everything ought to be possible in playing the Game of Glass Beads, even that an individual plant converses in Latin with Herr Linne." (VI, 220) However, its aim is to trace and rearrange complex deductive systems through which all these motifs are related. The Game of Glass Beads is both a universal language and a "symbolic logic" through which relationships among data gathered from all the arts and sciences can be compared and analyzed. But it is also a "game"—a music of life. The chief function of the Castalian Order is the preservation and perfection of the Game of Glass Beads, to which its elaborate educational system, its hierarchies and ceremonies are dedicated.

The institutions of Castalia and the Game of Glass Beads are given life through the biography of their greatest master and apostate, Josef Knecht. His first and last names indicate his position as an exalted servant, continuing the tradition of Leo in *Die Morgenlandfahrt*.[30] The master-servant's rise and "betrayal" are the ostensible motive for the chronicler's account. The largest part of the novel is devoted to the story of Knecht's ascendency in the Order, and his elevation to the position of Magister

[29] For a discussion of the relevance of Fichte and Hegel to Hesse's concept of the Game (as well as for the reference to Hegel noted in the text), see M. Schmid, *Weg und Wandlung,* pp. 163f.

[30] Hesse stresses the relationship between *Das Glasperlenspiel* and *Die Morgenlandfahrt* by dedicating his novel to the *Morgenlandfahrer; Dichtungen*, VI, 77. The Pilgrims to the Orient are said to have contributed an ingredient of the Game: "ein Tröpfchen Öl aus der Weisheit der Morgenlandfahrer"; *Ibid.,* p. 97.

For the meaning of Knecht's name, see von Faber du Faur, "Zu Hermann Hesses Glasperlenspiel," *Monatshefte,* XL (April 1948), 182ff. The name is seen as an intentional inversion of Wilhelm Meister. Josef, the great servant of Egypt, is the obverse of Wilhelm, the German apprentice become master.

Ludi, the highest functionary of Castalia and the Master of the Game of Glass Beads, It also deals with his doubts, which he masters until late middle age when he leaves the Order for the world. Since the chronicler's perspective is confined to Castalia, he relates this ending as an unsupported "legend." Having left Castalia to devote himself to teaching in the world, Knecht dies in the service of his pupil in an isolated mountain lake. The ambiguities which led to his decision are also expressed in various appended "documents." Although it was forbidden by the Order, the young Knecht had secretly composed some poems. As a student, he had been required to write autobiographies of his inner life in order to purge himself of its influence. (VI, 189–191) The chronicler includes both the poems and the "exercises" as evidence of Knecht's incipient apostasy, for they reveal his secret impulses toward sensibility and *Seele*. Within the framework of the novel, these appendices appear as part of its structure and meaning, mirroring as images the chronicler's account.

—— 3

The protagonist is replaced as the novel's center by a threefold constellation: Castalia, the Game of Glass Beads, and Knecht. The tension between *Geist* and *Seele* is portrayed on each level of this triad, which appears as an intellectualized version of the triad of *Der Steppenwolf*.

Castalia portrays the scheme of opposites as a system. On the one hand, it presents a formal figure rather than a world in time because it is insulated and rejects movement and change. Mathematical relationships take the place of a fluid historical world. On the other hand, it seeks to reconcile dialectically the individual world of the imagination and the universal form. Knecht's revered teacher, the Old Music Master, admonishes him: "Take note: one can be a strict logician or grammarian and still be full of imagination and music; one can be wholly a musician or Player of the Game of Glass Beads and still be wholly devoted to law and order. The man whom we mean and want, whom to become it is our aim, would be capable, at any time, to ex-

change his science or art with any other; he would be capable
of illuminating the Game of Glass Beads with the most crystallic
logic and grammar with the most creative imagination." Yet
this universal dialectic, which expresses the spirit of Novalis, is
directed toward the rational *center*. Man must strive toward
perfection, toward "the center, not toward the periphery." Passion must be expunged because it is "friction between the soul
and the external world." (VI, 156) Creativity and imagination
are directed toward the manipulation of *laws* within a system
both self-sufficient and self-contained. In its later degenerative
forms, this dialectical balance shifts in favor of a pure, unworldly,
aseptic rationalism.

By contrast, the religious orders form the bulwark of historical
recognition and social commitment—they are concerned precisely with the frictions between the soul and the external world.
Their opposition is epitomized by Knecht's successful mission
to a Benedictine monastery, during which he brings about a
modus vivendi between the religious and secular orders. His
adversary, Father Jakobus, rejects Castalia's secular monasticism
as a disavowal of responsibility. "You treat world history the
way a mathematician treats mathematics, as if there were only
formulae and laws, but no reality, no good and evil, no time, no
yesterday, no tomorrow, only an eternal, flat, mathematical
present. . . ." (VI, 251) But this correct assessment of Castalia's
idea also defines its dynamics. Pure *Geist* is immutable and unchanging. From its ceremonies to the arrangement of its build-
ings, to the organizations of its authorities and levels of command, Castalia is created as a formal figure. At the same time,
such a pattern of unity is opposed to the world of sense in which
it necessarily exists. It is a noumenal construct placed in a phenomenal order. Hesse deliberately constructed his Castalia on
the figure of the cycle, whose steps ascend in spirals but cannot
move forward in consecutive time.[31] But the fact remains that
this universe contains the very change it abhors.

[31] An important corollary of the cycle and the geometrical figure is
that of the *stairs* leading upward in the hierarchy rather than forward

The implied dialectic also defines the Game of Glass Beads, which demonstrates the Castalian dilemma in its function. It is a brilliant analogue in the realm of *Geist* to the psychological mirror of *Der Steppenwolf*. Rather than reconciling conflicts within the human personality, it seeks to harmonize an intellectual universe. "Spirits like Abelard, like Leibnitz, like Hegel have undoubtedly known the dream of capturing the intellectual universe in concentric systems, and of uniting the living beauty of the intellect and of art with the magical formulating power of the exact disciplines." (VI, 85) The Game is also conceived as a transcendental concept, leading to a recognition of God. In its most perfect form, it became a "select, symbolic manner of searching for perfection, a sublime alchemy, an approach to the spirit above all images and manifold elements yet uniting them in itself, namely, to God." (VI, 112)

Conceived in this fashion, the Game also exhibits an inner opposition to the very phenomena of sense which it requires for its material. Because it is confined, by definition, to the formulation of abstract laws, actual discoveries of nature or actual values concerned with human conduct do not fit into its mechanism. Private sensations are banned as incommunicable. Knecht relates that he can recall, at any given time, the simultaneous awareness of early spring, the scent of elder, and the first chords of a spring song by Schubert. But although in his own vision this association is constant, it cannot be communicated except by and to himself and therefore cannot be admitted into the Game. (VI, 251) Even the most resourceful player can apply his originality only to the creation of new laws. Moreover, as a game this intricate system of symbols also alludes to Schiller's theory of art as play, for it unifies opposites in detachment and freedom with seriousness and metaphysical purpose. But by excluding the most significant aspects of art—sensuous content and

in time. See the discussion between Knecht and his friend Fritz Tegularius about a poem called *Stufen,* which Knecht had written. A pertinent fact in their discussion is that the poem had been previously named *Transcendentieren. Dichtungen,* VI, 482–487. For the poem, *Stufen,* see *ibid.,* p. 556.

original creation—it converts a parallelism into a contrast. Finally, the symbolic construct exists within the flow of time. As Knecht makes clear in his letter of resignation, the Game had been created in time and is therefore only apparently timeless. Its forms may be immutable, but, as soon as it becomes history and "appearance" (*Erscheinung*) on earth, it becomes a *passing event*. (VI, 470) "The Last Player"—one of the appended poems —clearly establishes this point:

> Gone—even the temples and libraries
> The schools of Castalia are no more . . . the old sage rests
> In the ruined field, the beads in his hand,
> Hieroglyphs which once meant much—
> Now only colored splinters, beads
> Soundlessly rolling out of the aged one's hands
> Vanishing in the sand. (VI, 548) [32]

A construct of *Geist,* excluding rather than transcending elements of *Seele,* the Game of Glass Beads invites the opposition of time and change which it is fated to contain.

These oppositions are clearly shown in Knecht's biography. His life prescribes a cycle which mirrors the cycles of the Game but, moving beyond them, also completes their dialectical purpose. He ascends from the chaos of *Seele* (his physical birth) to the mysteries of *Geist.* His initiation into Castalia, his spiritual birth, recurs to him as the most significant event of his life. But, having obtained mastery of the world of *Geist,* he moves beyond it, eventually returning to nature or *Seele.*

Each phase of Knecht's development contains elements of its opposite. His problem, growing more acute as he reaches ma-

---

[32]   Sie sind dahin, und auch die Tempel, Büchereien,
        Schulen Kastaliens sind nicht mehr . . . Der Alte ruht
        Im Trümmerfeld, die Perlen in der Hand,
        Hieroglyphen, die einst viel besagten,
        Nun sind sie noch bunte gläserne Scherben.
        Die rollen lautlos aus des Hochbetagten
        Händen dahin, verlieren sich im Sand . . .

turity, is that of his double nature. Like the *Steppenwolf*-figure, Narziss-Goldmund, or H. H.-Leo, Knecht is a composite hero. A seer and master of the spirit and intellect, he nevertheless includes an awareness of the manifold of human nature. As the chronicler makes clear, the Order requires the person's submission without his surrendering entirely all distinct, individual traits. "For us, the only hero worthy of our interest is a man who has been enabled by nature and education to allow his person to dissolve almost entirely in its hierarchical function, yet without losing that strong, fresh, admirable drive which creates the flavor and value of the individual." (VI, 62) But in an eventual conflict between person and hierarchy, apostasy becomes tragedy. Justifying his lengthy account of Knecht's rise and desertion, the chronicler points out the dramatic implications of a dialectic in which the individual spirit and the universal spirit are engaged.

In Hesse's scheme, the tension between "person" and "order" also expresses a tension between two kinds of vision. The rational order, we noted, is an objective counterpart of the Yogi's intuitive trance. A man who submits to the Order and accepts its intellectual concentration can achieve a vision of the spirit—the detached gaiety or *Heiterkeit,* an apprehension of rational order without individual passion. But a man involved in the world of images may find his soul invaded by a sensual world which breaks up concentration into chaos. With the Game of Glass Beads, the Castalian surrenders his personal vision to an independent form.[33] This conflict between the individual vision and the objective concentration toward the center pervades Knecht's

[33] This idea is implied in the Music Master's admonishment to Knecht, *Dichtungen,* VI, 156, noted above. See, for example, Knecht's meditation on the occasion of his appointment as Magister Ludi. The vision proceeds in two stages, first that of a "dream" of pictures, secondly that of symbol and recognition (*Erkenntnis*), which leads the way out of the *Welt der Bilder; ibid.,* pp. 309–311. See also the Music Master's account of the effectiveness of the concentrated vision in returning the doubting soul to the order; *ibid.,* pp. 178–181.

entire life. He is secretly fascinated by apostates or those silently dropped from the Order's rolls. His love for his spiritual father, the Old Music Master, is balanced by an indistinct longing for his physical mother. His rational discipline is matched by the "world of images" he creates in his biographies and poems.

Knecht's life expresses the ambiguity of human identity in an order of the spirit. In a definitive article, Miss Hilde Cohn shows that the balance of the novel rests in the relationship between the worlds of *Geist* and of nature or *Seele*. With his decision to leave Castalia to become the tutor of Tito, son of his worldly friend Plinio Designiori, Knecht's personal cycle mirrors the universal cycle of the Game. His initiation into the world of *Geist* under the aegis of the Music Master is repeated as an initiation into the world of *Seele*. The immersion in water reflects the baptismal rite as well as the Jungian primordial matrix of life. He dies within life, outside Castalia, yet beyond life on an isolated mountain. He introduces his successor to the unifying matrix of *Seele* (water) as the Music Master had introduced him into the harmonious world of the spirit. But upon entering nature and initiating his successor, Knecht does not resolve the tension between the opposite realms of being. Rather, he sets up a new contrast between the rite of *Seele* and the Castalian rites of *Geist* and so introduces another cycle. Indeed, Knecht's return to nature is a further step on the spiral stairs of the Game's dialectic and its logical consequence.[34]

This conclusion—along with the appended poems and biographies which support it—demonstrates Hesse's manipulation of opposites, his counterpointing sense, soul, and nature on the one hand, with barren, masculine mathematics on the other. The

---

[34] Hilde D. Cohn, "The Symbolic End," XI (1950), 347–357. Anni Carlsson points out that Knecht enters the world of sense in obedience to the "real" function or *eidos* of Castalia, which is to include and transcend, not to exclude as the actual Castalia does, the hostile world of sense. "Hermann Hesses *Glasperlenspiel* in seinen Wesensgesetzen," *Trivium,* IV (1946), 200–201. See Knecht's "Letter to the Educational Authorities," *Dichtungen,* VI, 451–471.

close relationship between this vision and the narrative of *Der Steppenwolf* is shown by their similarities and reversals. In the earlier novel, the proscenium of the stage is enlivened by sense encounters which are mirrored in the Magic Theater. In the later novel—prepared for by *Die Morgenlandfahrt*—the Magic Theater is the novel's actual stage, whereas the allegorical progress appears as its evanescent reflection.[35] The legendary conclusion and the appended "fiction" and "poetry" demonstrate the tension between life and spirit which had been Hesse's theme since 1919. But they also translate into terms of temporal progression the tension between phenomenal and symbolic worlds —between image and cycle.

———4

Explaining the Game of Glass Beads, the pedantic chronicler writes:

But a glance at the pre-history of precisely this intellectual life, namely at the evolution of the Game of Glass Beads, shows us conclusively that each phase of its development, each addition, each change, each significant departure, whether progressively or conservatively interpreted, reveals not its unique and actual originator but rather indubitably shows its most distinct features precisely in the person who introduced the change, who became the instrument of its transformation and completion as a perfect form. (VI, 81)

The self and the formal Game *mirror* one another; as the "originator" submerges his individuality, the form adopts some of his features.

This type of mirroring is symptomatic of *Das Glasperlenspiel*,

---

[35] Hesse explicitly compares the intellectual unity aspired to by the Game of Glass Beads with the sensual *unio mystica* of *Der Steppenwolf* and indicates that an early expression for the ideal harmony aspired to by the Game during the early "feuilleteonistic epoch" (our own time) had been that of the Magic Theater; *Dichtungen*, VI, 109. Cf. Paul Böckmann, "Hermann Hesse," *Deutsche Literatur im Zwangzigsten Jahrhundert*, p. 289.

translating the actual mirroring of *Der Steppenwolf* into abstract, dialectical relationships. It also indicates the direction of a peculiar type of allegorical narrative. The apparently consecutive story conceals a deeper level on which all temporal relations are resolved in formal figures mirroring the dual character of Castalia, the Game of Glass Beads, and Knecht. This technique is particularly relevant to the development of characters who are conceived as mirrors reflecting the discrepancy between self and symbol as well as various aspects of the self.

Knecht is mirrored in a variety of figures, representing his conflicts at different stages of his career, which are absorbed into the larger scheme of Order and Game. Foremost among these is a trio of teachers—the Old Music Master, the Benedictine Father Jakobus, and the "Chinese" Elder Brother—embodying different ways to harmony. Although they exist partly to lend some substance to Knecht's life, their main function is to act as a composite ideal against which Knecht's progress is measured.

The Old Music Master—Josef Knecht's paternal sponsor—achieves self-detachment in pure *Heiterkeit,* a crystallic gaiety reminiscent of Mozart's, removed from the chaos of the world of sense. In his Nirvana outside time, he exemplifies complete control, rational insight, and "absolute direction toward the center." (VI, 347–357) He is only one step below the top rung of the hierarchy—the Game of Glass Beads—which signifies not only his own importance but also that of the art form he represents. Music, we noted, acts as a harmonizing art, reconciling the dissonances of life in terms of abstract laws which nonetheless reflect a noumenal freedom. For Knecht, the Music Master embodies the best of the Castalian spirit, its clear, rational "magic." He recognizes him as his godfather and initiator, and, by rising a step beyond him to the Master of the Game, he fulfills his teachings even more perfectly. But finally he also denies his teacher by realizing the inherent contradictions of the Castalian world and by acting upon his recognition.

Father Jakobus, on the other hand, acts as the paternal guide from the opposite point of view. As we have seen, he introduces Knecht to the time-bound laws of history, which can be overcome not by formal relationships but only by the transcendent Godhead. In their argument in the monastery, Jakobus makes clear that the Game of Glass Beads remains a game despite its sophistication. It cannot approach the power of the sacrament founded in human values and relevant to human action and experience. (VI, 273–275) Knecht, the exponent of a secular order isolated from the world, thus meets the defender of a religious order committed to the world. Between them, they reflect the novel's dialectic. But Father Jakobus' teaching also indicates the terms on which Knecht later breaks with Castalia and becomes its deserter.

The Elder Brother is chiefly an image of Hesse himself. A hermit whom Knecht visits as a student desiring instruction, he has devoted himself to the thoughts and habits of a Chinese thinker, and, though himself European, he speaks only Chinese and builds a Chinese bamboo island in an occidental world. His private isolation corresponds to the communal isolation of Castalia. The plants and rock garden in his bamboo grove are fashioned in meaningful figures which parallel the symbolic configurations of the Game. His reading is centered on the *Book of Blossoms* by Dshuang-Dsi, an interpreter of Lao-Tse, which teaches the self's surrender to the divine, its attempt to create unity by penetrating the world of appearances. This view opposes a transcendental quest for the self's elevation to the Godhead, Castalia's tendency to deny or exclude nature. When Knecht asks the Elder Brother whether he can build the latter's important principle, the *I Ging,* into the Game of Glass Beads, his host discourages him.[36] Later the sage also rejects the narrowly

[36] *Dichtungen,* VI, 204–206, 211. The Elder Brother's mystical *I Ging* is referred to by Hesse as early as his "Kurzgefasster Lebenslauf" (1925) as a way of recognizing and transcending the haphazard and changeable character of "so-called reality"; *ibid.,* IV, 486–487. For an account of *I Ging*

Castalian Fritz Tegularius, whom Knecht sends to him to learn Chinese. The Elder Brother's acceptance of Knecht, then, suggests not only an alternative solution but also a recognition of a cleavage within Knecht. His mysticism prefigures the final stage of Hesse's dialectic in the novel as a whole, in which nature and soul are reasserted as part of man's striving for unity.

Knecht's contemporary, Plinio Designori, exhibits most clearly the intellectual manipulations of the novel. His name—"One of the Masters" of the World—mirrors inversely that of his friend, the Servant (yet Master) of Castalia. Moreover, both men harbor analogous conflicts, enacting between them the implied dualism of the Castalian world. Early in the book they debate publicly the relative merits of Castalia and the World, encouraged by the authorities. In these debates their opposition is only apparently simple: Designori defends the World, Knecht the Order. But in brilliantly defending Castalia, Knecht also seeks to silence his own doubts, while in his equally astute hostile position Designori reveals both an intimate knowledge of the institutions in which he had been trained and his secret affection for a way of life he was destined to leave. (VI, 165–186) Later, Designori visits Castalia to study the Game as a hobby, but during this brief time the doubts of both men are repressed. (VI, 216–219) Their meeting in late middle age, however, results in complete understanding. Designori applies for admission to the Order just as the Magister Ludi decides to leave. (VI, 386ff.) In reversing their positions, each reveals a corresponding affection for the other's world. They are aspects of one another and reflect the inner contradictions of Castalia and World. Moreover, by entering the world as the teacher of Designori's son, Tito, Knecht cements this friendship as a *symbolic* relationship. As Hilde Cohn has observed, his death for Tito in the mountain lake confers a symbolic import upon the youth who now com-

and Dshuang-Dsi's *True Book of Southern Blossoms,* see Gnefkow, *Biographie 1952,* pp. 87–90. Gnefkow also indicates that the Elder Brother is an ironic self-portrait of Hesse; *ibid.,* pp. 90, 96.

bines within himself his spiritual and his physical father in a resolution of spirit and life.

In many ways, these figures perform functions familiar from Hesse's earlier novels; they are allegorical personages representing stages in the hero's quest, mirroring the conflicts of his divided nature, and acting as parts of a composite self. This is evident in most of the minor figures, such as the Castalian "hot house flower" Tegularius or Knecht's predecessor, Master Thomas von der Trave (whose name obviously and somewhat maliciously alludes to Thomas Mann). But the figures we have examined more closely also act in a further capacity. They mirror Knecht's conflicts but, in so doing, they also represent the dialectic of ideas underlying both Castalia and the Game. Mirroring, however, extends beyond the intellectual scheme into the world of *Seele* through analogous figures in the fictional biographies.

The biographies repeat in more broadly imagistic terms Knecht's search for the vision of unity through the teacher of salvation. In "Der Regenmacher," Knecht appears as the disciple of a primitive rainmaker and enacts his relationship with the Music Master in "magical" terms. His sacrificial death also foreshadows his own sacrifice for Tito. In "Der Beichtvater," Knecht appears as a confessor of the early Christian era who, dissatisfied with the results of his leniency, seeks out a Master renowned for his punitive methods. Joining the Master, he achieves fulfillment of his mission in combination with him but ironically discovers after his companion's death that each had searched for the other to complement himself. This search for unity and synthesis culminates in the concluding vision of "Indischer Lebenslauf." In this biography, an Indian prince, exiled in a society of shepherds since early childhood, murders his brother and becomes a fugitive. Prowling, like Haller, at the fringes of the "world," he is accepted by a Yogi, who teaches him isolation from the World of Maya. A vision of himself in the water of a brook arrests his last attempt to return to the "world." Under the influence of the Yogi's magic, his own features broaden into an image of life as a whole. The encompassing vision, apprehended in an instant of time, takes all past, present, and future as its province and shows him the horrors of the world. As an intuitive personal vision, in which time is reduced to an instant, it reflects Castalia's timelessness, but as a vision of nature and sense experience it is also its antithesis. The biographies thus reveal the dialectical conflict of ideas embedded in the novel as a whole, but they supply the counterpoint of *Seele* to the Castalian vision of *Geist*. Characters in the novel and in the biographies, then, mirror the oppositions of the Game, the Castalian World, and the human hero at the same time that they are also reflections of one another.

———5

As in Hesse's earlier novels, the fabric of *Das Glasperlenspiel* is woven of conflicting images. But, completing a development from subjective to objective lyricism, the novel does not always present its images in a vivid or even a sensibly accessible form. In the chronicler's account, they are nearly devoid of all pictorial surfaces (even Knecht is difficult to visualize). Landscapes are rendered in symbolic colors and formal figures. The most operative "images" are intellectual constructs, such as the Game, or abstract ideas revealing the oppositions of the novel. On the other hand, the journey into the "world" described in the conclusion presents nature in its vital diversity; its images resemble the pictures viewed by Knulp or Goldmund.[37] This contrast exposes the novel's dialectic in which creative, disordered nature appears as the obverse of Castalia's regular, harmonious forms.

Seen from this point of view, *Das Glasperlenspiel* contains profuse imagery; the mirroring of the characters extends into the

---

[37] The vividness of the mountain landscape described in the conclusion contrasts sharply with the monotonous green that characterizes the Castalian landscape. See Carlsson, "Hermann Hesses *Glasperlenspiel*," pp. 184–185. Knecht acts like the familiar vagrant, sitting on the back of a cart, playing a flute, recalling a poem by Rückert; *Dichtungen,* vi, 522–523.

novel's texture. One important way of conveying such images is that of the visionary trance, such as the Old Music Master's on the occasion of Knecht's first visit or Knecht's at the time of his appointment as Magister Ludi. Each such trance is an enactment of the Game, an attempt to order disparate ideas, snatching them out of time and the historical process, or an endeavor to refine the self. But these moments of vision are also mirrored in the "symbolic end" and in the fictional biographies. Here the reflections are reversed. The Indian prince apprehends multifarious nature in a single vision of *Seele*. Similarly, the disciple of *Der Regenmacher* sees a physical image of a harmonious universe which mirrors the harmony of ideas in the Castalian world. By contrast, the very notion of the "rational center" as the object of the Castalian's trance indicates a metamorphosis of the self into an instrument of knowledge. In the architecture of Escholz as in the symbolic flower beds of the Elder Brother's grove, such images create formally, often abstractly, an implied counterpoint between man and idea.

The relationship between hero and ideal expresses itself also in an opposition of consecutive movement, based on time, and of the cycle, based on geometric form (the mathematical equivalent of image and vision). As an allegorical quest, *Das Glasperlenspiel* conforms to a linear ascent. This progression is also suggested by the novel of education, which traces Knecht's development from a boy in the primary grades to the most exalted representative of the Order. Finally, the chronicle, by definition, employs consecutive time. But the world in which the hero actually functions presents a formal, timeless constellation. The "flat present" of an ahistorical Castalian mystique is matched by the circular movements of the Game, which, in turn, reflect the Castalian's ascent on the metaphoric circular stairway. Teachers and students are caught in a cycle which eternally renews itself, moving from the teacher's initiation to that of his student, who eventually begins anew by inducting a pupil of his own. (vi, 310–311) The idea is not only a caustic comment on academic circularity but also an echo of the Game's symbolic cycles. Musical harmonies, based on the succession of notes, illustrate the paradox which underlies the Game and its Castalian world.

These oppositions are also reflected in the psychic life; the tensions of *Der Steppenwolf* inhere in a symbolic scheme in which time and timelessness are telescoped. The conflicts dominating Knecht's personality are mirrored in the Game of Glass Beads, which, in its intellectual refinement, represents Novalis' idea of unity in multiplicity.[38] It reflects inner division as an opposition of ideas, i.e., of laws and their noumenal relationships. The analogy between human conflict and the transcendental dialectic is taken literally. The opposition within each of Hesse's composite heroes between the inadequate self in the world of sense and its ideal is absorbed by the novel's world as a whole. The ideal becomes a substitute for the hero; the novel's conflict is consequently dehumanized. This fact is evident in the relationships among Knecht, Castalia, and Game, but it also extends into the "nature" episodes of the "end" and the biographies. Deliberately avoiding human involvements as such, Hesse lends even the humanized episodes a stylized, philosophical quality. The opposition of ideas, however, is clearly stated: in the chronicle, men and institutions seek to follow rules above empirical laws; in the legends and appendices, they act through an intuitive awareness of the empirical world. Each realm is latent in the other; their opposition in the end opens another cycle presumably beyond the confines of the novel.

In Hesse's reshaping of the *Bildungsroman,* then, the tension between line and cycle becomes decisive. As in *Wilhelm Meister, Das Glasperlenspiel* is built around a central symbol, that of the Game, which parallels Goethe's theatrical world.[39] The protago-

[38] See Carlsson, "Hermann Hesses *Glasperlenspiel*," pp. 194f. Novalis, *Schriften,* III, 70.

[39] For descriptions of *Das Glasperlenspiel* as a *Bildungsroman,* and for the analogy with *Wilhelm Meister,* see Curtius, *Kritische Essays,* p. 217; Cohn, "The Symbolic End," pp. 348–350; Carlsson, "Hermann Hesses *Glasperlenspiel*," pp. 184ff.; von Faber du Faur, "Zu Hermann Hesses Glasperlenspiel," p. 182; Max Schmid, *Weg und Wandlung,* pp. 215–217.

nist seems to ascend in the Order, as well as to progress in time, but the cycles he prescribes as a teacher and a beholder of visions lend his progress an illusory quality. His life from nature back to nature, from the baptism of birth to the "baptism" of death by water, suggests such a negation of progress. Moreover, linear allegory itself is negated. Rather than viewing a hero's ascent toward the ideal, Hesse places himself within the ideal and from this vantage point measures his protagonist's progress— and eventual desertion. This position alludes to the stages of the hero's quest; at the same time it counteracts them, because it is identical with that of the ideal in which progression has already been resolved. A similar circularity is evident in the entire apparatus of the "educational province." The hero is so defined that he includes both its teachings and its inherent contradictions. In his service, he does not change but merely echoes its *eidos*. Deserting, he carries out a duality which had been implicit all along. The presentation of an educational motif and its subsequent negation is a final irony of the novel.

In an exhaustive analysis of *Das Glasperlenspiel*, Oskar Seidlin commented that Hesse's novel is really an extended short story. *Novelle* or *Allegorese* rather than the usual term, *Roman*, would most appropriately describe the work because it lacks a dimension in depth and the organic or psychological direction of a true biography, because it manipulates symbols rather than creating a world, and because it moves in a single unity.[40] This remark can be viewed in the light of Hesse's purpose of developing a

Although this notion has been usually held in critical literature, Joseph Mileck takes issue with the comparison; *Hermann Hesse's "Glasperlenspiel,"* University of California Publications in Modern Philology, No. 9 (Berkeley: University of California Press, 1952), p. 254. Nevertheless, various resemblances remain pertinent: the structure of the novel of development; the idea of the pedagogical province; the stress on apprenticeship and mastery; the idea of an essentially aesthetic unity suggested by Goethe's "schöne Seele"; the construct of the Game paralleling the puppet plays of *Wilhelm Meister*.

[40] "Hermann Hesse's *Glasperlenspiel*," *Germanic Review*, XIII (1948), 263–273.

dialectical scheme rather than a world of people. But these charges also indicate the attempt, distinctive of lyrical fiction, to convert the linear progression of the novel into one or several single situations portrayed as a pattern of images. In this instance, the novel's denouement is made only retroactively meaningful by the *pointe,* or, to use Hilde Cohn's term, the "symbolic end," which in its abbreviated action mirrors the inner contradictions of the novel as a whole and completes its dialectical movement. The trick ending, as Professor Seidlin observes, is indeed symptomatic of the short story and novella, but in *Das Glasperlenspiel* it also performs a poetic, albeit highly intellectualized, function. For the novel's meaning is contained in the subtle and *continuous* texture of dialectically opposed motifs.

Das Glasperlenspiel reduces various oppositions—time and timelessness, progress and its negation, *Geist* and *Seele*—to a single formula expressed by the figures of the line and the cycle. Their juxtaposition, however, illuminates an otherwise barren, inhuman novel as imagery of ideas which formulate the *issues* of lyricism. Like most of Hesse's fiction, it lacks a firm grasp of the machinery of the novel—conversations are elaborate and declamatory, characters are often puppets, the world, though ingeniously devised, is but a dialectical pattern—but in this instance it does not compensate for this absence of a fictional world by direct and sustained lyricism. The imagery in the appended biographies does not entirely relieve this impression of paucity. But, although the novel is chiefly expository, the problem it poses is the most advanced formulation of Hesse's poetic idea. Like music, the linear expansion through association and time is counterpointed by the immutable, circular form. In a dialectical movement of ideas, and in a harmony of counterpoints, these two elements are constantly contrasted and resolved. *Das Glasperlenspiel* is a refinement of a method which had matured since *Demian.* Consecutive narrative is reflected in an instantaneously apprehended form by which lyrical fiction is defined.

LYRICAL OBJECTIVES

Hermann Hesse's lyrical novels reconcile an inner vision with a universe of consecutive events. His success in creating an adequate form in the spirit of Novalis is his most important distinction as a modern writer and transcends many of his difficulties and imperfections. Combining allegorical narrative with psychological and philosophical self-portraits, he achieved a vision of man and ideas with an immediacy usually unobtainable in conventional narrative.

As a novel, his *Demian* is neither original nor particularly successful. The ideas are vaguely romanticized reproductions of Schopenhauer and Nietzsche; Hesse's original contributions had to await a later time. The mysticism of "light" and "dark" had already been worked out far more credibly in Thomas Mann's *Tonio Kröger* and *Der Tod in Venedig*. Many of the methods are still reflections of Maeterlinck and the post-symbolist romanticism which had pervaded German fiction. A large number of situations are sentimental, the flurries of intersecting images confusing, and the constant variations of a single theme appear from a perspective of forty years often wearying or dull.

Nevertheless, the sensation which the novel created in its time can be explained by its method. Fiction that appealed to the postwar malaise was not wanting in 1920, but Hesse created symbolically the feeling of the epoch. Enriched by obscure mystical references and modern, psychological recognitions—aloof from the political slogans of the day—his fiction achieved its tremendous effect precisely because of its weaknesses. Mann had portrayed the self in society; he had described the "outsider" against the image of a decaying universe. But Hesse expressed the desolation of the self facing a world in which society has been overcome, in which world and self are internal images. Novalis' allegorical form is turned wholly inward as metaphysical despair and psychological conflict are resolved in a celebration of the self. Expressing the sexual fears and fantasies of adolescents and young adults, Hesse converted trauma into a symbolic ideal. Through the use of emblems, pictures, and allegorical forms directed within, he fashioned both a portrait and a lyrical poem from the hopeless pilgrimage toward nothingness on which a generation of the educated young was embarked in 1919.

This approach served Hesse well in consolidating his reputation during the nineteen-twenties. The familiar fairy tales, nature idylls, and vagrant picaresques were now recast in allegorical fiction that sustained brilliantly Hesse's rejection of modern life. Knulp, his hobo of 1915, is a key figure in this form. Characters such as Sinclair, Siddhartha, or Goldmund echo his *Wanderschaft* as they move through space and time toward goals which eventually turn into their self-portraits. Visions and pictures chart the "Way Within" from the rural landscape of "Klingsors letzter Sommer" and the Indian world of *Siddhartha* to the medieval quest of *Narziss und Goldmund* and the fantastic transformations of *Die Morgenlandfahrt*. In this way, lyrical allegory as Hesse's principal form spanned the crucial German decade from 1919 to 1932.

An exception to this development is provided by Hesse's so-called "crisis" period of the mid-nineteen-twenties—the period of *Kurgast, Steppenwolf,* and *Krisis* poems. Feeling that his flight from urban life had become ineffectual, he found in expressionistic technique and in the dissolution of the hero's unconscious a new and, temporarily, more adequate manner. In *Der Steppenwolf,* the mirror was enlarged from a direct correspondence between image and subject into a means of portraying vividly the fluid unconscious and the divided self. But Hesse also used it as a method to provide a formal framework and thus created a more sophisticated scheme. Through psychological penetration and technical devices not available to Novalis, he rendered Novalis explicit: he depicted the implications of Novalis' symbolic allegory.

The contrast between the hero's progress and the contraction of self and ideal into a symbolic form also expresses the hero's ambivalence between dissolution and harmony described by the content. For this reason, *Der Steppenwolf* merits close attention. Rendering romantic allegory as both progress and contracted form, it defines the techniques and problems of lyrical fiction. Although the novel still bears the onus of the sentimentality Hesse sought to expunge and although it opens no strikingly original perspective, it exhibits skillfully and subtly the dialectic implied in romantic prose allegory. The mysterious changes of a self, for all their evasions and paradoxes, move the reader to ignore artificial triads and repetitive motifs to partake directly in a man's tragic divorce from reality caught in the prisms of humor, illusion, and play.

Das Glasperlenspiel extends this solution into a verbal and philosophical scheme. The image of consecutive time, on which linear allegory is constructed, is transcended by ironic oppositions. The novel is a vision of the future related in the past tense by an historian who describes a life in which time is artificially denied. Reciprocal mirroring is shown as a skillful analogue of human and universal experience. Drawing upon Buddhist and Confucian thought, Hesse translated the psychological resolutions of *Der Steppenwolf* into a dialectic of ideas. By reformulating the motifs of mirror and picture largely in abstract terms, the novel presents a kind of irony which is more rarefied, and occasionally more obscure, than are the more human and psychological ironies exhibited by the earlier novel. Yet the form as a presentation of a human and a universal idea, contrasting with the fluidity of life, is common to both works.

As they progress beyond the lyrical textures of *Demian* and *Narziss und Goldmund,* Hesse's novels seem flat and elaborately intellectual. Where poetic imagery is suppressed, as in the body of *Das Glasperlenspiel,* this lack of substance is particularly apparent because dichotomies of ideas cannot replace conflicts in a visual world. But few novelists have distilled the philosophical and lyrical essence of the romantic novel as purely as Hesse. If such a novel is found wanting, this is not wholly due to the author's obvious limitations as a writer. His chosen genre precluded the ordinary standards of narrative.

Although there has been a revival of interest in Hesse (particularly among young Americans, who may sense in *Der Steppenwolf* a kinship of revolt), most of his work has not penetrated too far beyond German-speaking audiences. Despite a Nobel Prize, his international reputation has never approached that of Thomas Mann, with whom, in Germany, he has been often compared as an equal. The reasons are not far to seek; they lie in his choice of the lyrical genre. In the English-speaking world, for example, this form appears alien to the novel, vaguely experimental, without the substance of character and plot required even of poetic novelists like Hardy or D. H. Lawrence. Nor does Hesse seem to be a "symbolic" writer like Faulkner or Joyce. Seen against the background of German tastes in the novel, however, his lyrical fiction is by no means unconventional.

Hermann Hesse's fiction develops into a significant variation of the modern lyrical novel. Neither wholly psychological nor entirely imagistic, it is built around the structures of the *Bildungsroman* and the allegorical picaresque—romantic forms which have taken deep roots in the German literary imagination. Yet Hesse penetrated further than the forms he used; his lyrical novels display a depth beyond that of older contemporaries like Hermann Löns or of younger emulators like Manfred Hausmann. His vision is Klingsor's self-portrait in the widest sense: Hermann Hesse's *persona* viewed as an image of contemporary European Man. With all of the accrued connotations of Taoism and Buddhism, of Freud and Jung, his novels evolved a sharp diagnosis of modern life, directly psychoanalytic in the work of the early twenties, tempered by more spiritually defined harmonies in the work of his old age. Utilizing the manner of Jean Paul and Novalis, he condensed the time-bound hero and the timeless ideal into a dual vision, embodying equally a dialectic of ideas and the physiognomy of the generation for which he wrote.

4

ANDRÉ GIDE

Lyrical Fiction and the Symbolist Method

PERCEPTION AND FORM: THE NOVELIST IN SPITE
OF HIMSELF

— 1

A READER of André Gide's fiction is easily mesmerized by the
spectacle of the artist donning his literary disguises in the
presence of his public. The close interrelation of Gide's fiction
with his various journals—themselves self-conscious enactments
of the literary personality—arouses curiosity about the real person behind the literary poses. But the self that reveals itself
kaleidoscopically in the pages of Gide's books wears the mask of
art: it is Baudelaire's fool at the pedestal of the figure of Venus,
bells, cap, and lonely awe. Ironic self-pity and an obsessive drive
for self-exploration, meeting with the hard limits of his art, have
created an image of Gide as the sincere hypocrite.

The paradoxical posture of confessor and prevaricator which
underlies the problem of Gide's "sincerity" determines his method
in the novel.[1] Whether Gide described his works of fiction as
récits, soties, or *romans,* all of his forms represent different manners of discovering formal analogues for subjective experience.
Detached and critically analytic, Gide has expanded and varied
the method of the prose poem in several disguises. His early
work was intentionally lyrical. Studies of his prose style, such
as Jean Hytier's, have shown his distinct commitment not only
to poetic language but also to poetic conceptions of material and
form. But when Gide deliberately denuded his language to affect

[1] See Jean Collignon, "Gide's Sincerity," *Yale French Studies* (Spring
1951), No. 7, pp. 44–50; Thomas Cordle, "Gide and the Novel of the
Egoist," *YFS* (Spring 1951), pp. 91–97; Kurt Weinberg, "Gide romancier:
la sincérité truqué," *Romanische Forschungen,* LXVII (1956), 274–287.

a sparse, "classical" rhetoric, the lyrical mood survived in the conceptions and structures of his works.[2] A confining form analogous to the abbreviating frame of the prose poem produced the simultaneous rendering and prevarication of confession which has remained typical of his art.

Gide only partially acknowledged the significance of lyricism to his fiction. For example, with *L'Immoraliste* (1902), he believed he had broken with his "lyrical" past; the loose effusions from *Les Cahiers d'André Walter* (1891) to *Les Nourritures terrestres* (1897) were now behind him. In 1905, he praised a German visitor for realizing that in *L'Immoraliste* he had ceased to be *un lyrique* and had achieved the ability to "glimpse through the gaps of culture." [3] But from his remarks about *Les Faux-Monnayeurs* twenty years later, we also know that Gide was still struggling to reach out toward an external world which for him was the only legitimate purview of the novel. This ambivalence between controlled confession and the external world resolves itself in a new conception of objectivity which Gide belatedly acknowledged. In a shift of focus, characters and events become part of schematic designs.

This shift defines Gide's method in the novel. Jacques Rivière contended, with considerable support from subsequent critics, that Gide's books "are not the books of a poet," because he does not "make the universe sensible to us." Gide's style does not recreate things.[4] But actually this attitude reflects a different kind of lyricism. As Gide turned away from a poetry of sensuous imagery, he utilized the consecutive function of prose to trans-

---

[2] Jean Hytier, *André Gide* (Algiers: E. Charlot, n.d.), pp. 13–14; 33–34 *et passim*. Note particularly Hytier's definition of the *ton poétique,* which he distinguishes from the *ton pittoresque* and the *ton éloquent,* and which he sees borne out in Gide's early work. Marie-Jeanne Durry pursues Gide's style in search of "poetic" elements up to the period of *Les Faux-Monnayeurs;* "La Poésie d'André Gide," *Hommage à André Gide. Etudes, Souvenirs, Témoignages* (Paris: Editions du Capitole, 1928), pp. 97–109.

[3] November 23, 1905; *Journal* (American edition; Rio de Janeiro: Gallimard, 1943), 1 (1889–1912), 218.

[4] *Etudes* (Paris: Nouvelle Revue française, 1924), pp. 180, 186.

form personal perceptions into their formal equivalents. This "objective" lyricism in the novel—sparse, analytic, often even discursive—employs new means of presenting a world. It creates the abstract hero and the stylized form as poetic methods of narration.

The personal cast of Gide's work, even when he wished most to escape into impersonality, establishes the hero as a disguised representative of the self. For this reason, the problem of his sincerity resolves itself into a question of the fictional presentation of the self, whatever its disguises may be, and eludes the moral stigma of hypocrisy so frequently applied to it. Nevertheless, it was Gide himself who raised his aesthetic preoccupation with himself as a moral issue. As late as December 1924, he suggested in a conversation with Roger Martin du Gard that some day a very knowing physician might discover that a gland of internal secretion, a *capsule surréale* opening him to the external world, had atrophied in him.[5] Moreover, from his earliest journal entries to his so-called "first novel," *Les Faux-Monnayeurs,* Gide had been haunted by the moral and aesthetic implications of his famous distinction between the sincere poet and the prevaricating artist. "Morality," he wrote in 1892, "consists of supplanting the natural being (original man) with a manufactured being which is preferred." The latter, he continued, the artist, cannot be sincere; only the former, the poet, can be sincere, and the artist will seek to supplant the poet. In the struggle between both the work of art is born.[6] This point was clearly expressed in Gide's *Traité du Narcisse* (1892). Here the self's symbol—Narcissus' reflection in the water—is objective and unwavering, enduring the flux of time, indeed, existing outside of time. As long as it is untouched by *awareness*—or its corollary, desire for possession—which destroys its existence as a pure form, harmony and innocence are possible, poet and artist are one. But after awareness (the Fall), and with the birth of time, it is only in art that pure form can exist and the real self can find its ex-

[5] *Journal,* III, 38.
[6] *Ibid.,* I, 31.

pression. Poet and artist are now distinct and the struggle between the sincere poet and the prevaricating artist becomes a
necessity.[7]

The conflict with superimposed control is formally conceived.
It has been remarked that Gide forced himself to use prose fiction in order to counteract his compulsion for lyricism or unfet-
tered self-projection.[8] But in effect this strained use of narrative
changed the terms of the narrative genre itself. As an enactment
of the struggle between the *révélateur* and his necessary limitation, it is symptomatic of the conflict between "poet" and "artist."
As late as the period of *Les Faux-Monnayeurs,* the novelist
Edouard, who often acts as Gide's mouthpiece, is made to remark: "I gladly believe that only the artist is in a position to
dominate the lyrical state, though, in order to dominate it, he
must have experienced it first." And he defines lyricism as a
state in which man allows himself to surrender to God. (XII,
445–446) In Gide's career as a writer, this domination of lyricism
takes on an almost obsessive quality. Although he would have
preferred to control it by means of conventional fiction and to
create heroes acting in society and world, Gide produced passive
heroes whose visions were depersonalized by forms. This tendency in his work is underlined by his ambivalent rejection of
symbolism and by his search for a classicism in which truth to
"inspiration" and truth to the confining letter can be identified.
Indeed, in Gide's fiction form takes the place of the external
world as a source of moral and aesthetic control.

The symbolist hero, through whose eyes the author could
legitimately view the world from his own perspective, reshaped
the universe in which he was placed; furthermore, he sought
adequate symbols, detached from himself, in which his visions
and perceptions might be manifested. Reality is conceived of as

[7] *Le Traité du Narcisse, Oeuvres complètes d'André Gide,* ed. L. Martin-
Chauffier (Paris: Gallimard, 1932–1938), I, 211–212 *et passim.* Hereafter
numbers in the text enclosed by parentheses will refer to this edition.

[8] See Thomas Cordle, "Gide and the Novel of the Egoist," *YFS* (Spring,
1951), pp. 91–92.

a strained juxtaposition of deformed worlds and corresponding masks donned by the hero as a tragedian or clown. Similarly, Gide constantly transforms the world with his poetic and critical intelligence, and his heroes assume masks which also mirror the distortions they project. This deformation of reality by the inner man is accomplished, even in Gide's late novels, in terms of Novalis, Schopenhauer, and Mallarmé. In his generally critical notice on Villiers de l'Isle Adam, Gide clearly defined the role of the symbolist artist: ". . . for life easily turns into a kind of parade, ironic and theatrical alike, sometimes in bad mummery; and it is the role of the artist, who does not believe in it, to cast on this nothingness a prestige, or better, to oppose to this nothingness, which must be avowed, another life, another world, a world created by the artist himself, an artifice made by him which he will pretend to be the revelation of the pure idea, which he will soon call the true world, the work of art." (III, 417) Despite the sharp, yet melancholy irony, this statement also betrays the role into which Gide himself had cast the poet and hero. As a self whose disguise mirrors the poet's perceptions, the protagonist also portrays these perceptions in constellations of images. A masked consciousness and conscience, he is an abstract artifice, a formed and forming intelligence who acts as the poet's *persona* in art.

This conception of the hero defines Gide's notion of formal objectivity. "That which passes today as 'objectivity,'" he wrote in his journal in 1924, "comes easily to novelists without interior landscapes. I can say that I am not interested in myself but only in the conflict of certain ideas of which my self is only the stage on which I function less as an actor than as a spectator, a witness." [9] Like Rimbaud's wood that cannot help it if it finds itself a violin, Gide turns the mind of the author into a stage on which his inner experiences and crises are enacted, then to be distanced from him in the novel's form. The very concept of "subjective objectivity," achieved, as Henri Peyre made clear in discussing

[9] *Journal*, III, 17.

La Porte étroite, through a successive or simultaneous incarnation in his characters, implies that in the shoes of his protagonists Gide stepped into a world which then became his own. This procedure issues in an act of highly personal depersonalization. It induces an objectivity wholly unlike that of the legitimate novelist, to suggest instead a kind of objectivity "so dear to symbolist poets," a formal or lyrical objectivity.[10] The hero masks the poet's intentions and only in this way becomes an autonomous figure whose world mirrors the author's inner landscape.

The formal prevarication of the inner man implies a version of idealism which survived Gide's most impassioned rejections.[11] Indeed, German idealism, with its tendency to telescope problems of value and problems of knowledge, had created that fruitful confusion of philosophically distinct relations which marked many of Gide's observations on the purpose and forms of art. In *Si le grain ne meurt* he may have cast aspersions on the vagueness of terminology and the overemphasis on the self in Fichte and Schopenhauer, who had "nourished" him as a young man, but in 1924 he was forced to admit that he had continued to live under Schopenhauer's spell.[12] His reading in Goethe and Nietzsche had led him to a concept of a Faustian man who rises above good and evil to become a supreme knower.[13] But although Gide subsequently questioned this notion, he retained a stylized conception of the poet-hero as the percipient whose visions are fashioned into art. As Lyncaeus in *Les Nourritures terrestres,* or Michel in *L'Immoraliste,* or Lafcadio in *Les Caves du Vatican,* this hero deforms the universe through his acts of awareness and so presents that cluster of ideas of which he is but the stage.

[10] *Hommes et oeuvres du XXe siècle* (Paris: Corrêa, 1938), p. 140.

[11] "De l'influence allemande," *Oeuvres,* IV, 413. See Peyre, *Hommes et oeuvres,* p. 112; Peyre, "André Gide et les problèmes d'influence en littérature," *Modern Language Notes,* LVII (1942), 558–567.

[12] *Oeuvres,* X, 301; *Journal,* III, 36.

[13] "Goethe," *NRF,* XXXVIII (1932); See Renée Lang, *André Gide et la pensée allemande* (Paris: Plon, 1949), p. 121–172 (Goethe) and pp. 81–120 (Nietzsche).

⟶2

An epistemological situation is created by Gide's concept of the hero's function and his relationship to the novel's form. This manner of viewing the problems of narrative had been a living issue for Gide since his earliest journal entries. His remarks particularly in the early 1890's abound with speculations about the self, its isolation, and its necessary relation to objects. The writer (subject) is opposed to the objects with which he works: "the writer must refuse himself to things." [14] But he is modified by them and by the work into which they fuse, so that work and objects are joined with their creator. This relationship of self and object, as the product of the imagination, defines for him the typical psychological novel: "The acting subject, that is the self; the retroacting object, that is the subject which one imagines. There is, then, an indirect method of acting upon oneself which I have thus presented, and that is simply a tale." [15]

This reciprocity of subject and object illustrates Gide's role as a writer and his concept of character and world. A formal projection of experience becomes an indirect method of "acting upon oneself." It may be argued that this statement of 1893 predates Gide's public break with the Symbolist Movement, that this very definition of psychological narrative suggests a method he was soon to satirize in *Paludes* (1895) and to explode in *Les Nourritures terrestres* (1897): the method of writers such as Huysmans and Dujardin. But the evidence of Gide's work and of his later reflections reveals that although this position was modified and renovated, it was never wholly abandoned. Even *Les Caves du Vatican* and *Les Faux-Monnayeurs* are "psychological" novels in which there is a sustained and subtle relation between each center of consciousness and its appearances in the perceptions of others. Indeed, art as an indirect method of acting upon oneself is not only evident in the novels or fictional "treatises" but also, as Germaine Brée has shown, in Gide's dialogues and

[14] June 3, 1893, *Journal*, I, 40.
[15] August, 1893, *ibid.*, I, 44–45.

plays.[16] It defines the tension between the self and its image from *Le Voyage d'Urien* to *Les Faux-Monnayeurs*.

The notion of reciprocity between a subject and an object of consciousness is implemented by mirroring. In the "Traité du Narcisse," for example, Narcissus before the Fall discerns no substantial difference between himself and his image, but after the Great Reversal the situation is changed. Loss of innocence has brought with it a conception of knowledge according to which the reflection exists apart from the viewing subject and is now an object of consciousness; the mirrored Narcissus is transmuted into an ideal or formed image. This shift in epistemological relations brings with it a moral meaning, for the distortion of sense content required by the form involves a falsification of experience which invites moral judgment. The knowing consciousness reflected in its ideal form is also a conscience.

Seen in this way, Gide's penchant for mirroring describes both a technique of writing and a moral vision. In the "play within the play" which Gide praised in *Hamlet* and in "The Fall of the House of Usher"—a situation set *en abyme* in a larger work—two transformed worlds are in turn mirrored in one another. This parallelism of aesthetic forms also leads to a reciprocity of moral perspectives, of clusters of ideas in which Gide professed a primary interest. But the insert obtains a deeper significance, for it becomes a symbolic representation of the work as a whole heightened as a significant image. Even in Gide's later novels, such formal mirroring suggests a *chiffre de la transcendence*—the key to an aesthetic and spiritual transcendence of the self—which Claude-Edmonde Magny noted in *Les Faux-*

---

[16] *L'Insaisissable Protée. Étude critique de l'œuvre d'André Gide* (Paris: Société d'Edition "Les Belles Lettres," 1953), pp. 122-155. Discussing Gide's early plays—*Philoctète, Saül,* and *Le Roi Candaule*—Germaine Brée sees the three heroes as a triad in which Gide's moral and personal dilemma is enacted and in which the recognition of his homosexuality—his awareness of a consequent exile—finds a dramatic and stylized portrayal. The chapter is significantly entitled "Je Est un Autre" and deals particularly with the representation of a moral scheme.

Monnayeurs. The mirrored image of a hero, or a world, expresses its own features formally shaped in an aesthetic and moral sense alike.[17]

What seems, then, to be confined to Gide's neo-romantic or symbolist beginnings, is actually a pervasive point of view which he held throughout his life. But his notorious ambivalence led to many different ways of describing the possible relations between awareness and form. In the early prose, the hero faces a world which owes its existence only to himself. The passengers in his symbolist *Voyage d'Urien* discover that their encounters are really only mirages of varying stability. In his *récits,* however, perceptual and moral awareness are fashioned into well-ordered schemata. Forms appear disordered in novels like *Les Caves du Vatican,* but an intricate system of ideas seems to control the satiric world manipulated by the skillful hand of a concealed narrator.

It is a truism of Gide's career as a writer that the mirror as a formal vessel is always matched by his "inquietude," his compulsion to reveal the incoherent impulses of the soul. Or, conversely, the Baudelairean passion for the quirks of the unconscious is ultimately always matched by the figure of the artist who checks impulses and imposes constraints. But, whichever way is chosen, a *limitation* of the impulse is introduced which derives from general artistic requirements and a classical tradition. For the music of Gide's violin is not entirely Rimbaud's nor is his sense of the "limits of art," his denial of the impulse, wholly that of Mallarmé. Although his heroes seem to remake their worlds in their images, the forms they seek are not completely suggested by symbols of inner states. Form was to be

[17] For the entry about the inset mirroring the work as a whole, see *Journal,* I, 44–45. Claude-Edmonde Magny recognized the intimate relationship between this early notion and Gide's technique as late as *Les Faux-Monnayeurs.* In her analysis of this novel she discusses " 'la mise en abyme' ou le chiffre de la transcendence," viewing the latter as a "Hièroglyphe de l'absurde constitutif de l'être . . ." of infinite depth and complexity. *Histoire du roman français depuis 1918* (Paris: Editions du Seuil, 1950), pp. 269–278.

"classical," and in Gide's vocabulary "classical" and "form" are taken in an aesthetic and moral sense alike. The Cartesian "I" as the rational knower submits his recognitions to Kantian forms of knowledge and morality. Experience is caught in limiting forms that displace the self, as in Racine's tragedies the self is effaced by a coherent and self-sufficient world. But, to compound the paradox, for Gide these qualities are ideally developed within the disciplined writer. In a brief reply to the editors of the journal *Renaissance,* Gide once said:

> True classicism is not the result of external constraint; that which remains artificial produces only academic works. It seems to me that the qualities which we like to call "classical" are above all moral qualities, and I consider classicism a harmonious vessel of virtues among which the first is modesty. Romanticism is always accompanied by pride, by infatuation. Classical perfection implies not the suppression of the individual . . . but his submission, the subordination to the word in the phrase, to the phrase in the page, to the page in the work.

Elsewhere, he cites Kant's famous remark about the pigeon that soars aloft only because of the resistance, or formal restraint, which the presence of air provides. Aesthetic and moral limitations are necessary to art, which perishes in total freedom.[18]

On one occasion when Gide described lyricism as a formal idea without the usual connotations of subjectivism and purple prose, he significantly did so in discussing another art form. After reporting on the performance of a Japanese dancer in his *Lettres à Angèle* (1900), he referred to "true lyricism" as the tempering of the "realism" of immediate experience in a manner acceptable to art. (III, 204–209) Through balance, harmony, limitation,

---

[18] "Réponse à une enquête de 'La Renaissance' sur le classicisme," *Oeuvres,* x, 25–26. Note also the phrase: "L'art naît de contrainte, vit de lutte, meurt de liberté." "L'Évolution du théâtre," *Oeuvres,* IV, 206–207. Note Justin O'Brien's discussion of this problem. *Portrait of André Gide* (New York: Alfred A. Knopf, 1953), p. 337.

through the submission of inspiration to the idea of preconceived beauty, true incarnation of the self in art is accomplished. But this notion of lyrical restraint is only partially realized in ready-made forms like the *récit*. Its chief virtue is precision, a kind of sincerity which, Gide noted as early as 1891, requires that the idea or substance of expression must command the word (interpreted as phrase, style, and even entire works). In this meaning of constraint, even the precise rendering of Gidean "inquietude" is not antithetical to a classical ideal. For the inconsecutiveness of the unmotivated act and the deliberately apolar novel are precise reflections of the poet's intentions caught in corresponding forms. Gide's searching self-analysis, and the intuitive falsifications he practiced, produces images in his heroes which become autonomous reflections of himself. To borrow Pound's famous phrase, the impulse is precisely rendered.

In Gide's world, formal relations signifying perceptions and ideas maintain a coherence of structure and design rather than a coherence of cause and effect. His figures reenact the drama of the Baudelairean prose poem. In this way, even Gide's classicism maintains its roots in the nineteenth century. The moral ideal and the formal stage of seventeenth-century tragedy are fused with a notion of the *objectified self*. Like the classicism of Pound and the early Eliot, Gide's classicism, too, extends and sharpens the peculiarly subjective notion of objectivity that describes the traditions of Baudelaire and Mallarmé. A "classical novelist," Gide also creates a version of symbolist poetry.

— 3

Any discussion of André Gide as a lyrical novelist must take into account his problematic ambivalence as a writer. A faithful and rigorous stylist, he demanded of himself both a complete rendering of the self, with all its distortions, and a precise rendering which might catch these distortions in corresponding forms. He was a *poète manqué* and yet, for all his protestations, a novelist in spite of himself. His refusal to project experience in the form of lyrical verse closed to him a rigorous manner of self-depiction which had been open to his contemporaries Valéry, Claudel, and even Jammes. But, on the other hand, a manifest difficulty in portraying a credible external world left him only the lyrical way of self-variation within ostensible forms of fiction. As a novelist, he never approached the richness of world and texture achieved by Proust. But the tragedy of his life became the substance from which he worked. The poetic crystallization and the subsequent detachment of the self reach in Gide's prose their most complete realization.

THE POET AS PERCIPIENT

———1

In the early phase of his career, Gide's work seemed to have been almost entirely circumscribed by his concern with self-consciousness and its relation to objective form. Two books of the eighteen-nineties, *Le Voyage d'Urien* and *Les Nourritures terrestres,* explore the act of awareness. *Le Voyage d'Urien* (1893) ironically projects a voyage in which each landing and each Homeric encounter is a symbolic way station. *Les Nourritures terrestres* (1897), on the other hand, obliterates these way stations and renders, instead, a flux of sensations—*la volubilité des phénomènes*—whose meaning is discerned by the percipient and reader.

In *Le Voyage d'Urien,* the reader embarks on an inverted Odyssey whose episodes are formal mirrors of a quest. It is a journey of dream-like, indeed often hallucinatory appeal, in which the landscapes encountered by the travelers are landscapes of the soul. The protagonists are a group of passengers on the *Orion.* Akin to the masters in Novalis' *Lehrlinge zu Saïs,* they are a chorus whose leader, Urien, is also the novel's first-person point of view.[19] All other people are essentially images in their minds, including the mariners on their boat, the "natives" they meet

---

[19] For the comparison with *Die Lehrlinge zu Saïs,* cf. Albert J. Guerard, Jr., *André Gide* (Cambridge: Harvard University Press, 1951), p. 67.

on their various landings, and imaginary figures who appear from nowhere. Moreover, the protagonists are wholly *passive* percipients, while landscapes, encounters, as well as figures are their collective content of sensibility and thought changing with their varying perspectives. In this way, the theme of self-liberation—the freedom to embark on the sea of desire while preserving one's purity—is developed through a contrast of the percipients' shifting modes of awareness with objects suggesting stability that they both seek and shun.

Gide's irony in this book lies partly in his deliberate play on the meaning of objects as the furniture of the external world and on their meaning as images in the interior landscape. In consequence, an odd universe unfolds before the travelers' eyes which reflects simultaneously an inner and an outer world. For example, a picture of their ship's submergence in "pure night" is rounded out by exclamations drawing a lesson:

> Changing aspects of massive cliffs and of long-drawn rocks jutting out into the sea. Cliffs! Metamorphoses of cliffs!

Urien, the narrator and hero, addresses the rocks directly:

> . . . we now know that you exist: it is in passing that one sees you passing, and your aspects change with the pace of your flight, despite your fidelity.

The Gidean question "what is out there?" is answered ironically. Changes in awareness become metamorphoses of objects. Although an external world is suggested, it is endowed with a movement projected by the self. "We learn," the narrator concludes, "to discern things which pass among the eternal isles." (1, 288)

This relationship of change and stability—based on the constant conversion of objects of nature into objects of the mind—is reflected in the ambivalence between the self's capacity for awareness and the changeability of objects which derive their existence from the perceiving self. For this reason, all things are subject to sudden and inexplicable changes. Even the "eternal isles" are inhabited by sirens; the North Pole reveals a majestic city shining unexpectedly through coats of glaciers; a lush island turns into the home of *Maenads* whose queen's demands on the heroes' purity exact ridiculous tributes; the blue-stocking, Ellis, appears in a boat reading *The Treatise of Contingency*. The mind, embarked on a sea of unpredictable sensuality, converts each appearance into a foil and object of temptation. The Platonic relationship of unchanging forms and of phenomena dependent on shifting perspectives is revealed through these visions of things symbolizing or embodying modes of awareness.

For this reason, descriptions are seldom ends in themselves. They usually suggest the percipients' visions manifested by the objects and their appearances. Whatever the descriptions of the bathing mariners may signify, they do not exist for themselves. The sailors are perceived objects whose changing shapes indicate forms of awareness, motions which contrast flux with the fixed beacon of the onlookers' perspective. Similarly, the more rarefied picture of Ellis—who becomes the intellectual counterpoint of the chorus—is a satirically distorted encounter mirroring the act of *connaissance*. (I, 327–333) Objects, events, or figures become symbols for sensations, transformed images of the heroes' quest. When one of the passengers falls ill with fever and snow must be fetched from the top of a mountain, both snow and fever instantly lose their sensuous import. The fever becomes a state of undefined longing and the snow a blue flower of fulfillment. In the later scenes of the *Mer des Sargasses,* this symbolic world is more loosely conceived, as experiences of objects are yoked with abstract concepts. A description of night is ironically translated into metaphysical terminology:

Majestic and profound night where our ecstasy has spread; texts of truth, where often a metaphysical flame shuddered; algebras and theodicies, studies! We have left you for other things, ah! truly for other things. (I, 331)

Concepts intermingle ironically with sensations to character-
ize symbolic objects and to give things specific weights. Or,
conversely, both ideas and feelings appear disguised as things
to furnish the baggage which the percipients must discard. But
since these objects are crystallized sensations and ideas, the protagonists cannot easily dismiss them; they are after all created
by their condition as percipients. In consequence, their very drive
for liberation becomes a ridiculously circular enterprise. Subject
and retroacting object are unified in a cycle which ends in the
percipient himself. The journey can lead only nowhere.

Satirically, then, this book points out the dilemma involved
in translating perceived reality into symbolic objects, because
the very nature of the perceptual act invites circularity. The voyage, as Gide tells us in his versified *Envoi,* was a dream journey
whose sole existence lies in an interior landscape. The very movement through this landscape demonstrates the function of objects as images appearing to a percipient for whom the world
dissolves, because he has created it. A linear counterpoint to this
implied circularity of theme is established by the fact of the
journey. Satirizing the *Odyssey, Don Quixote,* and other journeys of adventure, the seafaring sequence also suggests the Baudelairean voyage to *Cocagne,* the Rimbaldian dream voyage of
the *bâteau ivre.* In the later stages of the voyage, symbolist description appears with heightened intensity. Figures and objects
blend into one another with increasing fluidity, moving from
the fevers and crises of the *Mer des Sargasses* to the geometrical
purities of the *mer glaciale.*

Implicit in *Le Voyage d'Urien* is its sense of the concrete object as a crystallization of a moral and perceptual point of view.
For this reason, much of the book recalls the prose poem; perceptions converted into objects symbolize thematic points which
are arranged in a corresponding design. At the same time, this
closed form, in which the objects are manipulated as self-contained entities, is ironically juxtaposed with the unending and
therefore open voyage. It is a journey into a dreamland where

landscapes describe a picture of the soul. Ultimately, this soul is a universal content of consciousness which the poet portrays as an extension of himself. But this vision of an internal world with its unending vistas is simultaneously contrasted with a world of concrete symbols. The inner life is blended with capricious patterns of varying absurdities.

———2

During the five years which separated the conclusion of *Le Voyage d'Urien* and the publication in 1897 of *Les Nourritures terrestres,* Gide underwent his personal conversion. The satire *Paludes* (1895) had made evident many of the ironic asides against symbolism implied in the earlier book without the ambivalence which still marked *Le Voyage.* In *Les Nourritures,* however, the crystallic symbol is passionately discarded. The interior landscape itself is annihilated by a disordered flux, and objects are displaced by the "pure" sensations to which they give rise. The voyage through life, caught in the closed form, is replaced by a novel of education open to infinite flux, and the theme of self-liberation is actually demonstrated in its form.

The result of this change in method and in literary allegiances is a greater closeness to life, an often ecstatic demonstration of immediate experience caught in Whitmanesque exuberance, but at the same time the destruction of any recognizable narrative form. Whereas the wit of *Le Voyage d'Urien,* and indeed also of *Paludes,* had been the pretense of rigorous narrative as a counterpoint to symbolic absurdities, the point of *Les Nourritures* (on the whole a singularly unwitty book) is to suppress the story by a manipulation of sensations and the imitation of disorder created by sensuous flux. The *Bildungsroman,* underlying a seemingly irrelevant pattern, is broken into fragments, because immediate experience does not appear in continuous forms. The reader, the percipient, the disciple must be taught to supply these forms so that the projected development can be realized.

For this reason, the movement of teaching and implied learning has been intermingled with many seemingly disconnected elements: the inserted poems of free verse, the scraps of laconic dialogue, the vignettes of prose description, diary passages and moments of sensation thrust outward without apparent connection, brief stories and longer reflections which set the tone and suggest the theme of the book. Each of these moments is relevant to the idea of self-liberation, of breaking the bondage of social and moral institutions; it also always alludes to the converse need for form amid flux. In this conflict the interlocutor seeks to present all aspects of experience, all possible pitfalls and moments of enjoyment, the "infinite possibility of sensation." The narrator teaches his disciple; teaching him, then leaving, is his *raison d'être,* the single constant that pervades the book.

Three figures stand out in *Les Nourritures terrestres:* the protagonist or narrator as the continuous though changing self, the protagonist's previous master, Ménalque, and Nathanaël, his shadowy disciple. But neither Ménalque nor Nathanaël actually exists. The author's fictional "I" describes his book as being peopled by no one. (II, 103) Indeed, Gide suggests that all three figures are joined in the narrator and assume no independent existence. (II, 57)

Within this scheme, the book indicates the interlocutor's changing attitudes in the act of teaching.[20] In Book I, Gide not only defines the subject of the protagonist's teaching and the disciple's requisite attitudes but also gives the reason for his outlook. From the dependence and the dim and indolent perceptions of illness (II, 69), the convalescent reaches out toward independence which he hopes to find in sensations:

> My emotions have opened up like a religion. Can you understand this—every sensation is infinite in its *presence.* (II, 66)

or "To understand is to feel capable of doing." (II, 67) In growing health he is freed and proclaims his liberation in the prose poems constituting Book II. But, in the concluding passage of

[20] In the "Envoi," teaching is emphasized through a denial. *Oeuvres,* II, 223.

Book III, sickness and the need for stability are once more introduced, to be made fully apparent in the final phase of Book VIII.

As a character, Ménalque seems to serve as a savior, a kind of Platonic prototype of the protagonist's teaching, while at the same time assuming a particular personality as an object of fear. Ménalque interferes in the protagonist's teaching by removing the restrictions still felt by the latter on his expanding and asserting will.[21] Indeed, particularly in the opening pages of the book, Ménalque appears to the narrator as Mephistopheles appears to Faust or God to Moses. (II, 67) In the concluding book, through the vertigo of fever images, the poet's cry is for Ménalque: *"Je songe à toi!"* These moments are part of a narrative scheme which introduces the reader to Ménalque and then proceeds to establish parallels between the latter and the teaching poet's admonitions to himself. But while this scheme is an undercurrent that pervades the entire book, it is also broken up into individual moments which the percipient must trace. In each case the narrator is portrayed as longing for Ménalque, as being too weak to hold him, as being forcibly freed to find his own way. In each case the same course is suggested for Nathanaël, who is warned against similar pitfalls.

Within this movement, Ménalque's major appearances are concentrated at three crucial points: at the outset, the moment of liberation; in the center, opposing the ambiguous search for stability with the directness of his life history; and at the end, when the interlocutor calls for his aid. Nathanaël, on the other hand, is wholly mute; his presence is felt only through the narrator, who suggests his pupil's answers in the way he formulates his statements and questions. He is entirely ear, yet his importance lies not only in his identity with every reader who chances to open the book but also in his relevance to the protagonist as the latter's lover and pupil. Nathanaël thus mirrors the more fully elaborated relationship of the *moi* and

---

[21] For Wallace Fowlie's discussion of Ménalque's function, seen in terms of his genesis, see "Gide's Earliest Quest: *Les Nourritures terrestres,*" *Essays in Criticism,* II (1952), 293–294.

Ménalque. As aspects of a single self, Ménalque and Nathanaël are images of one another, determining between them the direction of the book.

—— 3

The fabric of *Les Nourritures terrestres* is woven by Nathanaël and, by implication, the reader, who create forms from apparently disjointed impressions. Both things and their meanings seem to depend on minds. "Let the *importance* lie in your look, not in the thing you look at" (II, 63), the narrator exhorts Nathanaël at one point, and at another he exclaims: "Before me, ah! let each thing be made to shine; let every beauty be clothed and colored by my love." (II, 78) In a familiar sleight of hand, Gide identifies sense perception with sensuality. The epistemological act of casting loose sensations into forms becomes a morally relevant celebration of the senses. Both are intermingled as the narrator exclaims: ". . . springs will flow where our desires bid them; for land comes only into existence as our approach gives it form." (II, 62; 12) [22]

Similarly, the opening scene in *Le Voyage en diligence* is not introduced by the physical objects—the carriage, the faces of the other passengers, or even their reflections in dark window panes. Rather, it is given through a sense of motion and discomfort, through the feeling of warmth engendered by a little boy sleeping at the narrator's shoulder. This scene illustrates Gide's procedure in directing the reader's attention toward the form in which sense experiences must be cast:

> He was there, up against me; I felt by the beating of his heart that there was near me a living creature, and the heat of his little body burned me. He fell asleep on my shoulder; I

[22] Page references given here are to both the French edition and, following the semicolon, the English translation used by the author, which was Dorothy Bussy, trs., *Fruits of the Earth* (New York: Alfred A. Knopf, 1949). Subsequent references to this translation in this section will be treated similarly.

heard him breathe. I felt disturbed by the warmth of his breath, but I did not stir for fear of waking him. His delicate head bounced with the violent jolts of the coach in which we sat, horribly crammed; the others slept too, making the best of what remained of the night.

The subject matter of this passage is not the boy but the feeling suggested by his presence: "the heat of his body burned me"; "I felt disturbed by the warmth of his breath." Everything else is in the shadow, relegated to vague outlines representing the moment of feeling. And we can divine, though in the description itself it remains unsaid, a further *inner form* of these feelings which narrator and reader share: protective tenderness above sensual love. This conclusion is then concentrated in a rhetorical question:

> Indeed, yes, I have known love . . . , but of this moment of tenderness is there nothing I can say? (II, 148; 102)

The "inner" conceptual form in which the narrator's feelings should be cast is explained by a "sign-post" statement. By yoking such direct comments with concrete images, Gide seeks to lend a particular perspective to sensations so that his disciple's manner of forming them will correspond to his intentions. This aim is achieved even as he questions the method itself, for the hero's ambivalence is an important aspect of the book.

Such reflections, presented as rhetorical questions, assertions, images, interpolated songs or scenes, break into the aesthetic situation and compel the reader to review his attitudes toward the book. These reflections create a thematic movement akin to a "lyrical process." A passage based on the swaying sensations of a seasick poet, for example, grows into a lyrical sequence through alternations of images and interlaced comments. In the initial picture, the *moi* perceives the rolling waves through his porthole. He observes: "Only their form continues to move; the water is given to them and leaves them and never goes with them. For a few brief instants only does the form occupy the same being . . ." (II, 106) The obvious, if unspoken, analogy to human life is condensed in this image of the constant form composed of fluctuating waters. The picture is then enriched by the interlocutor's exhortation to cast all thoughts to the winds. Together, the images of the waves and of the dispersal of thoughts demonstrate anew the pendulum between stability and motion which informs the book. Gide returns to the waves, but retains the thoughts: "Fluctuating waters; it was you who made my thought so shiftless." He also emphasizes the instability of the form: "You can build nothing upon a wave. It gives way beneath the slightest weight." (II, 173) In the final turn, he takes the reader back to the state of rest; the longed-for harbor is a counterweight of the mind's *errements* in the world of sense. But this port also includes a new source of perceptual power. Rather than looking through the unstable porthole, the soul will be "finally at rest beside the roving beam of the lighthouse," glancing "upon the sea." (II, 173) By opposing the shiftless self to the circumscribed motion of *le phare tournant* which lights up and thrusts into darkness the world within its beam, Gide transfers the focus of awareness from the individual mind to a center outside the mind. But however external to the self the power of knowing may be, it must still seek to approximate the light's perspective (it is *beside* the beam). Having jettisoned its intellectual burdens, the experiencing mind must be as near as possible to the center of awareness and, on the same solid pier, must seek its repose. The image of the waves has grown through expanding images based on a sick voyager's reveries.

The conflict between change and stability appears to be an opposition of the individual self and objective or universal form. In Book VI, the poet's power of apprehension is identified with Lynceus, who is called upon to descend from his tower and to look at each thing *de plus près*.

For have you not sensed that in this book there is *no-one?* And even I, I am nothing but *Vision*. Nathanaël, I am the guardian of the tower, Lynceus! (II, 183)

This theme is developed through various currents of lyrical sequences which occasionally mirror, often transform into its medleys of imagery, the underlying development of the story of education. The reality of both the vision and the protagonists, for example, is questioned as part of the theme of Book VIII. These passages convey a sense of the isolation of a self whose view of reality depends on its own awareness. The protagonist is cast into despair and concludes by calling upon objects and persons outside the self:

> A sob; close-pressed lips; overwhelming convictions; anguish of thought. What am I to say? *Things* that are true. The One-Other-Than-Self—the importance of *his* life. Oh to speak to him! (II, 218)

Despite the intense preoccupation with the self as a power of awareness, a contrary undercurrent is made fully evident in the end, and also forms a narrative climax of moving intensity. But this conclusion raises questions which have been thrown up by the flotsam of images throughout the book. Are there *choses véritables* apart from the impressions of the mind? Is it sufficient to decide whether one is exhilarated by or indifferent to the fact that two plus two makes four? (II, 92) Or is more needed: *true* facts in the world? These problems, already raised by Narcissus, dramatize the ambiguity of content and the negativity of form in a work shaped by a percipient whose existence is called into question.

———4

The combination of the aesthetic and narrative design of *Les Nourritures terrestres* is rendered not only by disconnected moments but also by several larger movements—pictorial scenes, bits of stories, and poetic and narrative idylls. Book V, for example, is composed of a continuous sequence of scenes. After descriptions of a rainy autumn in Normandy, attention turns to the scenes of roaming in *Le Voyage en diligence*. At the end of the coach journey, the focus shifts to a "picture gallery," *La Ferme,* and breaks again into movement in its final passage. In the "farm idyll" the narrator is given a key to eight doors, each of which leads to another scene representing a particular moment of sensation. Finally, he is led back into the plains through a ninth door. Since these scenes prescribe an arc from movement to rest and back to movement, the reader is reminded of the eight books and the epilogue of *Les Nourritures*.

Similar actions of scenes may depend on such devices as straight narration or the formal idyll. The history of Ménalque's life is perhaps the most important, for no matter how independent of *Les Nourritures* its genesis has been, in the context of the book it is pivotal. Connecting the travel notes of Book III (which include the wave image) with the Garden of Love of Book IV, this story acts as a thread whose straightforward narrative binds two such very different sequences together. But its central passage captures both the novel's content and its form in a single image. It shows Ménalque watching a bourgeois family through a window before he lures the boy away to become his disciple. Thematically, this scene suggests the obvious mirroring of Ménalque's attitudes toward the *moi* and of the latter's relationship with Nathanaël. The scene also epitomizes Gide's perceptual method. Observing the boy, Ménalque includes him as an image; the scene he views displays *en abyme* the rationale of the book as a whole.

The pastoral which follows poignantly illustrates the design of *Les Nourritures terrestres* by extending further the perceptual image central to Ménalque's biography. Its scenic arrangement of the Florentine Hills (and its Virgilian pattern) reinforces the sense that a formal design has been imposed on a concealed narrative. At first the scene still echoes the tone of narration: friends gathering in a garden and, after refreshments, breaking up into individual groups. But then this pattern is dissolved. Snatches of dialogue, songs, hymns of praise appear at first as a disordered medley of sounds. A union is achieved only by the narrator visualized as moving from group to group. Through him, the individual voices become part of one consciousness, his own, the reader's, Nathanaël's. A form emerges, indistinctly at first, then with surprising clarity, from words half understood. The combining consciousness—here the drowsy semi-awareness of a poet's intoxicated dreams—fashions the context in which these separate elements are joined.

Gide seeks to achieve such a choral effect in the entire novel. Like the figure walking in the garden, the reader gathers up all the disparate elements of sensation which he combines into form. Through an implied structure Gide can reflect the flux of sensations and celebrate their beauty not only by outright praise but also by the subtler method of forcing Nathanaël to inspect the quality of his feelings while making him aware of their ambiguity. Many contradictions remain, but the very contrariness of *Les Nourritures terrestres* emphasizes its theme and its underlying plot: the exultation of the convalescent returned to life combined with the anguished reminder of the ambivalence of flux in feeling, which may leave the searching mind aimless and, in the end, isolated.

———5

Gide's effort to project an implied form into the flux of the senses results in a portrayal of self-liberation. The controlling power of the will becomes an ethical act as well as an act of knowledge. By creating his forms, the hero functions as a single consciousness which includes himself as well as the figures he imagines. But this consciousness is also moral because it forces the reader to create not only shapes but also worlds of objects and others, as well as values, against which his impulses must be measured. Indeed, by mirroring perceptual in moral awareness, Gide has presented an involved confluence of lyrical and narrative forms. The figures that the narrator conjures on the scene do interact in their teaching, their doubting and singing. Conflicting statements, images, scenes gradually distill the theme that appears in the conclusion and is balanced by the *Envoi*. By means of the perceptual act, a pattern can be traced reflecting an underlying narrative in which moral choices are implied.

The poet is the percipient. Gide's inversion of the conventional novel in which sensations conceal a disjointed plot does not obscure the debate of the threefold character by which the theme of freedom versus stability is explored. Although the exuberant tone and loose imagery make clear that *Les Nourritures* shares in the tradition of the prose poem, its form is also firmly tied to the novel; a compound of both, it is a *lyrical* novel. Through discrete perceptions molded by thematic statements Gide created a deconcentrated type of lyrical fiction to which he returned at the climax of his career.

THE MIRROR OF NARRATIVE

—1

The disjunction between personal experience and an objective form besets any novelist who seeks to reconcile his craft with a compulsion to reflect variations of himself. The Gidean solution, particularly successful within its limits, rested on a balance between the poet, mirroring the perceptions and moral crises of a self in the work, and the dramatist, playing his role upon the stage of himself. Yet, despite his success, Gide resented the bonds within which his achievement was contained. His drive for different forms was motivated by his dissatisfaction with the limits of his art, by his search for an external reality through which, he felt, his work could be justified.

The egocentric predicament, which shaped Gide's epistemological point of view, sharply limits his scope. The hero's vision, whether continuous or momentary, had to remain a focal point of each scene or work. The problems raised in Gide's imaginative writing, as distinct from his critical essays, therefore tend to resolve themselves into particular forms of awareness and self-expression. The self seeks to break the fetters of external control or it submits to its requirements. This theme of expression or abnegation of the self in the service of superior commandments (God or *l'autrui*) pervaded Gide's writings from *Les Cahiers d'André Walter* to *Le Voyage d'Urien* until, in *Les Nourritures terrestres,* it is actually narrowed to pure sensation and percep-. tion. In *L'Immoraliste* (1902), designed to refute the latter's spirit and form, the introduction of an explicit moral situation unifies sensations and lends them a particular narrative direction.[23]

This moral theme is introduced through a dramatic conflict which is substantially absent in *Les Nourritures.* The hero of *L'Immoraliste* is not just an obvious reproduction of the *moi* in *Les Nourritures;* he is also given a specific personality and a place in the social world. Michel is a promising scholar, an unworldly archeologist who spent his life in unbelievable purity and devotion to his studies until, after the death of his father, he promises to take a resigned and devoted wife. In the course of the novel, he undergoes a series of transformations occasioned by well-delineated episodes. Although these episodes often mirror the loose collection of scenes in *Les Nourritures,* they are marshaled around a theme which is easily recognizable and fully explored. For it is one thing to exclaim about the self's need for absolute expression, for an absolute destruction of puritanical bonds, for total exultation in sensual freedom, and

---

[23] Gide himself felt that, with *L'Immoraliste,* he had finally achieved a vision of a world outside himself. Curtius, moreover, saw this attitude as a culmination of a drive which began with Gide's early work; "the breakthrough to life" starts in the early *traités* and in *Les Nourritures,* but in *L'Immoraliste* it is not only symbolically stylized or presented in abstract discussion but also treated in the narrative of a concrete human fate. Ernst Robert Curtius, *Französischer Geist im Zwanzigsten Jahrhundert* (Bern: A. Francke, 1952), pp. 46ff. Generally, *L'Immoraliste* is identified with the appearance of *l'autrui.* See, for example, Ramon Fernandez, *André Gide* (Paris: Corrêa, 1931), p. 95. On the other hand, Rivière clearly perceived that in the last analysis Gide still exposed himself: the hero of *L'Immoraliste* discovers the lives of others, but as he does so, he also discovers his own; *Études,* p. 234.

it is quite another to test the strength of such convictions against the contingent need to commit an immoral act.

The foil against which the hero's morality can be measured is created in the beatific wife Marceline. She is one of the few important figures in *L'Immoraliste* who is almost wholly absent in *Les Nourritures*. Although in his early work Gide usually assigned to the feminine figure a restrictive role, in an aesthetic as well as in an ethical sense, in this full-length *récit* she assumes a Christian role of renunciation as a person. This "rounding out" of the problem might be partially explained by Gide's marriage, which occurred after the experiences recorded in *Les Nourritures*. The change in his life, which involved at least the problem of social *engagement,* invited this new heroine through whom personal tragedy is converted into formal melodrama. For Marceline sets up the moral debate which introduces characters, however ephemeral, and the semblance of dramatic action.

Michel is the key to this action as a percipient. Indeed, in one sense he is wholly the focal point, in whose consciousness and conscience the action is embedded. This position is assured him through the frame-story device. He tells the substance of the novel to his friends after Marceline's death and at the same time establishes himself in his present way of life. This device ensures both immediacy of personal experience and formal detachment. It is reinforced by an artificial structure within the envelope which seems to arise from the author's compulsion to force a rigid coincidence of symbolic form and a content of ideas and experience. In *L'Immoraliste,* as in *Les Nourritures,* freedom of sensation is identified with North Africa, Arab boys, lush gardens, and implied homosexuality, while restraint is associated with womanhood, marriage, France, bourgeois order, and religion. Between these two poles Michel's choices are made to fluctuate in a pendulum movement. Recognition of illness is accompanied by a heavy burden of guilt and resentment for his dependence on his wife and, simultaneously, by an expanding awareness of the preciousness of sensation for its own sake. Having stated the double nature of his theme, Gide neatly carries his hero from one crisis to the next in which he first chooses morally acceptable solutions while entertaining morally reprehensible desires, and later chooses complete surrender to his desires, forsaking his wife and, with her, his moral force of control.

Inside the frame, a rigorous architecture mirrors Michel's choices and perceptions. Ostensibly divided into three parts, the novel actually unfolds in five movements and two parallel interludes. The first and last movements take place exclusively in North Africa. Despite their disproportion in length (the first sequence takes up nearly all of Part 1, while the last one encompasses only a few pages), they are obvious *pendants,* inversely mirroring one another. The book opens with Michel's discovery of his illness, his near-death, and recovery; it closes with Marceline's similar illness and her death. The first movement poses problem and conflict; the conclusion enacts their consequences.

Between this frame-within-a-frame, however, there exists a further triadic constellation. Two lengthy episodes describe Michel's attempt to become a respectable landowner in Normandy. North Africa, with its gardens and Arab boys, and Normandy farms, with their animal smells and rustic fellows, are both sketched in *Les Nourritures.* But in *L'Immoraliste* they are dramatized because they are identified with the protagonist's choices. The romantic compulsion to penetrate to the seamier side of life upsets Michel's precarious escape from his true feelings. Perceiving animal warmth beneath the settled rural exterior of his farm, he turns to the intellectual atmosphere of his Paris apartment. This phase forms the center and turning point of the book. As in *Les Nourritures,* so in *L'Immoraliste* the diabolic Ménalque appears and forces the issue indirectly. Preenacting the denouement, Michel deserts his wife to spend the night talking with Ménalque during the very time that Marceline falls seriously ill and is delivered of her still-born child. The book's cycle henceforth mirrors in a downward slope the upward slope that had led to its apex. Betrayal follows upon betrayal, and a helpless Marceline must suffer the obverse of her own solicitude. The second phase in Normandy permits the hero to act out his repressed desires: he joins poachers on his own estate to contribute to his own ruin. This phase is eventually followed by Marceline's death in Africa. Moreover, two intervening passages of *vagabondage* (also reminiscent of *Les Nourritures*) describe the hero's ambivalence. The first sequence of travels intervenes between Africa and Normany and includes the consummation of his marriage which cements the temporary decision for a moral commitment. The second phase, just before the end, acts out the opposite decision. Although at first Michel heeds the doctor's advice for a sojourn in Switzerland, later he insists on returning to Africa with a dying Marceline. Such a rigid scheme indicates less the choices of rounded characters dramatically impelled than artificially imposed movements ideologically propelled.

—2

The structure of *L'Immoraliste* is determined by forms which transmute epistemological into moral awareness. Such a change is made credible by the hero's persistent conversions of visual and tactile experience into moral meanings, a method which continues the tendencies of *Les Nourritures terrestres*. But in *L'Immoraliste* the moral implications of the hero's perceptions are introduced, not through a narrator's sign-post statements, but through the verbal and physical development of the novel. For example, Michel's ambivalence between sickness and health at the moment of convalescence is expressed in an awareness which shapes his life:

I was unable to sleep that night, so much was I disturbed by these new virtues. I had, I think, a slight temperature; a bottle of mineral water lay close by; I drank one glass, two glasses; the third time I drank I emptied the bottle in a single draught. I exercised my will, like a lesson one goes over; I understood my hostility; I directed it towards all things; I had to combat everything: my health depended upon myself alone.

At last I saw the night's passing; the day arose. This had been my night of taking up arms. (IV, 35)

This passage shows the conversion of perception into an articulated morality. The heightened perception of the self alone in the night becomes the self struggling to define itself in combat against all others. In a Baudelairean fashion, moral implications emerge from sensual awareness. The conclusion of these scenes portrays the dual point of the first movement of the book:

. . . the wall before me bore the streak of oblique shadow; the regular palm trees, without color or life, seemed to be forever immobile. . . . But one finds in such a slumber once more the palpitation of life. . . .

His awareness issues in supplication:

One day will come, I thought, one day will come when I shall not have the strength even to bear this same water to my lips. . . . (IV, 51–52; 40) [24]

The hedonism of *The Song of Songs,* which underlies *Les Nourritures,* is translated into a counterpoint associated with *Ecclesiastes.* Through the medium of perception—palm trees, shadows, feelings for sensations suggesting a capacity for life— Gide explores the equation of naïve hedonism and moral value as a further dimension of his attempt "to glimpse through the gaps of culture." Picking up the Bible, Michel reads in the moonlight from St. Matthew: "When thou wast young, thou girdest thyself and walkedst whither thou wouldest: but when

[24] Page references given here are to both the French edition and, following the semicolon, the English translation used by the author, which was Dorothy Bussey, trs., *The Immoralist* (New York: Vintage Books, 1959). Subsequent references to this translation in this section will be treated similarly.

thou shalt be old, thou shalt stretch forth thy hands. . . ."
(IV, 52) This counterstatement to *Les Nourritures* arises from
a sensuous recognition of inevitable decay. Sin and death involve one another, for the latter is the moral ground of the
former. Decay perceived, therefore, becomes sin perceived, and
the connection of morality and awareness is established.

This idea of sense perception as moral perception defines a
passive hero. A prone Michel observes the small Arab boy
Bachir, whose health and vivacity become symbolic of health.
Similarly, throughout all the stages of Michel's convalescence
he views the children passively, whether he sits with Marceline
on a bench in the public gardens or whether he wanders in the
parks. They appear to him essentially through their beauty or
color (Ashour is "as black as a Sudanese"). (IV, 40–41) Michel
observes the "golden glow of nudity," as one of the boys climbs
down from a tree.

The early episodes carefully intertwine the hero's penetration
to the depth of his sensuous life with the approach of a climax
in the novel's theme. The key is found in the public gardens
and especially in the forbidden "oasis." Obvious allusions to
Eden and the Fall emphasize the symbolic impact of these
scenes. The experience of the oasis is passive and perceptual.
As Michel, in the company of Marceline, approaches the river-
bed leading up to it, he notes: ". . . the walls are made of the
same earth as the path—the same as that of the whole oasis—a
pinkish soft gray clay, which the burning sun crackles, which
hardens in the heat and softens with the first shower so that it
becomes a plastic soil that keeps the imprint of every naked
foot." (IV, 44; 33–34) Readers familiar with *Les Nourritures
terrestres* and the extreme sensuousness conveyed by the image
of bare feet touching the sand realize the direct appeal to which
the fleshly color of the clay has been turned. Moreover, the
walk into the oasis proceeds wholly by visual and auditory discoveries. Michel hears a flute behind branches moved by a
gentle wind and, entering the sensual sanctum through a breach
in the wall, he perceives:

It was a place full of light and shade; tranquil; it seemed beyond the touch of time; full of silence, full of rustlings—the soft noise of running water that feeds the palms and slips from tree to tree, the quiet call of pigeons, the song of the flute the boy was playing. He was sitting, almost naked, on the trunk of a fallen palm-tree, watching the herd of goats. . . . (IV, 45; 34)

Michel's response to this sight is one of extraordinary peace. Passively, he lies on the ground and places his head in Marceline's lap. As he feels the burning sun and rejects thoughts, he begins to visualize his new self—*le vieil homme* or Adam before the Fall, as he calls it later. (IV, 55–57) Henceforth, he returns to the oasis alone whenever possible, reveling in taste, sound, and sight.

The moral consequences of the oasis are depicted in the scene with Moktir. One of the older and more criminal types among the Arab boys, Moktir (whose dubious character is revealed by his looks) is the very antithesis of Marceline, whose favorite he had been. The decisive scene is portrayed through observation, very much as the decisive scene in *Les Nourritures* is portrayed through Ménalque's observation of the boy. Michel views the Arab boy's theft of Marceline's scissors through a reflection in the mirror. The sight itself turns into an immoral act which delights him and moves him toward a decision in favor of self-expression at all cost. The contrary decision is also conveyed through perception. It has been much commented that the covert homosexual theme of the novel is made blatantly obvious in the first and probably only consummation of Michel's marriage. Showing his newly found strength by beating up a coachman on their *vagabondage* (the postillion of *Les Nourritures*), he evokes in Marceline, rather incredibly, the supreme admiration that sweeps them into their passionate bed and in himself the ability to consummate their union. But the conclusion of the sequence is more significant. Michel watches his sleeping wife at dawn, contrasting his pity for her great fragility with

an awareness of his own strength, and bestows on her the most
gentle and "pious" of kisses. The actual consummation lies in
this deliberate act of perception and in the condescending kiss.
(IV, 66–67) Moreover, this "picture" foreshadows two further
occasions when Michel comes upon his wife: her first illness and
her death. The passive hero is led to his choices, not by deliberate
acts, but by the subtle intertwining of inclination and perception that involves moral consequences.

Perceptual images and sign-post statements (mostly Michel's
lectures and Ménalque's monologues) depict the hero's gradual
estrangement from any sense of obligation or care for others. In
the first Normandy sequence, perceptions develop into pictures
of sensual temptation. Michel's unconscious attraction for
Charles Bocage, for example, is shown through extremely suggestive tactile sensations. Fishing for eels with their hands, he
"called to [Charles] after a moment to hold a big eel; we joined
hands in trying to hold it." Michel notes naïvely that he is
pleased that Marceline had not yet come "as though she would
have a little spoiled our pleasure." (IV, 79–80) Although, as the
estate manager's efficient son, young Bocage belongs in the sphere
of restrictive civilization, the actions which appeal to Michel
suggest the uncivilized freedom of the self. In a revealing scene,
Charles superbly imposes his will on a wild colt while Michel
and Marceline *look on.* (IV, 84–87) In the second Normandy
sequence, on the downward slope of the novel, Michel's far
more explicit yearning for freedom, sensuality, the criminal side
of life is also portrayed through sense perception. Indeed, here
his penchant for observation brings on his ruin. He is drawn
into the criminal activities of the Heurtevent brothers by watching their poaching on his own estate and eventually becoming
their accomplice. For the passive hero, the very fact of viewing
becomes a moral act.

Even in the narrative form of the *récit,* Gide cannot quite
manage without "sign-post statements." Here most of these
explanations are contained in Michel's professional lectures,
which he gives during the sojourn in Paris. Rationalizing his own

instincts, he seeks to show in these lectures that a parallel exists between the individual's search for health and the development of cultures. Civilizations grow by their secretions of health; they decay when life diminishes, when barriers are put up between mind and nature. But these statements, too, are converted into visually accessible motifs. The idea of the sick culture—the diminution of life under the appearance of life—is of course suggested by Marceline's disastrous pregnancy and its denouement viewed by an impotent husband. But it is also shown in the parties at Michel's Paris apartment. Following him from room to room we see a vivid demonstration of the false cultural life that covers a decaying civilization by watching with him his lounging friends amid littered furniture and ash-trays. Ménalque's appearance, which gives the novel its occult twist, introduces further verbal explanations—discussions in detail of the ideas heretofore pictured in image-scenes—but it also introduces visual motifs. In the first instance, Ménalque mysteriously produces the scissors Moktir had stolen in Africa as evidence of Michel's unconscious immoralism. In the second case, Michel's night of talk with him issues in the scene of Marceline's illness that pictures its consequences.

The brief conclusion, which matches Part I of the novel, concerns Michel's compulsive search for Moktir, a symbolic return to the "oasis." Significantly, both his betrayal and Marceline's death are shown through perceptions. Coming upon Moktir just out of prison, Michel feels as if he had reached the end of his pilgrimage. In the climactic scene, he takes Moktir's mistress in the former's presence. The importance of this scene lies not only in the further displacement of obvious homosexuality but also in the way in which Gide chose to cast his transparent veil. Michel sinks passively into the mistress' arms while Moktir plays impassively with a white rabbit whose anxiety he tames. Echoing Michel's observations of Charles' taming the horse, it reverses the perceivers while it retains the theme of taming as an act of the strong or liberated self. The inversion of the percipient's roles is similarly important—Moktir's indifferent presence makes possible Michel's release—because it reenacts his view of Moktir's theft with opposite roles and so completes the novel's cycle. But chiefly this scene vivifies Gide's method: through the reflection of a vision in the consciousness of another, the hero's own action is observed, mirrored, and objectified.

————3

Among the images in *L'Immoraliste* which involve moral consequences, those concerned with blood are especially pertinent to the formal and dramatic development of the novel. In the early phases, Michel's illness is ushered in with a profusion of blood. During a coach journey in Africa—echoing the coach scene in *Les Nourritures*—he suffers the novel's first hemorrhage. Napkins, shawls, nothing can stop the blood from draining his body except a miracle and Marceline's devotion which save him. (IV, 24–25) During his convalescence, blood appears again, this time introducing a growing life. He *observes* Bachir at play as the boy cuts his finger, and he is impressed by the rich flowing of the child's *living* blood. (IV, 30–32)

After the novel's reversal, the blood motif is transferred to Marceline. Indeed, her decline and death are portrayed through perceptions of blood. In the first scene, Michel penetrates the semi-darkness of her room until his glance is finally arrested by the crucial, blood-stained object:

The room was darkened and at first I could make out nothing but the doctor who signed to me to be quiet; then I saw a figure in the dark I did not know. Anxiously, noiselessly I drew near the bed. Marceline's eyes were shut; she was so terribly pale that at first I thought she was dead; but she turned her head towards me, though without opening her eyes. The unknown figure was in a dark corner of the room, arranging, hiding various objects; I saw shining instruments, cotton wool; I saw, I thought I saw a cloth stained with blood. . . . (IV, 116; 97)

In the final scene, there is no such gradual revelation. Lighting the room, Michel sees her half raised in agony, covered by the blood of her hemorrhage. If in the early scene Marceline's devotion had arrested Michel's flow of blood, no such devotion saves her in the conclusion. As blood streams from her, the helpless husband only searches for an unsullied spot to kiss. The experience of her death, and the flow of her blood, are conveyed as a cruelly vivid sense perception. And with penetrating irony, the hero's search for a place to "put the horrible kiss" recalls the pious kiss of their night of love.

The scene of Marceline's melodramatic death unfolds the novel's theme through its action as an image. Lighting up the figure of renunciation bathed in blood, it also illuminates the hero's liberation. The irony of the novel is shown in this double-edged conclusion. Death is revealed to Michel's senses with the intensity of those visual and tactile sensations he had learned in the service of the joys of life. Within the progression of the novel, it also signifies Michel's successful quest for the sensualist's "oasis." But Michel is not only freed by Marceline's death, he has also scored his most outrageous point. The rosary which he had refused Marceline in her first illness, and which had been her weapon against his incredible hedonism, now seems to be useless. She appears to be stripped even of her God.[25] The epilogue, in which Michel combines his somber confession with unmistakable references to a "liberated" life, opens this resolution to further questioning.

The scheme of *L'Immoraliste* is presented through a passive hero's creation. It portrays Gide's obsession with the moral implications of sense experience and creates a philosophical tale from a constellation of image-scenes held together by rapid transitions. Through such scenes and perceptions within an artificial structure, it enacts the conflict between an "immoralist" and a symbolic "woman" as the bearer of Christian love. For Dostoyevsky, the outcome would have been a foregone

[25] For the first rosary scene, see *Œuvres,* IV, 117–119; for the second, *ibid.,* pp. 167–168.

conclusion, but Gide's hero succeeds in his quest and even destroys the heroine's confidence in her values. This resolution is portrayed through sensuous awareness, in which the reader is invited to share.

———— 4

Both the movement and the ideas of *L'Immoraliste* are viewed in symbolist as well as in Christian terms. For the symbolist, the evanescence and inadequacy of the senses necessitate their transcendence and eventual denial through artifice. For the Christian, sensations entail their obverse, decay, sin, and death —the fruits of the Fall. These two implications are telescoped in *L'Immoraliste* as the lover's kiss, celebrated in *Les Nourritures,* becomes the kiss of death. Something of this sort touched the tortured conscience of Huysmans' Des Esseintes, who recognized that the degeneracy attendant upon a surfeit of sensation signifies the bankruptcy of the world of sense but who refused the Christian sacrament with which to transcend it.

Whatever may have been the psychological significance of Gide's vision, either for himself or his hero, the key to his method in *L'Immoraliste* is a skillful exploitation of his protagonist's visual compulsion. In his quest for the "oasis"—a pilgrimage past symbolic way stations suggested by the gardens and the scenes of *vagabondage*—Michel alludes to the transcendental hero. He also recalls Rimbaud's *Voyou* in the literal sense of the term. He is essentially a prototype of the passive hero who transforms the universe of nature and social relations into an inner world and converts inaction into tragedy. Despite its concern with events, Gide's novel retains many distinguishing characteristics of his symbolist *traités*. The protagonist creates a world of his own, whose images bear a primary relation only to his passive choices.

Although he had rejected the thinking of Mallarmé, Gide retained crucial features of the symbolist hero: the passive apprehension, the deformation of the world, and the conversion of perception into symbolic ideas. Gide sought to avoid the artifice and intellectual insularity of the symbolist novel by establishing a universal moral scheme as part of his culture. But in narrowing this scheme to the passive hero's orbit, he vitiated his critique of symbolism and retained the artificial framework he had sought to avoid. Mirroring both ideas and narrative in a design of significant perceptions, he created not only a well-made *récit* but also a form in which a hero's inner life is rendered with the immediacy of a lyrical poem.

THE PROTESTANT CONFESSIONAL

———1

The identity of formal and moral commitment, which marks *L'Immoraliste,* is sharpened considerably in Gide's subsequent work. Beneath his attempts to preserve the *récit* as a traditional form, there remained as a persistent motif his need to find the means of creating objective analogues for intimately personal awareness. It would not violate Gide's reputation for an unusual technical versatility, or do an injustice to his constant struggle for new forms and greater maturity, to suggest that the continued survival of his symbolist beginnings matches only the consistent impact upon him of the Calvinism of his youth. Indeed, form as the neutral embodiment of the self became the Protestant confessional. The self as the stage of its own mental and emotional process was crystallized, perhaps in its purest form, in his two most Protestant novels, *La Porte étroite* (1907) and *La Symphonie pastorale* (1916).

Gide's fiction is dominated by a tension between a loosely symbolic conception of the novel and rigorous adherence to traditional forms. The difficulty of reconciling such forms with his familiar leaning toward confession and identification with his characters led to the impressive experimentations of *Les Caves du Vatican* and *Les Faux-Monnayeurs.* To resolve this tension, Gide frequently resorted to the journal and first-person narrative as the most suitable devices with which a self might be objectified. Following the eighteenth-century tradition of the epistolary novel and the Rousseauistic confession, the journal could serve in both its functions of preserving the appearance of verisimilitude and of unconscious prevarication. It can *formalize* the most intimate and personal experience without requiring an outer world. In *La Porte étroite* and *La Symphonie pastorale* the journal looks forward to this experimentation with its form.

The introduction of the journal as a technique of fiction is a fresh departure for Gide. To be sure, it had played an important role in *Les Cahiers d'André Walter,* Gide's first novel in 1891. The hero writes a book in the form of diaries whose protagonist not only resembles the fictional writer but whose death coincides with the "author's" madness. In these later two books, however, the journal is used in a less artificial and more sophisticated context. It becomes that "internal stage" on which a crisis of conscience can be enacted by various figures who reflect the poet's point of view.

—— 2

The themes of *La Porte étroite* and *La Symphonie pastorale* continue the Gidean debate. It is the conflict between self-expression and submission to external control which had marked Gide's efforts in the cycle that led from *Le Voyage d'Urien* to *Les Nourritures terrestres,* and ultimately to *L'Immoraliste.* Alissa's journal begins with her realization of her love and her need for sacrifice; her subsequent disintegration is mirrored both in the content and the manner of her journal. In order to pass through the Strait Gate she must divest herself of her love, her fondness for art, her taste, her very humanity, even the support of her God, until, at the moment of her pitiful death, she is faced with herself. In its course, Gidean self-examination has done away not only with a self that thinks and therefore is but also with a self that derives its very existence from denying that it is anything more than a minute reflection of an inscrutably perverse divine will. The Pastor of *La Symphonie pastorale* also loves, but in order to pass through the Strait Gate with his questionable confusion of love and passion he transforms not himself but the divine word until, having lost everything, he kneels to pray with his burdened and devoted wife. The world the good pastor had set askew is put to rights again, not by himself but by the sacrifices of those around him whose tragic acts he dutifully records.

This relation of the self to divine commandment, enacted in journal passages and first-person narrative, is linked with the point of view through which it is expressed. Protestant emphasis on individual conscience gives rise to the solipsism through which the characters' misguided actions can be understood. Neither Alissa's deluded self-sacrifice nor the Pastor's equally deluded refusal to accept evil even in himself would have been possible without that crisis of conscience which is their subject: the awareness that too much granted to the individual self may lead to a distortion of truth, virtue, and law. Furthermore, the irony in both novels lies precisely in Gide's remarkable feat of turning their moral and religious solipsism into an aesthetic one. Each in his own way reenacts the dilemma of the symbolist hero. Each deforms his universe if not in terms of his or her hallucinations, at least in accordance with a conscience, and reconstitutes it in journals which become "tragic masks" of a "perfect as well as of a rational humanity." In both novels the theme is enacted through self-deception, through a kind of delusion, willed or unconscious, in which the protagonists deform not only the external world but also the substance of their experience by mistaking a counterfeit universe for a true one.

————3

In its use of the journal, *La Porte étroite* employs both a first-person narrator who supplies part of a perspective and an intimate journal which contrasts effectively with the foregoing account. Interestingly, Jerome's *récit* is the formally closed unit in which the entire narrative—that is, its characters, side-plots and complications—is embedded. Alissa's journal, on the other hand, while more meaningful in its poetic beauty and psychological penetration, is an open form. In constant juxtaposition with Jerome's otherwise uninspiring account, her journal takes the reader on a voyage of discovery into the recesses of a strangely endowed and inexplicably haunted mind. Here Alissa's rationalizations for not marrying her lover, which in Jerome's story become the more incomprehensible to him the clearer they become to the reader, are laid bare in the internal physiology of her mind. In Alissa's notes, chance remarks, events, encounters, even symbolic motifs suggested in Jerome's account are enlivened by a new, an interior meaning. Many crucial scenes in the *récit,* for example, take place in gardens whose sensual lure and classical form are familiar to readers of *Les Nourritures terrestres* and *L'Immoraliste.* In a garden Jerome overhears Alissa discussing him with her father; in a garden he experiences the denouement with Juliette; his most crucial meetings with Alissa occur in gardens. But in Alissa's journal the garden is made explicit as an inner landmark of great importance which decides her course. In the unfamiliar surroundings of the home of her married sister, Juliette, and embarked on the first journey of her life, Alissa is impelled to think of nature no longer as God's handiwork, but as an embodiment of pagan mythology suggested to her by Jerome's letters from Italy. In a panic of the senses, she scurries into the house.

Even more directly, the Fall of Alissa's mother, which sets the tone and theme of the novel, is channeled from Jerome's account into Alissa's journal until the reader at last understands that the mother's sexuality has been turned into its passionate obverse in the daughter. In the *récit,* Jerome views the mother on a couch, surrounded by her lover and children; then, with masterful irony, Gide leads him to view Alissa in a scene which turns the mother's sensual bed into the daughter's pew. In the journal, this scene is reenacted when Alissa's father views her lying in a posture of rare abandonment (her feet protruding from the self-enclosed severity of her gown) and is at once reminded of the mother. Immediately following this scene, Alissa experiences a fierce sense of panic when she feels Jerome's body close to her own as he bends over her to share her book. In the loneliness of her room she merges both scenes into one and prays to God to preserve her from "even the appearance of evil." (v, 87–88, 222–223)

The many passages of direct and moving prayer which address to God what Alissa does not wish to address to herself (the analysis of her motives and actions) are rooted in the pastor's sermon on the occasion of the mother's elopement early in the book. In Jerome's account the direct statement of the passage from Luke, "Strive to enter in at the strait gate," is used as a dramatic climax, but in Alissa's journal it becomes the text for her evocations of inner torment that lead to her renunciation. Alissa's prayers continuously reemphasize the motif of aloneness which communicates itself from Jerome's narrative to the intense portrayal of the moral need for isolation in Alissa's journal. They correspond to Alissa's conversations with Jerome in which she insists on aloneness and to her dream image of Jerome's death. The motif of death as another aspect of complete personal isolation runs through the entire novel and culminates in the obsessive preoccupation with death which permeates Alissa's notes. In the journal, death becomes more and more the visible counterpart of the Garden which encompasses beauty as well as the Fall. "See the lilies of the field. . . . But oh Lord, where are they?" (v, 229)

It is easy to see how Gide came to consider Alissa's journal one of the best and most moving of his writings and Jerome's *récit* as its uninteresting though necessary preface, but nonetheless the novel's irony and form are contained in a relation between them both.[26] Alissa's world, created from her deluded conscience, comes to life in her journal, but it requires the juxtaposition of Jerome's perception of her with her self-perception to crystallize this world in aesthetic perfection. Mirroring the incoherence of the self in the closed form of the *récit*, the novel as a whole retroactively produces a double exposure through which its power is revealed. The objective vision of a narrator

[26] See Guerard, *André Gide*, p. 122. Guerard cites from the journal entries of Nov. 7, 1909, and March 1913, *Journal*, i, 333; ii, 7.

who cannot see the real cause of human suffering in the jungle of his misplaced sensibilities, and the subjective vision of a correspondent and diarist who gives voice to this suffering behind a screen of misleading rationalizations, provide the poles between which the work's form is suspended.

———4

In contrast to this delicate balance of two first-person accounts, *La Symphonie pastorale* exhibits a very different use of the journal. Advertised as the "formation and development of a pitiful soul" (IX, 5), the book appears primarily as a confession. The deformation of reality by the confessor and hero, unconscious in *La Porte étroite,* cuts with a moral edge it did not possess in the earlier novel. First unwittingly, but soon deliberately, the Pastor remakes the world and the word of God, emphasizing the goodness of nature and the non-proscriptive passages of the Gospels at the expense of evil in nature and the sternness of Pauline prohibitions. For the Pastor seeks to raise a Galatea of exceptional ability who is not to know that the world is no longer the Garden of Eden.

In *La Porte étroite,* the Fall is the *fait accompli,* the condition by which its heroine is defined; in *La Symphonie pastorale,* it is the pivot around which the novel is made to turn. More than this, it becomes the reversal where one world collapses and another must take its place. At the same time, this reversal is prepared for by a scene of recognition to which the Pastor is led by his wife and by the declaration of love professed by a deluded Gertrude. Thus, translating the classical terms of "recognition" and "reversal" into Biblical terms of "awareness" and "fall," Gide, in a manner reminiscent of *Le Traité du Narcisse,* channels his story into a classical structure. Unity of action is facilitated by the journal of confession which, by the very nature of the genre, must suppress, or press into its service, all that is not germane to its subject. Symmetry of form is rigorously maintained through the balance between the two notebooks, which, though disproportionate in physical length, neatly divide the action at the point of the Pastor's first recognition. The Pastor, furthermore, becomes in Gide's subtle interplay of Biblical motifs and classical structure a passive counterpart of the tragic hero. Although his deliberate blindness brings down tragic consequences far less on himself than on those, such as Gertrude and his son Jacques, whom he uses for his purpose, he is not only the narrator but the protagonist as well. True, he is, if anything, an inversion of the classical hero. He is no Prometheus or Philoctetes, no Oedipus or even a Gidean Saul. Yet the measure of his fall is not taken by his stature but by the enormity of his descent from grace.

At the same time that Gide implies the structure of classical tragedy, he also presents his story as an internal confession. Both recognitions, that of the Pastor in the geometrical center of the novel and that of Gertrude in the end, are arrived at through an inner progression whose stages are marked by Gertrude's process of learning. As she rises from a condition of literal blankness—her mental universe a veritable *tabula rasa* —first to an innocent awareness of nature, then to a search beneath the perceptual surface, the moral implications follow close behind.

This internal development toward recognition and reversal is made perfectly clear in the Pastor's record. At first the "wall of darkness" between them grows less opaque as Gertrude's experiences begin to take shape. But soon she seeks to go beyond her sensations. Sound seems flat; despite her blindness, she probes into the meaning of light and color. "We always used things," the Pastor records, "[which] she could touch or feel in order to explain what was beyond them. . . "[27] She increases her understanding and so prepares for the reversal after hearing a concert of the Beethoven symphony from which the title is drawn. The eighteenth-century "organ of color"—like the eighteenth-century "savage child"—is explored in its religious implications and made into a symbolic motif. The aware-

[27] ". . . car nous nous servions toujours de ce qu'elle pouvait toucher ou sentir pour expliquer ce qu'elle pouvait atteindre. . . ." *Oeuvres*, ix, 29.

ness of multiple harmonies of sound prepares Gertrude's intelligence for their correspondence first with harmonies of light and color, then with their moral implications. Is there, she inquires after the concert, a deeper perceptual as well as moral level to correspond to that world of sound she had just witnessed? (IX, 32ff.) The process of her growing awareness, then, becomes gradually imbued with a moral meaning. It leads to her discovery of beauty, of its sensual implications and, therefore, to her knowledge of Eve's transgression. Moreover, as her perceptual horizon expands with the help of Dr. Martins and Condillac, the Pastor's rationalized passion for her is correspondingly increased. As Dr. Martins had wisely predicted, her deepening knowledge of the potentialities of her senses bore within it the seeds of the Fall. (IX, 19–22)

The motif of "light" toward which a blind Gertrude probes from the surface of increasingly intelligible sounds also becomes the subject of her "moral and intellectual development." Throughout her religious education, the most dominant feature remains the Pastor's exploitation of the sensual and moral ambiguity of "light" and "love." Christ of the Gospels is love and therefore hallows their passion. Christ says in the Gospels that the world is light, and therefore this part of the doctrine alone is suitable for the sightless. (IX, 34–35) These ambiguities, related to the novel's reversal, are first made explicit in the Pastor's interchange with his son on texts from St. Paul's Epistles to the Romans and in their discussion of happiness as restraint. For the "light" and "love" of the father's misdirected vocabulary, rationalized through one part of Scripture, are opposed by the son's contradictory interpretation of Scripture. Indeed, the true nature of the documents which the Pastor had suppressed in his education of Gertrude (such as the Epistles of St. Paul) is not revealed until after his challenge by Jacques, who represents less a sexual than a religious rival. The final discovery that his son had clandestinely acquainted his charge with these "forbidden" passages restores the counterpoint of "sin" to the Pastor's carefully nurtured phantom of Eden. Authority and law, the hitherto suppressed opposites of self and conscience, are now revealed through Jacques' and Gertrude's conversions.

  Gide's use of Scripture, his employment of contrapuntal motifs and figures within the framework of a predetermined classical form cast the Pastor's journal of confession in an objective mold. Yet the story within this form is entirely embedded in the narrator's consciousness. Other figures, even Gertrude, Jacques, and the incredibly understanding Amélie, are seen as reflections of the Pastor's inner record. Vivid images of nature and unusually lavish descriptions which punctuate the narrative are bent to conform to the purpose of his confession, that is, to reflect upon his relations with Gertrude. Through its form, the journal of *La Symphonie pastorale* indeed becomes an objective stage on which a moral crisis is enacted through the internal denouement of its protagonist.

—— 5

  Both *La Porte étroite* and *La Symphonie pastorale* utilize first-person accounts not only to convey a sense of intimacy but also to provide an "internal stage." The journal represents the platform on which the self's subjective deformation of reality can be enacted. In *La Porte étroite,* it aids in creating the tension between two points of view in which the novel's substance and irony is implied. In *La Symphonie pastorale,* the journal converts all points of view except that of the diarist into an inner drama which in its structural symmetry and reversal suggests the model of classical tragedy. Both novels intensify the transformation of sensible into moral awareness, which had been Gide's method in his earlier work. But in each case, the hero's commitment to moral action is formal. From the well-made *récit* of *L'Immoraliste* to the journal presented in the form of classical tragedy evident in *La Symphonie pastorale,* the hero's choices infer a moral universe from a poetically presented inner world.

THE INNER LANDSCAPE

—— 1

"Precision," writes Edouard, Gide's double in *Les Faux-Mon-nayeurs,* "is not obtained through the details of a narrative, but in the reader's imagination, through two or three strokes exactly at the right place." (XII, 133–134) Although this remark was meant to stress the need for rigorous selection, it also describes Gide's intentions in two novels of his maturity, *Les Caves du Vatican* (1914) and *Les Faux-Monnayeurs* (1926). Both books present a variety of important characters related to a theme whose manifold perspectives they embody. In both books, persons and scenes are stylized images to be ordered in imaginative appre-hension.

Gide's notion of the mind as an "inner landscape" harks back to *Le Voyage d'Urien.* In *Les Caves du Vatican,* however, and more fully in *Les Faux-Monnayeurs,* this landscape developed into an inner stage, described by a detachment akin to that of drama. For Gide contrived to expand the inner world beyond that of a single, present consciousness into a panorama of inter-acting figures perceived by a consciousness which is largely effaced. In his attempt to replace an egocentric predicament by a critique of his time, Gide transposed the self-portrait onto a larger scale, mirroring individual traits in a collective physi-ognomy. The intellectual and social landscape is a broadened image of the personal consciousness and conscience.

Comments on *Les Faux-Monnayeurs* have usually taken Gide's own intentions at their face value, and have accepted his ex-planation that this work reproduces the essence of the novel's form in experimental terms. The juxtaposition of time sequences, the simultaneous rendering of action and symbolic motifs, the contrasting and complementing figures and points of view, can be seen within a scheme designed to broaden Gide's narrative into a stylized portrait of the external world.

The original plan had probably been to create a world comparable to that of *Tom Jones*. Jacques Rivière's theory of the *roman d'aventure,* which in large part reflects Gide's, insists on the novel as the precise opposite of poetry: deconcentrated, gradually revealing characters and ideas to the reader's glance. But Gide's refinements indicate the ambivalence of his theory and deepen the perceptual implications which had been evident since *L'Immoraliste*. He rendered an analytic commentary as well as a portrait of psychological conflict by juxtaposing various monologues. This method, which had been successful in *Les Caves du Vatican,* turns into brilliantly conceived, if loosely ordered, lyrical fiction.

Gide's obsession with the relationship of inner experience with "world" and "form" found its most varied reflection in *Les Faux-Monnayeurs*. His admission of failure to penetrate to the external world was made in the early nineteen-twenties; the idea of the self as an "interior landscape" became the workable concept of the "inner stage" in 1924, at a time when his work on *Les Faux-Monnayeurs* was nearing its end. An entry in 1920 in his self-conscious commentary, *Le Journal des Faux-Monnayeurs,* concerns itself with the relationship between confession and the novel. The writer should use personal experience to create the novel's texture, but he should then depersonalize the self by concentrating on the novel's figures who would reveal themselves to the reader. (XIII, 17–18) The precarious balance between subjective awareness and its form is now viewed in a somewhat different light. Gide formulates an answer through the fictional novelist Edouard. The subject of the novel is a "rivalry between the real world and the representation we make of it ourselves. The manner in which the world of appearances imposes itself upon us and the manner in which we try to impose on the outside world our own interpretation—this is the drama of our lives." (XII, 297; 189) [28] This statement elaborates the notion of the "psychological novel" Gide had enunciated as a

[28] Page references given here are to both the French edition and, following the semicolon, the English translation used by the author: Dorothy Bussy, trs., *The Counterfeiters with Journal of the Counterfeiters (Journal*

young man. The identity of subject and retroacting object is maintained even on a panoramic stage.

The reciprocity of subjective and objective experience applies to Gide's conception of character and action. Despite the discrepancy in emphasis between Gide's novel and the plan of the *Counterfeiters* devised by his character Edouard, the notion of appearance and reality—affecting the social and psychological compulsions of the characters—pervades the entire book. If we analyze Edouard's statement concerning the "drama of our lives" more closely, we note that in direct perception appearances impose themselves on the percipient as an index of reality. But we also *create* a counterfeit world by imposing upon external reality our own interpretation. *Les Faux-Monnayeurs* portrays this relationship between actual perception by a passive self and deformed perception by the self as a creator.

Both the meaning and the technique of the novel are suggested by the implications of the counterfeit coin. Introduced in Book II, the coin recalls the false Pope and his delayed entrance in *Les Caves du Vatican*. But though it obviously refers to counterfeit values, it also signifies an epistemological motif. In the palm of Bernard Profitendieu, the coin is symbolic of his own awareness and of the way in which he is viewed by others. (XII, 276–278) In the same way, each of the characters subtly deranges his vision, deforming reality through his perception, and at the same time is himself viewed as a counterfeit of his "real" identity. As a subject and as an object of consciousness, each self is caught as a prevaricating percipient and as a deformed mask viewed by others.

The two stories, which, by Gide's testimony, inspired the book, formulate the manner in which visions and masks are deformed. The story of the literary counterfeiting ring neatly combines the theme of moral degradation with that of intellectual deceit. The story of the gratuitous death of the little boy supplies the interest in the perversion of innocence in children and

translated by Justin O'Brien) (New York: Alfred A. Knopf, 1955). Subsequent references to these translations in this section will be treated similarly.

the rationale for renewed explorations of the gratuitous act. The first indicates commerce with deliberate falsification; the second celebrates freedom from social and psychological determinacy.

The social setting is sharply limited to the upper reaches of the bourgeoisie and to a high-class Bohemia. The novel's structure is composed of different stories and scenes, each of which is dominated by a particular percipient, whether he be character, narrator, or author. These individual passages render particular fields of vision which, in turn, appear as typical "exterior colors" of the percipients. Gide carefully refrains from using visual imagery. Indeed, in one of the opening passages of the book the ridiculous speech of the pompous school boy Dhurmer and the pathetic musings of the "poet" Bercail satirize the use of imagery. (XII, 241) But Gide's disconnected sequences created by perceived and perceiving selves function as intellectually conceived images defining the novel's form.[29]

———2

Viewed in this light, each important figure in *Les Faux-Monnayeurs* becomes a prototype of Mallarmé's Hamlet. Exemplifying a "symbolic reciprocity of types among one another and in relation to a single figure," each character reveals within the scope of his "image" a coherent *récit* set *en abyme*. But he also wears a mask of madman, actor, or clown, deforming his perceptions by critical rather than hallucinatory acts. Each major figure thus arrives on the novel's scene as a passive percipient, exposing himself and others through willed or uncon-

---

[29] For the "network structure" akin to that of a poem, see Claude-Edmonde Magny, *Histoire du roman français,* pp. 241–242, 268. The analogy to music, which has been often suggested, also seeks to explain the partly ordered, partly disordered structure. Note Ramon Fernandez' explanation: "Plutôt qu'à romancier, au sens ordinaire du mot, il [Gide] fait songer à un chef d'orchestre qui décompose pour ses musiciens les mouvements divers de la partition." Fernandez sees the novel as a pattern of repetitive and interlocking *passages* (in the musical sense) which are dominated by the characters and themes they express; *André Gide,* pp. 152–154.

scious perceptions and receiving his distinctive features through the degree and subtlety of his detachment.

The novel opens with Bernard:

> "This is the moment for believing I hear a step in the passage," said Bernard. He raised his head and listened. Nothing. (XII, 21)

At this moment Bernard had just been "liberated." Spying in hidden papers, he had discovered that he was really his mother's illegitimate child, that the man he had believed to be his father was counterfeit not only in spirit but also in fact. Detached, he now regards himself in a fresh perspective: the spy who had viewed the evidence of his own identity is observed, in turn, by the ironist who can look upon himself as an object in melodramatic flight. (XII, 21–22) For though he avoids a particular perception—a visual or auditory image—Bernard ironically refers to the perception which would be most appropriate to the melodramatic moment. Hence, the mysterious "demon" who makes his first appearance in this passage for the moment embodies the ironist in Bernard himself (the family respects his solitude but the "demon" does not). Bernard can confuse the sensation of tears and sweat with impunity. This attitude typifies Bernard's self-imposed vision of himself, his family, and his friends, to be exposed as a further disguise later on. As a mirror of ironic perception, it defines the initial contours of his "image."

Olivier Molinier, with whom Bernard seeks refuge, is seen first as part of Bernard's image and later from his own point of view. In both these encounters, the reader has no sense of the ironic self-awareness which had initially defined Bernard. Olivier appears as wholly unfree; his perceptions are falsified not by design but by scruples. His passivity is succinctly expressed in the sentence with which his "image" is introduced:

> "Olivier is lying on his bed to receive the kiss of his mother." (XII, 49)

Ironic distance is here supplied not by the character but by the narrator speaking in the present tense. But even as the reader moves from Olivier's passive pose to the perceptions the latter communicates to Bernard, he finds a self-conscious sense of foreboding which shows him that Olivier plays his melodrama straight. Indeed, the worlds opened up during the night for the benefit of Bernard and the reader reveal Olivier as one of Bernard's counterpoints. Olivier's account of his first sexual experience focuses on a lively albeit ridiculous image through a report of irrelevant perception ("It was her talk that was the most loathsome. She never once stopped jabbering."). (XII, 53) Bernard's reaction to Olivier's story is less perceptive than that of the least knowing reader, but his understanding of himself indicates his need for a voluntary commitment to sensation and voluntary control (". . . I'm biding my time. In cold blood, like that, it doesn't appeal to me."). (XII, 53) Olivier, however, uses his own experience as a pretext for a further report on a perception, his eavesdropping on the pitifully unreal interchange between his brother Vincent and the abandoned Laura. He is touched by Vincent's melodramatic rejection and by her pleas. The unknown woman is left behind Olivier's door, but the latter listens to her sobs, unmoving. When challenged by his puzzled friend why he had not opened the door, Olivier expresses fear of his brother. "You're never afraid of anything," he tells Bernard. "You do everything that comes into your head." (XII, 53) Even the sensitive report of Olivier's uncle, Edouard, underlines his passivity. Although Olivier resolves to meet his uncle at the station the next day, he will be content to shake his hand. As the reader is soon to discover, Bernard decides upon more drastic measures. The contrast between the two friends emerges through reports of and comments upon perceptions—accounts of scenes from memory, eavesdropping, accounts of sensations. Counterpoints, then, arise not only in the musical sense as taken up by Aldous Huxley in *Point Counter Point* but also in an epistemological sense in which different sets of consciousness lend one another distinctive colorations.

The sentences introducing Edouard are similarly revealing:

"In the Paris express Edouard is reading Passavant's book, *La Barre fixe,* fresh off the press. . . . Without doubt his copy will await him in Paris, but Edouard is impatient to find out." (XII, 103)

Most of the characters are introduced as observing or being observed by others; Edouard views his rival Passavant through the mirror of his book. Both his vagueness as a character of fiction and his incisiveness as an observing and reflecting point of view can be traced to this posture of the analytic knower whose perceptions are filtered through the word. His thoughts on the debacle of Laura and on the reality of his feelings for her are fused with musings about his novel and with the presentation of his feelings in his diary. In both novel and diary, Edouard emerges as an intelligence, deforming experience to fit preconceived plans. Set down in his notebook, which Edouard reads on the train, his experiences assume arranged features which he views quite in the manner of Narcissus admiring himself in the water of the brook.

Edouard's assessment of his feelings for Laura in the self-conscious pose of his diary, for example, defines a rationale for *Les Faux-Monnayeurs* as a whole. As he debates the truth or falsity of psychological fact, he adds a new dimension to the counterfeit motif by applying the question of appearance and reality to the very nature of experience itself: "Psychological analysis lost all interest for me on the day I convinced myself that *a man experiences what he imagines he experiences.* From this to thinking that one imagines one experiences what one experiences. . . ." (Edouard's ellipsis; italics mine.) (XII, 110) [30] This question strikes at the heart not only of Edouard's personality but of Gide's entire concept of the hero. Imagination and experience (like subject and object) are reversible. A man's

[30] In the preceding paragraph Edouard notes that nothing exists for him except the *poetic* element, which he identifies with "beginning with oneself"; *Œuvres*, XII, 110.

thought or image fashions his modes of awareness in terms of his interpretation; conversely, experience itself may refashion a content of consciousness. In this form, the unanswered question also enters Edouard's own thinking about the novel and becomes the plumb line by which all his relations are measured the moment the train reaches the station. Responding to this way of thinking, his diary is an internal point of view, matching from within the seemingly disconnected involvements of the novel, but it is also the record of an eavesdropper who deforms clandestine observations to suit his intentions.

Edouard's diary is a monologue which defines his image. It is developed in a series of interspersed but coherent episodes that shed light on several characters in the book, including Edouard himself. Yet this journal is not an intimate confession used as an objective stage, like the diary in *La Porte étroite*. Alissa's evocations of Jerome and herself had been truly visionary, conveying feelings with mystical intensity. But Edouard shows how, in *Les Faux-Monnayeurs,* such expressions are deliberately and purposefully suppressed. Edouard is an apparent bystander—a professional mentor—who views La Pérouse and his wife, the lamentable Pastor Vedel and his family, Georges Molinier and his school-fellows, even Bernard and Olivier, with an analytic detachment that betrays his personal involvement only by implication. In other words, he becomes a masked narrator as well as a protagonist, an intellectualized version of the *moi* of *Les Nourritures terrestres,* whose comments direct experience toward the creation of meaningful wholes. A symbolist hero *manqué,* Edouard remolds experience to deliver it as a substance of consciousness deformed by critical introspection.

The ideas which form Edouard's perceptions and diary are crystallized in his theory of the novel and in his much-discussed plans for his own *Counterfeiters.* As a matter of fact, since Edouard's novel exists only as a theory and a plan (except for the few pages he shows to Georges Molinier), his project is not so much an image of an actual work as an analytical commentary upon it. (XII, 135–139; 275) An abstract mirror, it relates to

Gide's novel as a whole in the same way as Bernard's awareness of the appropriate perception relates to his actual perception of tears and sweat. Edouard's own position is described by his discussion of his "ideal" novel in his conversation with Laura, Bernard, and the psychologist Sophroniska at Saas-Fée. The novelist, who should circulate in his work as a character, reflects "that very struggle between what reality offers and what he himself desires to make of it." (XII, 271; 173) As an index of such a reality, the world of appearances apprehended by the writer and his figures is subject to their falsification, just as a gold piece, even if counterfeit, is worth the amount people believe it to be worth. Moreover, this imaginative deformation of reality also suggests an ideal reality. In the same conversation Edouard said that the novel's subject presents "the struggle between the facts presented by reality and the ideal reality." (XII, 273) This statement identifies the theorist Edouard with his fictional counterpart; it also suggests that his projected novel is a theoretical rehearsal for the "real" novel written by Gide. The conflict between the facts and the ideal of reality informs Edouard's aesthetic and ethical position in *Les Faux-Monnayeurs*.

Edouard renders intellectual formulations of perceptions—present and past—which examine the very nature of experience on which all modes of awareness are based. He is *defined* by his novel and notebooks as the other figures are defined by their physical perceptions. Like the others, he is also *perceived:* Bernard clandestinely reads his notebooks; Laura, the psychologist Sophroniska, and Bernard later listen to Edouard's espousals of his theories; the reader views all relevant sections from Edouard's journals.

On the other hand, his rival, Passavant, is a caricature of all those elements by which Edouard's "sincere" position is defined. On the surface, Passavant is, of course, a stage villain, the sincere hero's hypocritical counterpoint. A false *pervertisseur* opposed to the truly Socratic mentor of youth, a counterfeit of the hero of unassailable integrity, he is the despicable homosexual opposed to the mature homosexual lover. But as a less pleasant

Julius, Passavant's pragmatic nature and intellectual opportunism allow him to exploit for his own ends those moral and artistic ambiguities which define Edouard's position as a deforming critic. Plying his trade of willful corruption, he achieves exaggerated versions of Edouard's critical act. For Edouard, the pose as diarist and novelist had created a platform for legitimate deformations of reality rendered with the observer's detachment and irony. He had fashioned experience into critically controlled imagery. The clash of the two men sets them off against each other vividly and dramatically, but, in so doing, it also betrays their opposite ways of viewing reality. Edouard's and Passavant's "colorations" are determined by their modes of perception and by their moral intentions, by the degree to which a deformation of experience is a critical act or an act of moral corruption.

Perception, without sensuous color, defines many characters in *Les Faux-Monnayeurs*. Passavant is first seen by his two-dimensional companion, Lady Griffith, who goads his vanity by commenting on his thinning hair. (XII, 75) Vincent had been the object of Olivier's eavesdropping, just as the latter's conversation with Bernard had been overheard by his younger brother, Georges. At another point, the reader views Vincent in the depth of his satisfied slumber, while his corrupter, Lady Griffith, ponders his bare foot. (XII, 95) As Bernard spies upon Edouard and Olivier at the station and later uses the purloined suitcase to read the notebooks, so Edouard spies upon Bernard when the latter confesses his love to Laura. (XII, 194–199) These intersecting perceptions, in which characters contain one another, extend from physical perceptions to perceptions of scenes, from contemplations of theories to notebook passages which present observations in a first-person perspective. They expose characters and their actions as *images,* to be joined with other images in a non-logical, inconsecutive sequence.

————3

Gide's emphasis on perception extends to all levels of *Les Faux-Monnayeurs,* involving theory and characterization as well as social criticism. Its relevance to the counterfeit motif ensures that the subject of actual and distorted awareness is explored both in a formal and a thematic dimension. Moreover, the vision of a character or scene caught by a further percipient joins Gide's epistemological bent with a dramatic technique. As the picture viewed by the reader is vivified, it takes on the appearance of a dramatic stage not only for the reader but also for the character whose vision the reader shares.

An example of this technique is the scene in which Sarah's brother, Armand, views his sister in bed with Bernard. This scene was brilliantly analyzed by Albert Guerard in both its psychological and critical dimension, but it can also be considered as startling evidence of Gide's dramatic sense.[31] The night before, Armand had locked the lovers in the bedroom and had kept the key. In the morning he opens the door while they are still asleep. He had placed his sister on the "stage" containing her bed of corruption and now regards the effect of his action with the relief that attends a dramatic resolution.

The most moving part of the novel—Boris' illness and suicide—is similarly "staged" from the psychologist's probings to the dramatic denouement. Although the death scene is described by the omniscient narrator, it is focused in the horrified stare of the paralyzed grandfather, La Pérouse. (XII, 544) This vision, rather than the melodramatic machinery which surrounds it, defines Gide's technique. As in Hesse, the dramatic stage is actually a vivified picture, a vision viewed or overheard which is animated like a film. Laura's wedding to Douviers is contained in Edouard's journal as a scenic picture. The Argonaut dinner, drawn by the narrator and perceived by many of the participants, becomes a fantastic and farcical affair—a Brueghel canvas set into motion. Earlier in the book, the reader views with Gontran Passavant the laid-out body of his father, sharing—somewhat ironically—the boy's grief-stricken pose in obvious contrast with his indifferent brother. This technique, though it involves eavesdropping and vicarious viewing, is not merely a quirk, a tend-

[31] *André Gide*, pp. 158–159.

ency which requires only a pathological explanation. The very way in which the author circulates among his characters and directs the reader's attention to this scene or that indicates an aesthetic plan based on observation. Gide's method equates each "image" with a stage on which the percipient becomes a protagonist, and the reader, however briefly, turns into the audience of a play.

Individual moments or scenes—presented either directly, in conversations of the protagonists, or in comments passed on by the narrators—elicit responses from the reader as images of a perceived reality. But these images are continuous only within individual chapters or sequences, such as consecutive episodes from Edouard's diary, or complementary conversations such as Olivier's meeting with Bernard and Armand. Often they are *faits accomplis* which sum up a character's development. Bernard returns to his father, but the reader is made to piece this change together from a number of references (his rejection of Edouard and his love for Laura, for example) and is permitted to view the change indirectly in Bernard's struggle with the "angel" (as his departure from home had been signified by the "demon"). Finally, in his conversation with Edouard after the fact, he reveals himself fully. Using continuous sequences, scenes, or images of varying length, Gide creates a version of a pointilist painting, leaving a progressive development to the reader's imagination.

Gide realized a continuous form by utilizing the dramatic possibilities of an individual image or scene within a framework based on the extended nature of prose. He accomplished his end by engaging the reader at disconnected points at which he either explored a perception pictorially or dramatically or, frequently, described its portent analytically. This notion turns "inconsecutiveness" from a psychological recognition to an aesthetic criterion for the novel. "Never establish the sequence of my novel by prolonging lines already traced," Gide reminded himself in the *Journal des Faux-Monnayeurs*. "Like a constant surge, each chapter must pose a fresh problem, it must be an overture, a

direction, a new point jutting out—ahead of the reader's mind."
(XIII, 53) And elsewhere in the same book he tells himself that
the rules of his game is "never to profit from an acquired élan."
(XIII, 50) In the true novel, as distinct from the drama or the
well-made *récit,* purity is obtained by a dissipation of images
and potentially dramatic scenes to force the reader to turn from
a particular perception to an instantaneous understanding of the
whole.

These remarks on the problem of *succession* in the novel illuminate Gide's way of converting ostensibly "pure action" into
a panorama of images. The pattern of interacting percipients—
and their roles as objects of perception—is to be achieved without "successive illuminations" (XIII, 18–19) but rather through
involved juxtapositions of time sequences, tenses, and the narrator's renderings. Simultaneity is attempted primarily through the
characters who *create* events by exposing themselves gradually.
(XIII, 18) [32] These exposures to perception account for the many
contradictory movements of *Les Faux-Monnayeurs* which the
reader's imagination is required to combine. The author weaves
"threads about the characters" whose total network is perceived
by the reader. (XIII, 14)

Edouard's theory of the novel, which elaborates these points,
gives an important clue to Gide's intentions, but it is supplemented by a psychological point of view whose decisive version
is supplied by Sophroniska. In his journal. Edouard declares that
the novelist should "strip the novel of every element that does
not specifically belong to the novel," and he goes on to suggest
that purity akin to that of drama can be achieved only by a
stylization which leaves the main task to the reader. (XII, 113–
114) At Saas-Fée, he expands this point into a more mature
notion of the psychological tale. He suggests a massive vision
of reality in which the lengthwise slice of life would be supple-

---

[32] On the other hand, Gide writes later that the main characters should
be left shadowy, to be realized by the reader's imagination. The minor
characters, however, should be described with precision; they should be
"led boldly to the fore" ahead of the others. *Oeuvres,* XIII, 39–40.

mented by many different slices cut at many levels by various scissors in several directions. (XII, 270–271) But a conversation with Sophroniska about little Boris, held earlier, had defined for Edouard and the reader a further notion which contrasts with Edouard's theory. Speaking of Boris' cure, Sophroniska reports that she keeps her charge in a state of semi-consciousness for certain hours to permit images to escape the usual control of reason.

[These images] no longer group and associate themselves according to ordinary logic, but according to unforeseen affinities; above all they answer to a mysterious inward compulsion —which is the very thing I want to discover. . . . (XII, 260; 165)

This is the "logic" of *Les Nourritures terrestres,* but the inward perception is also a counterpoint to the cerebral perception which defines Edouard. Yet it is this logic of unforeseen connections, this imaginative comprehension of wholeness which even in *Les Faux-Monnayeurs* the reader is asked to trace. In fact, Sophroniska expresses the challenge to Edouard, which is part of the novel's point. "Most of your characters," she tells him, "seem to be built on piles, they have neither foundations nor subsoils. I really think there's more truth to be found in the poets; everything which is created by the intelligence alone is false." (XII, 261; 165) No doubt Gide also implies a criticism of Sophroniska, whom as a person and as a psychologist he finds ultimately wanting, but it is equally evident that he means to convey a similar critique of Edouard, who is a critical prevaricator as a novelist, and a *pervertisseur* (however "honest") as a man.

Gide's intention, expressed in the *Journal* and through Edouard's conversation and pen, is to render a comprehensive portrait of life by presenting a stylized picture of lives to be apprehended by the reader. Alluding to the anxiety of creation, Gide notes that he finds himself "peculiarly exhausted" by the effort to "externalize an interior creation." The task of objectifying the subject before having to "subjectify the object" appears to him novel and difficult. (XIII, 15–16) This statement points out a change in Gide's intentions, but it continues his problem of seeking an objective analogue for subjective experience. His solution leaves him with a form which in its general outline returns him to his most inconsecutive early work—*Les Nourritures terrestres*—although its individual elements represent not feelings but attempts at external creation.

Depending on the reader to supply both unity and meaning to deliberately fragmented appearances, *Les Faux-Monnayeurs* renders a more complete version of *Les Nourritures terrestres*. To be sure, the more reflective nature of the later work changes the epistemological position without disturbing the basic pattern. As in *Les Caves du Vatican,* a deceiving demon—questioning reality through the counterfeit motif and the themes of intellectual, social, and moral corruption—interposes itself between the act of awareness and its object. Moreover, in *Les Faux-Monnayeurs,* several percipients are juxtaposed, although all of them finally defer to the ultimate apprehension of the reader. But in Gide's *chef d'œuvre,* ideas, figures, and scenes create the kind of choral effect which in *Les Nourritures* is achieved by combinations of feelings and statements. Celebrations of bare feet on the sand or of ocean waves become Lillian Griffith's corruption of Vincent or Robert Passavant's of Olivier. Allusions to stylized narrative substitute for directly presented emotions; conversations replace songs. The sign-post statements become narrators' interpolations or inserted discussions and theories. But although in *Les Faux-Monnayeurs* diaries and perceptions deal with recognizable persons and coherent ideas, they are similarly stylized and allusive, representing various points of view as part of a pattern of images. Voices have received names and sign-post statements have been converted into scenes and articulated values. *Les Faux-Monnayeurs* is determined by perceptions from which sensuous content has been largely expunged. But its form depends nonetheless on an apparently disjointed pattern of images from which meaning and form—the idea as well as its aesthetic and moral distortion—are expected to emerge. The "form" so conceived becomes like that cluster of images or ideas of which the self is but the stage. It organizes the novel as a network of images perceived by the reader, a form which lends it the quality of a poem.

—4

It seems paradoxical that a novelist as self-consciously intent on pure narrative as Gide should have written a supremely poetic novel, but such was the nature of his problem as a writer. The figures in his work function as *images* rather than as rounded agents of a story. His narrative is deliberately stylized and loosely formal. This ambivalence between his intentions and his practice is reflected in the elaborate theories of both the novel and the *Journal*. His aim was not only to reach beyond himself toward the external world, as we have initially observed, but also to present a *classical* form of the novel.[33]

Theoretically, Gide required of the novel a purity of genre in its own terms equivalent to that of classical and seventeenth-century tragedy. "It is worthy of note," he wrote in his *Journal des Faux-Monnayeurs,* "that the English who have never known how to *purify* their drama in the sense that Racine's tragedy is purified, yet achieved at the very outset a much greater purity in the novels of Defoe, Fielding, even Richardson." Therefore, the novel should be "purged of all elements that do not specifically belong to the novel." (XIII, 41) As Edouard notes in his journal, among these are all matters which concern the outward appearances of characters, realistic conversations, or external

[33] Gide indicates that the epic is closest to such a form: "Pourquoi me dissimuler: ce qui me tente, c'est le genre épique. Seul, le ton de l'épopée me convient et me peut satisfaire; peut sortir le roman de son ornière réaliste. Longtemps on a pu croire que Fielding et Richardson occupaient les deux pôles opposés. À dire vrai, l'un est autant que l'autre réaliste. Le roman s'est toujours, et dans tous les pays, jusqu'à présent cramponné à la réalité. Notre grande époque littéraire n'a su porter son effort d'idéalization que dans le drame. *La Princesse de Clèves* n'a pas eu de suite; quand le roman français s'élance, c'est dans la direction du *Roman Bourgeois*." *Œuvres,* XIII, 38.

events. (XII, 114) Although in his journal Gide adds ironically that Edouard will "never write his pure novel," the drive for purity is uniquely part of his intention. In Edouard's extensive conversations at Saas-Fée, he elaborates the novel's need for means of stylization so that it may obtain the universal scope and depth of the great tragedies. Details of life should be obscured; the novel as a painting of illuminations should reflect the struggle between actual reality and the ideal. (XII, 273)

Why, then, did Gide not attain his goal, creating instead a great intellectual lyric in prose? There is little doubt that his model for much of the structure of *Les Faux-Monnayeurs* had been *Tom Jones:* in the author's survey of his characters, in his intrusions, and in the ironic insertions of theories.[34] But Gide himself recognized that, though it is often loose and unconsciously stylized, *Tom Jones* is a realistic novel. (XIII, 38) The "anti-realism" through which he sought to lead the ideal form to its triumph destroyed the "pure" novel's realistic base. Gide's cursory remark in the *Journal* that the "epic tone alone suits me," because "it alone can free the novel from its realistic rut," indicates the direction of his thinking. Similarly, Edouard's journal excludes from the novel and assigns to the motion picture "all outward events, accidents, traumaticisms." (XII, 114) What remains for the novel is an idea of action in the widest sense— evolving for the reader with the constant surprises of the *roman d'aventure*—and a cast of figures who shed light upon one another, illuminate the scene, and who are in turn revealed as each one steps to the foreground of the stage. Gide's demand for stylization, for the "erosion of contours" to present a universal idea, led to an overdependence on the reader's imagination. It also entailed a lack of emphasis on an *independent* world. As in Rivière's theory, so in Gide's practice, the transfer of the percipient from poet to reader still left the novel as an act of imaginative apprehension. Whatever analogy is chosen to describe the structure of *Les Faux-Monnayeurs*—painting, music,

[34] See William B. Coley, "Gide and Fielding," *Comparative Literature,* XL (1959), 1–15.

or the motion picture—its deliberate disruption of any acquired continuity, its constant motion within and beyond scenes, creates the poetic network of images which Claude Edmonde Magny criticized for destroying any particular world.[35]

Enlisting the imagination to penetrate to the "real" patterns which the mind is to perceive through the veil of appearances and multiple perceptions, Gide has met both his needs: to express immediately the content of an inner landscape and to establish a formal framework of perceptions and dramatic moments that appears to the viewing intelligence. In this sense, *Les Faux-Monnayeurs* adopts the character of a poem: it dissolves external reality into a world open to instantaneous apprehension, reaching toward the level of unique and formally accessible meaning.

THE POET IN PROSE

Gide's work as a whole presents the paradox of a writer who seeks to broaden a narrow range of experience into an intellectual portrait of his time. During the period of his early work, this attempt was predominantly lyrical in intention and language. Whether he expressed himself in the loose diaries of André Walter or developed a theory of symbolism, as in the treatise on Narcissus, his forms remained recognizable variations of lyrical prose. Even *Les Nourritures,* we noted, while eschewing the tight symbolic forms he had developed since *André Walter,* "sang" of the quality of experience in tones hardly compatible with classical prose style.

Yet, paradoxically, as Gide became more and more successful in finding adequate forms in which the image of the self could be contained, he emerged as one of the most accomplished writers

---

[35] Claude Edmonde Magny criticizes *Les Faux-Monnayeurs* on two counts: (1) that it divorces its movement, form, and subject matter from the "real" world, i.e., from a credible external world of narrative, without evoking human sympathy; (2) that both the statement through hyperbole and the attempt to reproduce the network structure of a poem are unsuccessful. *Histoire du roman français,* pp. 241–242, 268.

of classical prose. Indeed, it is no contradiction to say that as Gide approached his "plundered" classical style,[36] he also evolved into a more perfect writer of lyrical novels. This choice was compelled by his limitations as a writer. For essentially Gide was neither a perfect novelist (his difficulties and stratagems attest to this fact) nor was he a poet in the ordinary sense (he rarely created images as the substance of experience). Rather, he was a great critic, expressing himself in imaginative forms.

As a critic Gide recognized both his limitations and his possible aims. While avoiding the term "poetry," he developed a formal portrait of inner experience which resembles the definition of a poem.[37] Gide's prose, as lucid as that of Swift and Stendhal, could not employ itself in the development of consecutive action. Rather, it utilized the *idea* of the formal portrait as imagery. As a result, Gide lessened his use of imagery but turned to discussions of images.[38] Indeed, the notion of perception, which defines the relationship between a self and the images it reflects, becomes part of the subject matter and themes of his books.

In this sense, Gide can be defined as a poet in prose. The method he used is basically the method of the prose poem. Baudelaire's choice of prose as the medium in which the movements of the soul are mirrored most succinctly suggests a standard by which Gide's accomplishments can be measured. In many of Baudelaire's prose poems, the poet is actually the narrator, the analytic commentator who presents ideas and themes which have been evoked in his verse. The struggles between the divided aspects of a single self, the presentation of a self in art by a detached, partially effaced self in life (that of the narrator or poet), reflect within the narrower limits of *Les Petits Poèmes*

---

[36] See Peyre, *Hommes et oeuvres,* p. 134.

[37] See Edmond Jaloux's excellent summary of Gide as a moralist and a lyricist. "André Gide et le problème du roman," *Hommage à André Gide,* pp. 111–121.

[38] Cf. Stephen Ullmann, *The Image in the Modern French Novel: Gide, Alain-Fournier, Proust, Camus* (Cambridge, Eng.: Cambridge University Press, 1960), pp. 79–81.

en prose a method which Gide developed more fully in his fiction.

The success or failure of Gide's "classicism" in fiction, grafted on a symbolist conception of the hero, is not easily determined. Certainly, his characters, precisely because their motives are not plausibly rooted in the external world, lack a conviction which, despite all their subjectivism, the characters of James and Proust possess. Gide's experimentations in *Les Caves du Vatican* and *Les Faux-Monnayeurs* show his persistent attempts to come to terms with the external world and at the same time to develop forms from within a created experience that would be adequate to their tasks. But Gide's strength as a writer lies precisely in his weakness as a novelist, in the formulation of personal "inquietude" in terms of a controlling form that fashions experience into an act of aesthetic imagination.

5

AWARENESS AND FACT
The Lyrical Vision of Virginia Woolf

THE ACT OF CONSCIOUSNESS AND THE POET'S VISION

1

Mᴏᴅᴇʀɴ lyrical fiction has been accompanied by a genuine concentration on the inner life and on its distillation in spiritual or aesthetic forms. The passive hero, recreating his perceptions symbolically, dominates the world of images for whose existence he is responsible. Even two writers as different as Hesse and Gide struggled under immense psychological stress with a similar need to identify themselves with their worlds and to transmute them into forms. But lyrical novels can also emerge from situations in which the author's point of view is the aesthetic key to a formal representation, not of himself or of his hero, but primarily of the world on which his vision has been trained. Gide moved in this direction in *Les Caves du Vatican* and *Les Faux-Monnayeurs,* but Virginia Woolf went further and developed this tendency into a unique method. Despite her well-known preoccupation with inner experience, she maintained her important toe-hold on the earthy substance of Liverpool.[1] She used the imposition of poetic techniques on the novel as a method to redefine rather than to supplant traditional concepts of fiction.

Such a dual allegiance explains both the appeal and the antagonism which have surrounded the reputation of Virginia Woolf. By blending poetry and prose with increasing success, she challenged deep-seated prejudices about the form of the novel, but

[1] "Notes on an Elizabethan Play," *The Common Reader,* First Series (7th. ed., London: Hogarth Press, 1948), pp. 73–74. See David Daiches, *Virginia Woolf* (Norfolk, Conn.: New Directions, 1942), p. 36.

she never abandoned an underlying commitment to the native conventions of her craft. Her famous essay, "Mr. Bennett and Mrs. Brown" (1924), which sets forth her "new novel," is usually viewed as a description of all novels portraying inner rather than outer experience. But it was much more clearly a personal testimony of Virginia Woolf: it established the points at which she felt traditional requirements of narrative art should be modified.

Beneath Mrs. Woolf's critique of her elders lies an implied suggestion that the tradition of the English novel itself is at issue. She knew that English fiction, as represented by Jane Austen or Trollope, had sought to deal with character and scene in their broadest temporal relations on a varied stage of events. On the one hand, she accepted this tradition, and, indeed, she saw in the work of Jane Austen the English novel most successfully realized. But at the same time Jane Austen represented for her the climax of this method, the point beyond which the English novel could not go without the infusion of new techniques.[2] The sharpness of "Mr. Bennett and Mrs. Brown" does not conceal Virginia Woolf's search for such a mediating form through which she could convey simultaneously a picture of life and manners and a corresponding image of minds. She sought to represent the essence of character, and the quality of experi-

---

[2] Note Virginia Woolf's remarks in her essay on Meredith: "When he [Meredith] wrote, in the seventies and eighties of the last century, the novel had reached a stage where it could only exist by moving onward. It is a possible contention that after those two perfect novels, *Pride and Prejudice* and *The Small House at Allington,* English fiction had to escape from the dominion of that perfection, as English poetry had to escape from the perfection of Tennyson. George Eliot, Meredith, and Hardy were all imperfect novelists largely because they insisted on introducing qualities, of thought and of poetry, that are perhaps incompatible with fiction at its most perfect. On the other hand, if fiction had remained what it was to Jane Austen and Trollope, fiction would by this time be dead." "The Novels of George Meredith," *The Common Reader,* Second Series (5th ed.; London: Hogarth Press, 1948), p. 234.

ence, without indulging in superficialities.[3] Her essay opened
the doors of the novel to fresh conventions, foreshadowing a
lyrical manner for English prose narrative through the conversion of character and scene into symbolic imagery.

This outlook identifies Virginia Woolf as a novelist and critic
beset by an allegiance to the English novel yet stirred by excitement for new artistic possibilities in the novel form. But her
attitude also emerged from her impatience with the purely subjective writing that pervaded the literary atmosphere in which
she lived. Her path toward lyricism had been marked not only
by a genuine and faithful concern with the inner life but also by
her consciousness of the artist's egocentric predicament and her
intense anxiety about the dangers of solipsism. In "How It
Strikes a Contemporary," she analyzed this problem as the
dilemma with which "our contemporaries afflict us." Unlike
Wordsworth, Scott, or Jane Austen, who never needed to question the general pertinence of their values, twentieth-century
writers "cannot make a world, cannot generalize," because they
have ceased to believe. "They cannot tell stories, because they
do not believe that stories are true." Although contemporary
man must begin his quest for reality with what he knows—his
personal awareness—he has been seriously incapacitated in his
attempt to penetrate to worlds beyond himself. Such a position
undermines the possibility of lasting, generally accessible works.
The writer may have to be content to "write notebooks rather
than masterpieces" which a future generation might evaluate.
But Virginia Woolf's way of stating the problem points out
her awareness not only of the dilemma's existence but also of
the writer's need to find appropriate avenues of escape. "To believe," she wrote, "that your impressions hold good for others
is to be released from the cramp and confinement of personality."[4] Her attempt to translate the traditional forms of the novel

[3] "Mr. Bennett and Mrs. Brown," *The Captain's Death Bed and Other
Stories* (London: Hogarth Press, 1950), pp. 96–97, 103–105.

[4] *The Common Reader,* First Series, pp. 300–301, 302.

into organized explorations of consciousness represents her contribution to this task.

───2

Although Virginia Woolf's ideas of lyricism and narrative are deeply connected with her concepts of the self, and with an analysis of the inner life, her notion of lyrical writing is by no means identified with psychological projections. Her main emphasis—despite many equivocal pronouncements to the contrary —was placed on the need to combine both inner and outer experience in art. This combination extends from private awareness to external "facts" and ultimately to general ideas and values. In its formal action, poetry begins with the self but leads to its *depersonalization*. A similar process takes place in lyrical prose narrative. Worlds in time and space are not precisely reproduced but are rearranged in aesthetic designs which become universal and symbolic.

In a brief essay devoted mainly to the poetic drama, "The Narrow Bridge of Art" (1927), Virginia Woolf proposed one of her several ways toward the depersonalization of the self in the novel. Since the conventional novel of motive and environment had proved insufficient, she suggested that it give way to a form that provides, like poetry, "the outline rather than the detail" and that stands "further back from life" in order to achieve the symbolic distance of impersonality. Human relationships—the unremitting business of falling into and out of love— are to be abandoned for subtler, simultaneously more private and more impersonal relationships with "such things as roses and nightingales, the dawn, the sunset, life, death, and fate." Such a novel would "give the relation of the mind to general ideas and its soliloquy in solitude." It would be neither psychological nor social; rather, it would render a vision of the mind's conversations with life. "The psychological novelist has been prone to limit psychology to the psychology of personal intercourse . . . We long for some more impersonal relationship. We long for ideas, for dreams, for imaginations, for poetry."

"Poetry," then, is firmly identified with *impersonality*. Impatient with the probing instruments of the conventional novelist, Virginia Woolf rejected the analysis of motives and substituted for man's relations with himself and others his impersonal relationship with life as a whole—his soliloquy in solitude.[5] Her view of poetry appears to be one of increasing abstraction. The "poetry" of *Wuthering Heights,* as she noted in her essay on the Brontë sisters, rendered a universal portrait of life in its essential or archetypal forms. The Brontës are poets, because the emotion they project "wings . . . its way past the daily conduct of ordinary people and allies itself with the inarticulate passions." In *Wuthering Heights,* Emily moves from personal emotion to a universal feeling of the human race and its relations with the "eternal powers." Life is freed from its "dependence on facts." "With a few touches [Emily Brontë could] indicate the spirit of a face so that it needs no body." [6] Similarly, Hardy's symbolism was poetic because it dealt with Fate, Gods, the impersonal element.[7] Meredith was not a psychologist like Henry James or Stendhal. Rather, "he is among the poets who identify character with passion or with the idea, who symbolize and make abstract." [8]

Nevertheless, it is part of Virginia Woolf's seemingly contradictory credo that both poets and novelists build upon a sub-

[5] *Granite and Rainbow* (New York: Harcourt Brace and Company, 1958), pp. 18–19. In an essay on "Women and Fiction," Virginia Woolf comments that "it is in poetry that women's fiction is still weakest." She attributes this fact to women's greater involvement in the details of life, and in private sensibilities, which prevents them from obtaining a truly impersonal vision. The statements clearly identify poetry with *impersonality,* which, with the acceleration of emancipation, she hopes women will soon achieve: "The greater impersonality of women's lives will encourage the poetic spirit. . . ." *Ibid.,* p. 83.

[6] " 'Jane Eyre' and 'Wuthering Heights,' " *The Common Reader,* First Series, pp. 200–202.

[7] "Phases of Fiction," *Granite and Rainbow,* p. 137.

[8] "The Novels of George Meredith," *The Common Reader,* Second Series, p. 232.

stance of *facts*. When her work on an essay about De Quincey forced her to rethink the relationship between the genres, Virginia Woolf gave an explanation of poetry in which facts are prominently stressed. In a letter to her friend, V. Sackville-West, quoted in Aileen Pippett's biography, *The Moth and the Star,* Mrs. Woolf wrote that "one test of poetry . . . is that without saying things, indeed, saying the opposite, it conveys things." Facts may have to be remolded into a symbolic vision, but the poet must begin with them. Instead of giving "accurate descriptions of buttercups and how they're polished on one side and not on the other," the poet should "deal seriously with facts." "What I want is the habit of earthworms; the diet given in the workhouse—anything about a matter of fact—milk, for instance. From that proceed to sunsets and transparent leaves and all the rest, which, with my mind rooted upon facts, I shall then embrace with tremendous joy." [9] To obtain his "liberation" from facts, the writer must first focus on his relations with facts.

Impersonal values and concrete facts, rather than pure subjectivity, define a poetic method which Virginia Woolf also applied to the novel. When she set out to remodel her art in 1919, the relationship between consciousness and artistic form impressed itself upon her with great urgency. Her famous definition of the stream of consciousness in "Modern Fiction" (1919) did not limit itself to private feelings. Rather, her comparison of life to a "luminous halo," a "semi-transparent envelope surrounding us from the beginning of consciousness to the end," represents a serious attempt to examine the structure and conditions of consciousness itself and their effects on the novel. Even though the form of the "new" novel was to be molded by the self's "uncircumscribed spirit," with "as little admixture of the alien and incompatible as possible," Virginia Woolf did not mean to dissolve all external relations into symptoms of the inner life. Indeed, an important point of this essay had been to criticize Joyce's *Ulysses* for its failure to penetrate to life beyond the self. Was not reading Joyce, Virginia Woolf asked, like "being in

[9] *The Moth and the Star* (Boston: Little Brown, 1955), p. 209.

a bright, yet narrow room, confined and shut in rather than enlarged and set free?" Did not Joyce's then fragmentary novel
force us to be "centred in a self which in spite of its tremor of
susceptibility, never embraces or creates what is outside or beyond?" Toward the end of her essay, Virginia Woolf demonstrated in a few remarks about Chekhov's story "Gusev" how
the furniture of life is illuminated by a vision in which consciousness and things require one another to create a scene of wider
symbolic dimensions.[10] Whatever changes Virginia Woolf's
views underwent during the following decades, this interaction
between self and scene remained characteristic of her vision.

The process of awareness registers the impact of the external
world upon the inner life. It also yields a method through which
the knowledge of facts can be symbolized and rendered abstract.
In her "Letter to a Young Poet" (1932), Virginia Woolf defined the writer's problem as such an analysis of the mental act.
The writer's task, she wrote her poet, is "to find the right relationship . . . between the self you know and the world outside." The poet can be occasionally content to focus on his own
awareness, for his is "a self that sits alone in the room at night
with the blinds drawn." This definition of the poet's way recalls
a technique she had applied brilliantly to a novel she had published only one year earlier—*The Waves*. ". . . Stand at the
window and let your rhythmical sense open and shut, open and
shut, boldly and freely, until one thing melts in another, until
the taxis are dancing with the daffodils, until a whole has been
made from all these separate fragments." [11] Facts and relations,
rendered formless by the deceptive time sequences of the external world, are brought together in the artist's apprehension, in
his "rhythmical" or "formal" recreation of life in abstract or
"symbolic" forms.

As her thoughts crystallized during the nineteen-twenties,
Virginia Woolf became quite specific about the way in which

[10] *The Common Reader,* First Series, pp. 189–193.
[11] *The Death of the Moth* (New York: Harcourt Brace and Company,
1942), p. 221.

acts of awareness can be formally portrayed. A "poetic" picture of the world, as she showed it to her correspondent in 1932, allowed her to reject pedantic realism yet to insist on facts as the components of an ultimate symbolic vision. These recommendations to a poet also shed some light on the opposition and rapprochement of the "inner" and the "outer" which beset her throughout her life and most clearly expressed her anxiety about solipsism. "And what is my own position towards the inner and the outer?" she wrote in her journal in 1928. "I think a kind of ease and dash are good;—yes, I think even externality is good; some combination of them ought to be possible." This fusion is most obviously present in the act of awareness, particularly in the artist's unique apprehension in which atomic facts can be absorbed and recreated as a meaningful whole. "The idea has come to me," Virginia Woolf added, thinking of *The Waves* on which she was then at work, "that what I want now to do is to saturate every atom. I mean to eliminate all waste, deadness, superfluity: to give the moment whole; whatever it includes. Say that the moment is a combination of thought; sensation; the voice of the sea." And more emphatically: "That is what I want to do in *The Moths* [the working title of *The Waves*]. It must include nonsense; fact; sordidity: but made transparent." [12]

The *moment* emerges as Virginia Woolf's key to her theory of apprehension as well as to her concepts of poetry and the novel. The moment is the artist's awareness of significant conjunctions between his private sensibility and appropriate facts in the outer world. As a mental act, the moment is indeed internal, but it does not reduce experience to private images alone. Rather, it consists of an analysis of the act of consciousness into its components, i.e., mental awareness and the objects of awareness. Thus, the moment also includes the mind's relations with a multitude of facts. The facts, however, do not belong to the moment due to haphazard accidents of time and space—de-

[12] Nov. 28, 1928, *A Writer's Diary* (London: Hogarth Press, 1953), p. 139.

scribed by that "appalling narrative business of the realist: get-
ting from lunch to dinner"—but by virtue of an artist's significant apprehension. Pure poets select too severely: "The poets
succeed by simplifying; practically everything is left out." But
the novelist includes all that is germane to the moment: "I want
to put everything in; yet to saturate."[13] "Transparency" or
"saturation" are, of course, not definite terms, but they suggest
that novelists must recreate their visions in peculiarly significant
forms. The rendering of the "moment" as an act of awareness,
and its distillation in poetry or fiction, solve the dilemma of
solipsism by compelling the self to come to terms with the objects of its world. At the same time, as we shall see, it liberates
the novelist from photographic realism by allowing him to fashion novels of facts and manners, as well as of inner experience, in
a *lyrical* form.

—3

In its *literary* function, the moment is linked to the various
distinctions between novel and poem. Among these, Virginia
Woolf's repeated definition of "extended" prose and "concentrated" poetry is pertinent. "The novelist's way is spun out at
length," she wrote, "while the poet's way is condensed and syn-
thesized."[14] And in "How Should One Read a Book?" she insisted that "the illusion of fiction is gradual," while the "poet
is always our contemporary."[15] This *contemporaneousness* of
the poet's world is an important source of Virginia Woolf's poetic
vision of the moment from which her later novels have evolved.

One of her most decisive essays illuminating the issue between
novel and poem was stimulated by Elizabeth Barrett Browning's
novel in verse, *Aurora Leigh*. The imposition of verse upon a
work of narrative fiction forced Virginia Woolf to reassess her
attitudes and to redevelop her distinctions. Her initial position
is conventional enough. Mrs. Browning is chided for "poaching

[13] *Ibid.*
[14] "A Letter to a Young Poet," *Death of the Moth,* p. 221.
[15] *The Common Reader,* Second Series, p. 265.

on the novelist's terrain." A novel should be a book in which "the relations of many hearts [are] laid bare" and a story is "unfalteringly unfolded." [16] Poetry is identified with verse. Mrs. Woolf's chief criticism appears to be that the distinctions between characters and forms of speech were leveled by the metered monotone, that world and word were reduced to Aurora Leigh. But she also turns to a subtler concept of poetry. While criticizing *Aurora Leigh* as a novel, Virginia Woolf calls it a "masterpiece in embryo," whose incipient value lies in its poetry. The poet can compress time-bound plots into significant moments. Characters can be "snipped off and summed up with something of the exaggeration of the caricaturist" to "obtain a heightened and symbolical significance which prose in its gradual approach cannot rival." Mrs. Browning's way of proceeding through the "compressions and elisions of poetry" might have led to a masterpiece,[17] had she also heeded the requirements of the novel and expanded her heroine's soliloquy into a true "soliloquy of silence," a "conversation with life."

The "compressions and elisions of poetry" constitute another way of describing metaphor. Aided by verse and other linguistic devices, the poet contracts the manifold world into a momentary image. In a recently republished essay, "The Phases of Fiction" (1929), these distinctions are also applied to writers of prose narrative. Poet-novelists, as Mrs. Woolf occasionally calls them, remold consecutive prose to achieve precisely those contractions and elisions which Mrs. Browning could approach only in verse. Among their efforts, she distinguishes between poetry of language, as in Laurence Sterne, and poetry of "situation" or "scene" which she finds exemplified in various novels, including those of Emily Brontë, Hardy, Meredith, and even Tolstoy. The former actually reproduces in prose some of the linguistic idiosyncrasies of verse; the latter creates its poetic effect through individual scenes.[18]

Although poetry of situation emerges from consecutive prose,

[16] "Aurora Leigh," *The Common Reader,* Second Series, pp. 210, 212.
[17] *Ibid.,* pp. 212–213.
[18] *Granite and Rainbow,* pp. 136–139.

its effect on the reader is instantaneous, presenting an image of a mood or an experience as a unified whole. The definition Virginia Woolf gropes for in a jungle of contradictions is undoubtedly that of the "moment" as the significant scene. In *Wuthering Heights,* the scene in which Catherine pulls the feathers from the pillow (a moment to which Mrs. Woolf repeatedly refers) draws disparate elements together and integrates them into a vision divorced from the actual plot but blended with the poetic texture of the entire novel.[19] A similar contraction of experience, she felt, determined Meredith's attempt to "destroy the conventional novel" and to "supplant the sober reality of Trollope and Jane Austen with a new and original sense of the human scene." In *The Ordeal of Richard Feverel,* she notes that landscapes become features and emotions symbolizing characters and drawing their contours with descriptive imagery. Seen in this way, moments congeal into scenes that portray states of mind.[20] They introduce a relationship between sensibility and scene that inverts the positions inner and outer worlds usually occupy in the novel, because they transmute landscapes and objects into mental acts.

Similarly, in Hardy's novels, vivid scenes, which Hardy himself called "moments of vision," stand out in the flow of the narrative. But these individual scenes appear against too general a backdrop of life; their emphasis vitiates the traditional function of the novel. Hardy's psychology, as Virginia Woolf sees it, is simplified; his figures are seen large, being shown not in detail but responding to or doing battle with a universe of elemental passion. As in Meredith, whose characterizations also lack concreteness and depth, the poetic spirit defeats itself, if individual moments or scenes exist in too general or symbolic a world. To be effective, the poetic novelist must also measure up as a novelist.[21]

[19] *Ibid.,* pp. 136, 137–139.

[20] "The Novels of George Meredith," *The Common Reader,* Second Series, pp. 228–230.

[21] "The Novels of Thomas Hardy," *The Common Reader,* Second Series, pp. 247–248. Writing of both Hardy and Meredith, Virginia Woolf notes:

These judgments, which reveal Virginia Woolf's ambivalence between the poetry of life and the novel of observations and manners, also point out her shrewd appraisal of the dangers of poetic fiction. One such difficulty she notes is that of the discontinuity of individual moments. Each character, she points out in her discussion of Meredith, terminates at his moment of illumination; he becomes incapable of being subjected to further development or analysis.[22] Narrative continuity is displaced by concentrations of individual scenes—a problem which becomes especially acute if the narrative background is pale or abstract. This problem is inherent in any conception of the novel as a sequence of illuminations. Proust, too, had recognized this danger and had ultimately overcome it.[23] Virginia Woolf's essay on Sterne shows that she was fully aware of this difficulty even in her favorite English poet-novelist. His "light attachment to the accepted reality, [his] neglect of the orderly sequence of narrative, allows [him] almost the license of a poet." And poetic license it is. In *Tristram Shandy,* feelings and sensations rendered as "images" become the fabric of the novel, depicting brilliant moments through witty compressions and verbal play.[24]

Coherence is supplied, and discontinuity eliminated, by the mind of the omniscient poet whose "poetry" suffuses scenes and even entire books with an aura of mystery or "lyrical recogni-

"This would seem to prove that a profound poetic sense is a dangerous gift for a novelist; for in Hardy and Meredith poetry seems to mean something impersonal, generalized, hostile to the idiosyncrasy of character, so that the two suffer if brought into touch." "Phases of Fiction," *Granite and Rainbow,* p. 137.

[22] "The Novels of George Meredith," *The Common Reader,* Second Series, pp. 231–232.

[23] For this distinction, see Maxime Chastaing, *La Philosophie de Virginia Woolf* (Paris: Presses Universitaires de France, 1951), pp. 145–146. For Virginia Woolf's comments on Proust, see "Phases of Fiction," *Granite and Rainbow,* pp. 124–126, 138–141.

[24] "The 'Sentimental Journey,'" *The Common Reader,* Second Series, pp. 79–80, 82–83. Cf. "Phases of Fiction," *Granite and Rainbow,* pp. 134–136.

tion." Seen from this perspective, *Wuthering Heights* and *Moby Dick* are successful, because in both novels the emotions of hero and reader are caught in an atmosphere of poetry to which "the characters of Catherine or Heathcliff, or Captain Ahab give expression." Hardy and Meredith, on the other hand, were inadequate poet-novelists. In their novels, the writer's "sense of poetry, of youth, of love of nature, is heard like a song to which the characters listen passively without moving a muscle." The song can be separated from the hero; when it is done "[the characters] move again with a jerk." [25] The author's "world" and the atmosphere expressed by his heroes must coincide. The poet's vision, of which his characters are instances, is analogous to the act of apprehension which is portrayed in the novel and supplies its poetic unity.

—— 4

In her search for a form in which the "inner" and "outer" can be combined, Virginia Woolf conceived of the moment as a contraction of the manifold elements of life into significant images or scenes. In addition to such a literary use, the moment also serves the *epistemological* function of clarifying the implications of consciousness for the artist's experience of life: a version of the imagination.

The moment involves the relationship of the self-conscious mind with its body (including its physical organs of perception) as well as with the world of objects it apprehends. The first of these relationships Virginia Woolf indicated in a brief, remarkable essay, "On Being Ill" (1930), in which she actually re-examined the concept of the "semi-transparent envelope." Literature, in describing illness, had always acted as if the body were "a sheet of glass through which the soul looks straight and clear" and which, with some notable exceptions, is "null and negligible and non-existent." Actually, however, "[the] creature within [the body] can only gaze through the pane—smudged or rosy."

[25] *Granite and Rainbow,* pp. 137–138.

The self "cannot separate off [from the body] . . . like the sheath of a knife or the pod of a pea for a single instant." [26] By reemphasizing the difficulty of distilling a clear image of the mental act from its involvement with the body, Virginia Woolf focused sharply on the implications of the "semi-transparent envelope." She noted an almost classical dualism, extending from the relationship of mind and body to the philosophically distinct relations between self-consciousness and its world.

This dualism supplies an important key to an understanding of imagination as Virginia Woolf conceived it. In the essay "The Moment: Summer's Night," illumination is described as a higher state of awareness, revealing a vision of the act of cognition itself. Poetic imagery evokes meaningful intersections of mind, objects, and associations to portray the various stages of awareness through which the moment is created. The scene is a night in the country before a summer house, involving four people, the observer among them, who are desultorily gathered as separate entities. The darkness surrounds them like an envelope nearly opaque, penetrated only by a few appearances. Sense impressions—voices, shuffling feet, a match striking, glimmering ends of cigarettes— are the starting points of a vision which evolves from the periphery of consciousness to its center (the group of percipients), to radiate again outward and encompass the universe as a whole. In this way, the entire process of awareness is exhibited, from the first moment of striking up an acquaintance with the facts of the world through sensation, to an awareness of their universal implications.

From disparate elements combined by a consciousness, the moment moves to associations and memories which expand perceptions into scenes. But, throughout this process, the conscious self remains aware of the objects which feed its cognitions—the lamps being lit, the night sounds, and the words of companions —and realizes that for the duration of the moment these "things" are freed from their time-bound existence. At the same time,

[26] *The Moment and Other Essays* (New York: Harcourt Brace, 1948), pp. 9–10.

the objects and words remain potentially distinct. The mental act strikes at *relations:* words turn into objects; appearances suggest the objects behind them protruding from the sheath of darkness. Although vivid scenes are created by association and memory—the terrier catching a rat, the farmer beating his wife—the reader is constantly aware that these scenes are occasioned by objects and acts, things and words. In its final stage, the moment obtains an independent existence of its own, combining both physical and mental worlds and engulfing the self in brief, ecstatic recognitions before it collapses into its components and burns out like the significant match of Mrs. Woolf's description. Then things become once more external and limiting as the mind is wrenched away from objects which it again views as alien and apart from itself.[27]

In Virginia Woolf's imprecise, eclectic way, this essay demonstrates not only a mystical ecstasy in which all disparates become one but also a shrewd analysis of the components of consciousness. Equating the subject and the object of awareness with the "inner" and the "outer," Virginia Woolf suggests that both are included in a single whole. The mind recognizes relations between experience and its objects, isolated from the stream of experience upon intense concentration but incapable of enduring in time. Within this moment, the mind reflects upon its own activity as it lights up the world and constructs it as a distinct pattern of existence, only to see it fall apart at the point of its clearest insight.[28] It is part of Mrs. Woolf's supreme eclec-

[27] *Ibid.,* pp. 3–8.

[28] This analysis of consciousness is reminiscent of G. E. Moore's famous essay in epistemology, "The Refutation of Idealism" (1903). Moore concludes that upon intense concentration we can become briefly aware of our awareness of the content or objects of our consciousness. Such states are "diaphanous" and cannot endure in time. See *Philosophical Studies* (London: Routledge and Kegan Paul, 1948), pp. 1–30. How far Virginia Woolf was affected by Moore's epistemology, if at all directly, is a question. J. K. Johnston has shown the impression made upon the Bloomsbury circle by Moore's *Principia Ethica; The Bloomsbury Group* (New York: Noonday Press, 1954), pp. 20–45.

ticism that at this juncture, she also envisaged the artist's intervention to recreate simultaneously, in an almost Crocean sense, the fleeting recognition and the permanent form. The moment becomes the work of art, requiring only words or scenes, colors or shapes, to endure in time.

Seen in this light, Virginia Woolf's views appear as variants of traditional concepts of the imagination. Her analysis of mental experience sometimes recalls Wordsworthian definitions—the artist's conscious reconstruction of unconsciously assembled impressions recollected in tranquility.[29] It is also reminiscent of Proust's "involuntary memory"—a union created by the interaction of time-bound physical and timeless mental worlds—or, on a different level, of Coleridge's primary imagination. In some respects, Mrs. Woolf's eclectic mind undoubtedly also included in her concept of the moment Bergsonian ideas. All of these sources have left clear marks in Virginia Woolf's work and have haphazardly fashioned her thought. But while the "moment of illumination" seems to exhibit that "esemplastic power" through which, in Coleridge, self and object are brought together, the vision itself is focused on the impact of mind upon objects; an autonomous act, it creates not so much a fusion as an elevated awareness of their relations. Rising from within the flow of experience, Virginia Woolf's moments thrust themselves into consciousness as the passively borne stream finds itself conjoined with particular objects in the external world: trees, waves, and human figures on the beach creating significant forms for Lily Briscoe in *To the Lighthouse;* Isa converting a teacup into a wishing-well in *Between the Acts.* While they unite present and past, image and experience in a "pure" aesthetic vision, these moments also include the recalcitrant facts of outward existence which retain their independence. They may be present in memory or be converted into symbols intensely meaningful to an inner consciousness, but they also represent that substance of factual life which belongs in the province of

---

[29] "The Leaning Tower," *The Moment,* p. 134.

the conscientious novelist. This duality of imagination and fact defines the ambivalence Virginia Woolf discerned in Conrad's novels between the sea-captain enamored of "simple facts" and the brooding Marlow for whom the world was always at bottom symbolic.[30] It suggests an ambiguity she found in all her poet-novelists, and, most deeply, in herself. But this distinction also became the source of her method, reconciling the novelist's need for a concrete world with the poet's heightened insights.

Virginia Woolf's mature concept of "imagination" is explained in her essay on Turgenev (1933). A truly symbolic vision, she held, must represent two incompatible efforts in an ideal form: that of "observing facts impartially" and of "interpreting them symbolically." Emotions remain indeed important, but they have a specific function. They obtain their existence from a vision of "incompatible things" drawn together in single instances of illuminated perception. Radiating from "some character at the center," a succession of these emotions replaces the succession of events to create a form embodying life as a whole. The "fact" and the "vision," the "photograph" and the "poem," as Virginia Woolf calls them, are united in a symbolic self. Rising above individual selves, the "character at the center" transmutes "hot" particular emotions into an ordered image of universal experience. In this way, Turgenev achieved, as Meredith, Hardy, or Conrad did not, a peculiarly poetic continuity in which the novelist's pursuit of facts is integrated in a symbolic form.[31]

Virginia Woolf's conceptions of form and self owe a great deal to ideas she had absorbed in her wide reading of both the English romantic poets and Proust and the *fin de siècle* French writers. Her readings enriched her ambivalent conscience, which strained simultaneously toward a projection of the world as a symbolic image and toward its vision as a distinct entity with

[30] "Joseph Conrad," *The Common Reader*, First Series, pp. 286–290; "Mr. Conrad: A Conversation," *The Captain's Death Bed*, pp. 76–77.

[31] "The Novels of Turgenev," *The Captain's Death Bed*, pp. 56–58, 60, *et passim*.

which the self must come to terms. For this reason, her fusion
of novel and poem did not lead, as might be expected, to a dilu-
tion of the novel. Rather, it intensified the novelist's task of making, with Jane Austen, "the moment to glow." The elements
of each novel became images in a picture that reflects "facts" in
their universal dimensions.

—5

Virginia Woolf's lyrical narrative depends on a design in which
various contents of consciousness are juxtaposed. David Daiches
defined her method succinctly: it is to ". . . distill a significance
out of the data discovered by the personal sensibility and, by
projecting that significance through the minds of others, to
maintain an unstable equilibrium between lyrical and narrative
art." [32] Whatever may be the limitations of this definition of
lyricism (and Daiches identifies it too closely with the personal
sensibility), it shows how the poet's awareness can be the focus
of a work that is also composed of the individual "moments"
of its characters. Indeed, the "unstable equilibrium between
lyrical and narrative art" shows Mrs. Woolf's brilliant achievement of telescoping the poet's "lyrical self" and the novelist's
omniscient point of view.

The novels of the nineteen-twenties, which develop the new
design, are composed of carefully distributed mixtures of indi-

[32] *Virginia Woolf*, p. 153. The strongest statement identifying Virginia
Woolf's poetic method with subjective effusion was made in an unsym-
pathetic review of her novels from *The Voyage Out* to *The Waves* by
Robert Peel: "The abnormally acute inner emotion [in *The Voyage Out*]
dissolves the outer world into a dream, an hallucination; the habitual self,
as part of the outer world, shares its isolation and helplessness before the
released emotion streaming up from the unconscious. *This is the method
of poetry;* we accept such a poetic interlude as Richard's and Lucy's meeting in *Richard Feverel,* but it remains to be seen whether a whole novel
can be successfully constructed on this method." "Virginia Woolf," *Criterion,* XIII (1933), 79, 82, *et passim.* (Italics mine.) On the other hand,
Leon Edel describes her method approvingly as that of a "lyric poet";
The Psychological Novel, pp. 190ff., esp. p. 194.

vidual images or illustrative descriptions and motifs with *monologues* of particular characters. The motifs are the products of the author's sensibility, the monologues his projections through the minds of others. These soliloquies are of necessity interior, but as poetry they serve an additional purpose. They are the *forms* in which moments—the meeting of association and memory with the facts of the external world—are caught to reflect content and coherence in lyrical narrative. They act as units, both lyrical and dramatic, to supply the instances of perception and recognition of which the novels are composed. These monologues deal with the matter of experience and infer the substance of speech and action from a postulated point of view behind the figures. But they do not render a stream of consciousness directly; rather, they present moments of awareness in set speeches which convert the subterranean flow into poetic imagery. Like Gide, Virginia Woolf identifies herself successively or simultaneously with her figures to translate their various monologues into formal patterns. They are *dramatic* monologues in which psychological drama and common speech are replaced by lyrical drama and inner speech.

Such a method also requires a *structure* in which the monologues are utilized. Despite her concern with the musical form of poetry, Virginia Woolf saw this design chiefly in terms of an analogy with painting, precisely with impressionist and post-impressionist art. Her "paintings" were visual illuminations, like Lily Briscoe's in *To the Lighthouse,* namely, forms in which all elements fall into place, artistic equivalents of the recognition of the moment. As language depicts the visions caught by each perceiver's eye, the image becomes that form of awareness which corresponds to the figure on the painter's canvas. The resulting design is not instantly recognizable. In her fervent concern with relations, Virginia Woolf constructed her pattern of images and monologues in constellations which showed abstract relationships rather than bodily movements or forms. A distillation of this method is shown in the short sketch, "Kew Gardens" (originally in *Monday or Tuesday,* 1921), which shows all the ele-

ments of subtle design later brought to fruition in the full-length
novels.

Like a symbolist prose poem, this story develops a description of a summer afternoon in a London park into a drama, setting off the ordered nature of the park from the plight of human
beings and unifying both as a poetic image. The key to the
design is a colorful world in which objects are enlivened by the
impact of light:

> The light fell either upon the smooth, grey back of a pebble
> or the shell of a snail with its brown circular veins, or falling
> into a raindrop it expanded with such intensity of red, blue,
> and yellow the thin walls of water that one expected them to
> disappear.[33]

Brilliantly anticipating *The Waves,* Virginia Woolf projects
these images through her own as well as her characters' consciousness to create a coherent pattern. A middle-aged family,
an old man and a bored younger companion, a pair of lower-
class women and a couple of working-class lovers are joined as
images by a flower, a snail, and the light. Occasionally dipping
into monologues—and the associations and memories of her
figures—the omniscient poet paints her canvas by selecting a
few details in the external world to which her human characters
relate. Sweeping across her scene in an encompassing arc, Virginia Woolf mirrors the broad image of nature in smaller images,
yielded by individual monologues, in which awareness is ultimately portrayed as a picture of the world. The design of this
sketch consists of "points" of awareness, intersecting with other
"points," with images and objects, to convert a drama of moments and relationships into a continuous design.

This process translates into literature terms which were used
about painting by Virginia Woolf's close friend, Roger Fry. The
concept of *transmutation* is most pertinent in this context; it
prescribes that "any visual datum" be incorporated in a spiritual

[33] "Kew Gardens," *A Haunted House and Other Stories* (New York:
Harcourt Brace, 1944), p. 28.

whole, determined by plastic and spatial values.[34] In fiction, such visual data are the novel's figures as they are viewed by the reader. They include a character's awareness, his monologues as well as his perceptions of objects and other figures, all of which intersect with a variety of other characters similarly conceived to provide a pattern of sensibilities composed of figures, images, and scenes.

The creation of scenes as moments from images and monologues, the use of these moments to provide binding threads between characters in such a way as to fashion a pastiche of life, these are also the techniques Virginia Woolf developed in her fiction. These forms render a vision of experience in its relations between objects and selves. But, as we noted, there remains in the poet-painter's endeavor the novelist's concern with the world of facts. The poet's imagination becomes the novelist's task of representing moments precisely and of gathering them in adequate forms. Imagination in prose narrative unites the formal awareness of isolated moments with the outer universe and the portrait of manners.

This approach enabled Virginia Woolf to join the traditional

[34] See Chapter 1 of *Transformations: Critical and Speculative Essays on Art* (London: Chatto and Windus, 1920), "Some Questions in Esthetics," in which Fry summarizes his views more fully developed in his *Vision and Design* (1920). The relationship of Fry's aesthetics to Virginia Woolf's technique has stimulated a great many critical responses, but the basic treatment of the subject remains that of John Hawley Roberts, " 'Vision and Design' in Virginia Woolf," *PMLA*, LXI (1946), 835–847. The subject is placed in the more general context of Bloomsbury in Johnstone's chapter, "Bloomsbury Aesthetics," *The Bloomsbury Group*, pp. 46–94, and is also treated in a discussion of Virginia Woolf's ideas, *ibid.*, pp. 136ff. The "spatial" view of fiction, which involves a relocation of temporal sequence in the novel, was a primary point of criticism in William Troy's pioneering essay, "Virginia Woolf: the Novel of Sensibility," *Symposium*, III (1932), 53–63, 153–166 reprinted in Morton Dowden Zabel, *Literary Opinion in America* (2nd. ed.; New York: Harpers, 1951), pp. 324–337. Taking issue with Troy, an essay by Dean Doner shows how a fictional world can be created from repetitive and expanding motifs. "Virginia Woolf: the Service of Style," *Modern Fiction Studies*, II (1956), 1–12.

novel of "facts" and a prose poetry of symbolic forms. Contradictory, often evasive above a core of firm convictions, she mirrored the "rainbow" of her illuminations in the "granite" of a world which had been fashioned by a Victorian past. Sensibility is the most cultivated form of human awareness and its communication is largely aesthetic. Mrs. Woolf's conception of the self, though intuitively personal, was primarily shaped by a vision, poetic and symbolic alike, which reached from an awareness of the self's immediate relations to an image of man's enduring struggle with the facts of his existence.

DEFINITIONS OF THE SELF

—⁀1

Virginia Woolf's comprehension of poetry as a symbolic relationship between person and life makes the self a crucial term in her concept of the lyrical novel. The relationship between the individual self, and its range of experience, and the omniscient self of the poet-novelist is the core of her poetic method. As she gradually refines an impersonal image of the self, individual monologues become more and more absorbed into the omniscient point of view whose vision is rendered in a formal perspective. This is Virginia Woolf's approach to poetry: the evolution of the self toward a depersonalized image. Its development culminates in *The Waves,* but its beginning is clearly reflected in *Jacob's Room* (1923). In this early work, Mrs. Woolf's manner is by no means wholly poetic; rather, it illuminates the precarious balance between lyricism and narrative. A self is placed in a changing world of facts and events to be viewed both as an object and as a source of consciousness.

Three impulses determine the direction of the novel. A primary impulse is Mrs. Woolf's desire to depict life as she saw it. Accordingly, she reproduced the postwar generation of young men of her class, their pursuits as students, lovers, enthusiasts, social and literary rebels, and, occasionally, didactic fools, whose promise was cut short by the war. The second impulse is to experiment with the stream of consciousness, to develop new modes of transition replacing the sequence of a plot with the requirements of the moment. But, as it is used in *Jacob's Room,* this method is connected with the traditional point of view of the omniscient author. The narrator is not effaced, like Proust's Marcel in "Un Amour de Swann," nor is he a source of memory like Marcel of the overture. Rather, having achieved her distance from the characters by seeing them only in their most pertinent relations, the hidden author herself draws an arc around her figures. Like the concealed observer in "Kew Gardens," she develops a stream of associations of her own which constantly plays off the external perception of characters against their inner awareness of themselves and each other. From this method, there emerges a dense network of relationships, which is raised from the level of mere "intricacy" to that of tragedy and pathos by the larger symbolic image in which they are reflected. This image, provided by Jacob's *room,* creates a point of reference for the self and its interactions with the world.

The third impulse is the familiar concern with inanimate objects, which involves the larger purpose of illustrating the workings of consciousness both within and without the protagonist.[35] As Bernard Blackstone has shown, Virginia Woolf looked for objects as the expression of a truer reality concealed by the changing perspectives in the world of appearance and deception. But, in the context of a novel recognizably bearing the imprints of personal interaction, these things also obtain an epistemological significance; they define the self. Virginia Woolf may have considered *Jacob's Room* an inadequate early experiment, but it renders most precisely the image of a self through relations of minds with objects and other minds, including that of the author herself. Indeed, the plot resembles the progress of "The Moment:

[35] See, for example, "Solid Objects," *A Haunted House,* pp. 79–86. Cf. Bernard Blackstone's discussion of this story in *Virginia Woolf. A Commentary* (London: Hogarth Press, 1949), p. 153. Throughout my analysis of *Jacob's Room* I have found Blackstone's treatment of "things" in relation to the "human world" particularly suggestive.

Summer's Night," in which a center of consciousness draws to itself various objects and minds, to be divorced from them in the end.

Jacob's significant experience is focused on *things*. They illustrate and counterpoint, reflect and deepen his relationships with people—his mother, teachers, friends, and mistress—and at the same time they illuminate the necessary apartness of man and his world. After Jacob's death, his things are symbolized in his room, meaningful to no other human being. Things illustrate the relations between consciousness and its objects; Jacob's "internal stream" is modified by the objects he views and possesses. His awareness consists of these relations as they are caught by the omniscient consciousness of the author. Yet he, too, is an object—as the potentially non-sentient thing which is his body and as an object of consciousness for others. The relation between being aware and being an object of awareness, between perceiving and being perceived, provides the underlying scheme of the novel.

Jacob is described by his relations with the different things he observes. Like the poet whom Virginia Woolf advised in her letter of 1932, Jacob in Greece stands at the window, his mind focused on the world outside:

> Jacob went to the window and stood with his hands in his pockets. There he saw three Greeks in kilts; the masts of ships; idle or busy people of the lower classes strolling or stepping out briskly, or falling into groups and gesticulating with their hands.[36]

Thus seen, people are like figurines: impersonal, discrete. This image stands for the character's behavior in the novel as a whole. Since the inanimate objects in his room make for a more constant relationship than do people, Jacob tries to convert other minds into things. This way of thinking, however, prevents the

[36] *Jacob's Room* (New York: Harcourt Brace, 1923), p. 238. The letters "JR" followed by the page number, which will appear henceforth in parentheses, will refer to this edition.

possibility of intimate relationships. It not only disrupts communication but also compels the dissociation between the mind
and the objects of its world.

There appears to be a genuine connection between Jacob's
abortive relationship with the dubious Florinda and his more constant association with things. Both lay bare the self's capacity
for perceiving and knowing others. In the scene of the Guy
Fawkes bonfire in London, the reader's perception of Florinda
is that of a *thing:*

> Of the faces which came out fresh and vivid as though painted
> in yellow and red the most prominent was a girl's face. By
> a trick of the firelight she seemed to have no body. The oval
> of the face and hair hung beside the fire with a dark vacuum
> for background. (JR, 122)

Barely illuminated by the flames, a male hand, soon revealed
to be Jacob's, thrusts a harlequin's hat on her head. Significantly,
while assuming the form of the stream of consciousness, this
description actually approaches its object from the outside. Jacob
and Florinda are equally illuminated; we see them both as objects of perception just as later we are allowed to see now the
one, then the other, from their opposing points of view. The
omniscient observer shows clearly Jacob's innocent acceptance
of her as an object, not callously, but in the naïve confidence
that woman as an object of beauty, pure and faithful like a thing,
can be illuminated by consciousness. (JR, 124)

As the relationship progresses, Florinda and Jacob are treated
as separate moments, now containing each other, then isolated
in their respective worlds of Shelly and chocolate creams. (JR,
130f.) But especially their brief moments together reveal that
there is no "illumination" except at that evanescent point when
Jacob is the knower of beauty and Florinda his "brainless" object.
But soon both are dissatisfied: Jacob realizes that objects do not
make relationships. Their separation destroys entirely the illusion of their relationship as knower and object. When Jacob
sees her "turning up Greek Street on the arm of another man,"

light once more sheds its luster upon the scene. This time, it is caused by street lamps accentuating her shadow. Through a brilliant use of external association, moving from an observation of the scene into Jacob's mind, Virginia Woolf illuminates both body and mind as objects:

> The light drenched Jacob from head to toe. You could see the pattern on his trousers; the old thorns on his stick; his shoe laces; bare hands; and face.
>
> It was as if a stone were ground to dust; as if white sparks flew from a livid whetstone, which was his spine; as if the switchback railway, having swooped to the depths, fell, fell, fell. This was in his face. (JR, 158)

This intimate relation between objects and consciousness dissolves into a novelist's contemplation of her hero. Virginia Woolf now becomes the omniscient narrator stepping out of her role: "Whether we know what was in his mind is another question," yet we do know "that destiny is chipping a dent in him." Jacob is treated like an object, a moving statue. In one of the rare passages in which Mrs. Woolf treats her hero as a patient whom author and reader may conspire to help, she wonders whether to follow him to his *room:* ". . . —that we won't do." "Yet that, of course, is precisely what one does." (JR, 158–159) We now see Jacob's external actions as he enters his room, shuts the door, knows the presence of things which had remained unchanged by the experience. The omniscient poet can concentrate on the abiding, hence truly faithful things in his room, which maintain their existence apart from any beholder. At this point in the novel, the hero still exists for his things to bestow their comfort upon him: ". . .—yet all the while, having for centre, for magnet, a young man alone in his room." (JR, 160) At its conclusion, the magnet is removed and he becomes an object himself. In this way, Jacob's attempt to convert other minds into things involves him precisely in those barren relationships which he seeks to overcome.

The paradoxical situation created by the definition of a self as, simultaneously, a subject and object of consciousness lends the "picture of life" into which Jacob is fitted a particular significance. The narrator-poet projects Jacob's experience as a variety of disconnected moments in which his character is portrayed in relation to the lives and manners of others. In one sense, all characters are indeed things which survive him, but, being people, they are also sources of consciousness and share some of Jacob's own problems. *They intersect with and create his world.* Some of these lives are stories in their own right, reflecting—like the vicissitudes of Jacob's mother, the distraught widow, Betty Flanders—a painfully satiric portrait of manners. Mrs. Flanders' abortive attachment to Captain Barfoot, and the offer of marriage by the Reverend Mr. Floyd, who had laboriously helped educate her children, recall the deft hand of Jane Austen. This is true of many of the lives and worlds we briefly encounter on our quest with Jacob, such as the Wentworth Williams in Greece, or Timmy Durant and his family in a Cornwall summer, or the crowd of young men and women in London. But, like Jacob's life, indeed, like life itself, these stories lack Jane Austen's neat conclusions. Their conclusion lies on a different level. Mrs. Flanders' life, satirically portrayed, has the completeness of an image. The relationships and "stories" moving in and around Jacob, affecting him, determining him, often passing him by, also move within and beyond one another to be contained in the ordering imagination of the omniscient author.

For this reason, the underemphasis of plot in *Jacob's Room* is not in itself significant. To be sure, Virginia Woolf opened up forms which were never completed: both her satiric sketches in the vein of Jane Austen and her Dickensian scraps of realistic scene. Even character is not fully explored except as it illuminates certain moments of experience, although these moments draw milieu minutely and express characters' impulses with accuracy. But the development of the story is more fully apparent than the anxious author often persuaded herself to admit. The theme consists of man's struggle for mature visions of himself and his world which turn out to be elusive. In the beginning this vision is simple—Jacob's sheep skull and Betty Flanders' widowhood—but as the young man grows, his world grows and, with both, the complexity of the author's vision increases. Viewing the changes of relationships between selves—and of their perspectives of each other—Virginia Woolf renders simple ideas more complex as the naïve thing is mirrored in a consciousness that includes others as well.

Mrs. Woolf's remarks about "Gusev," already cited, illuminate this deepening of the novel. She admired in Chekhov's story the desultory manner in which a picture is created from the interchange of various consciousnesses. The passage is sufficiently prophetic to deserve full quotation.

> Some Russian soldiers lie ill on board of a ship which is taking them back to Russia. We are given a few scraps of their talk and some of their thoughts; then one of them dies and is carried away; the talk goes on among the others for a time, until Gusev himself dies, and looking "like a carrot or a radish" is thrown overboard. The emphasis is laid upon such unexpected places that at first it seems as if there were no emphasis at all; and then, as the eyes accustom themselves to twilight and discern the shapes of things in a room we see how complete the story is, how profound, and how truly in obedience to his vision Tchekov has chosen this, that, and the other, and placed them together to compose something new.[37]

Virginia Woolf continues that such a story fits into no fixed form, neither of tragedy nor of comedy nor of the short story, the sketch being "vague and inconclusive." Yet this is indeed the method she had chosen in *Jacob's Room* and, more profoundly, its theme. Like Gusev, Jacob, killed in the war, has indeed become a thing. Others survive him to carry on the vague networks of life indefinitely, dying and recreating themselves, while the things, now lacking their "magnet," soon to

[37] "Modern Fiction," *The Common Reader,* First Series, pp. 192–193.

be scattered, retain a meaning of their past relationships with the hero. But at the same time this thematic resolution—inconclusive only on the level of dramatic plot—is delivered in the typically impressionistic manner Mrs. Woolf had praised in Chekhov. No prescribed emphasis or rigid formula mars the reflection of the picture; it is the image in the impressionistic painter's eye and that of the beholder.

The combining of disparate movements of life in an author's concealed perspective approaches a poetic method which Mrs. Woolf was to work out more fully in her later novels. It underlines the suspicion that although she agreed with some of the negative judgments of her book, she was also aware of the fact that they actually pointed out the beginnings of a purposeful technique. Although it is not yet a lyrical novel, *Jacob's Room* is the first important example of her "new" method; it marks the point at which she had at last discovered "how to begin [at 40] to say something in my own voice." [38] Her voice is that of the soliloquist acting as the omniscient author of conventional fiction. It describes the act of cognition in which awareness unites with objects and other selves, or separates from them, to create a world of imagery that directs the flow of the novel. In her following two books, *Mrs. Dalloway* and *To the Lighthouse,* Virginia Woolf sought to reconcile this poetic insight with the novel's form, until in *The Waves* she found herself fully as a poet in prose.

—2

Mrs. Dalloway (1925) is the first among Virginia Woolf's "new" novels to accommodate the poet's vision to a well-devised story. "The narrative technique," Bernard Blackstone observed, "has become more *serré*. The gain in intensity is a corresponding loss in expansiveness and allusion." [39] The poet has come to terms with the novelist's craft; the picture viewed by the poet-

[38] July 26, 1922, *A Writer's Diary,* p. 47.
[39] *Virginia Woolf,* p. 97.

painter of "Kew Gardens" and *Jacob's Room* is more selective, concentrating its design on two primary and several subsidiary figures.

The development of Virginia Woolf's technique reveals a fuller conception of personality, society, and manners and a deeper insight into their relation to poetry. On the one hand, the book's function as a *novel* is made fully apparent. It reinstates a coherent plot made up of intricate motives and manifold relations. Proper dispositions of times and places are given careful attention. The stream of consciousness, filtering life through inner experience, serves to lay bare many hearts within a panorama of life. Even the evident symbolism exists within a narrative framework of time and cause. But, on the other hand, a poetic pattern is at least partially imposed, impressing itself upon the novel with disproportionate strength.

As a work of *narrative, Mrs. Dalloway* goes beyond a depiction of society. Its theme, if not its method, is an indictment of society and its superficial values. The intricacies of social experience are shown to be on trial, losing out against fate, "the greater passions." But essentially this indictment proceeds through relationships, through the awareness of the protagonists, their author, and the minor figures. A "comedy of manners" centered in Clarissa Dalloway, whose foibles are treated with penetrating irony, is matched with a "tragedy of life" compounded of the illness and suicide of Septimus Warren Smith. It is one of the novel's further dimensions that ultimately the upper reaches of London society—the social world in which all the figures finally meet—is counterpointed by the inner world of a single protagonist who symbolizes life, death, the European war.

The relationship between the comedy of manners and the tragedy of life is illustrated by the constant interweaving of these two plots. On one side of the scale there are the manifold characters of Clarissa Dalloway's world; the friends of her youth like Sally Seaton, Peter Walsh, and even Hugh Whitbread; her husband and daughter; the servants; Lady Bruton and her comic passion for emigration; and even the finely chiseled minor figures who turn up now and then and are gathered at the party in the end. On the other side, there are essentially only Septimus and his hapless Italian wife, Lucrezia. They are impinged upon by the two evil assailants of society, Dr. Holmes and the majestic psychiatrist, Sir William Bradshaw; but in their self-contained suffering they are quite alone. Septimus encompasses the world in huge symbolic recognitions; he is like Conrad's figures of fate, like Hardy's Jude. His world is wholly internal; he is the romantic hero in reverse. Having absorbed the world, he must be its victim. Clarissa and Septimus, as the two protagonists, do not complement one another only because they are aspects of a divided personality in a clinical sense, or even because they share a divided point of view, as we have observed it in Hesse and occasionally in Gide. Rather, they are components of an impersonal insight in which they are briefly united in the end. The goal of *Mrs. Dalloway* as a novel lies in this impersonal *moment* in which Clarissa is liberated and brought into a union with life, in which she is "defined."

The *external plot* is centered on an increasing awareness of failure, of malaise, of falling short of one's expectations. The war has not created these failures in Clarissa's world: although we meet many male characters, the war duties of Richard or Hugh or even of Peter Walsh are scarcely mentioned. But the war has created the significant abyss in Septimus' world. Here it becomes crucial and symbolic. Failure, then, in Clarissa's world is of a different kind: it is the usual surrender to the seasons or to the changes in life (later to become the central issue in *The Waves*). For this reason, youth is stressed in the novel as hope contrasted with the "failure" of middle age. Sally Seaton had promised to be a great, warm, illuminating rebel, but she married a bald millionaire in Manchester and had five boys. Peter Walsh was to be a brilliant poet, but he was a "failure" in India. Clarissa, too, had lost her youthful capacity for love and compassion and struggled to recapture it through the haze of her parties. This theme is also illustrated by the emphasis on Elizabeth, who, although she bears within her the compromises society will exact, is still alert to the possibilities of life.

In Septimus' world, however, failure has a totally different meaning. Suffering a delayed mental shock from his war experience, Septimus specifically fastens on a deeper failing which is echoed in Clarissa's world. He feels guilt at having been unable to feel sadness at the death of his closest friend. Septimus' entire life is engulfed by this disease from which even his marriage cannot save him. He cannot feel; he cannot "connect." Although he is a potential poet like Peter Walsh, his incapacity for reaching outside himself—in contrast with Peter who can still fall in love—renders the poetry he dictates to Rezia hallucinatory, indrawn, with only patches of beauty. His disordered mind rambles; his images are occasioned by objects which he distorts into a world of his own.[40] He is the counterpoint of Jacob's undaunted optimism, because the war has intervened and the shell-shocked mind has drawn into itself.

These two plots, and their respective worlds, reflect Virginia Woolf's vision of the "inner" and the "outer." The novel as a whole is internal only in the sense that the action is filtered through minds. Its substance lies in the opposition of an external world of manners and an internal symbolic world. For example, "beauty" is a frequent word in Clarissa's vocabulary. She admires the beauty of jewelry, the beauty of women in the past. Once she had wooed Sally Seaton's spiritual beauty with her own gown of pink gauze. Beauty, indeed, is the standard by which her world is measured. But for Septimus, sitting in the park and mistaking the airplane advertising *Toffee* for a message from another world, beauty has a more basic meaning:

> So, thought Septimus, looking up, they are signalling to me. Not indeed in actual words; that is he could not read the language yet; but it was plain enough, this beauty, this

---

[40] *Mrs. Dalloway* (Modern Library, 1928), pp. 212–213. Hereafter "D" followed by the page number will refer to this edition.

exquisite beauty, and tears filled his eyes as he looked at the smoke words languishing and melting in the sky and bestowing upon him in their inexhaustible charity and laughing goodness one shape after another of unimaginable beauty and signalling their intention to provide him, for nothing, for ever, for looking merely, with beauty, more beauty! Tears ran down his cheeks. (D, 31)

This contrast reveals the gulf between the two worlds, between Clarissa's or Peter Walsh's knowledge of horror or selfhood—as sensitive people experience these terms in a social context—and Septimus' symbolic comprehension, which surpasses any interaction among people or even communion with oneself. Part of the novel's irony lies in just such semantic discrepancies, such differences in shades of meaning which at the same time are part of its poetry.

This irony also functions on the narrative level, determining characters in their various relations to one another and to life as a whole. To achieve the continuity of a novel, Virginia Woolf required narrative links between her divided worlds. All of the familiar connecting threads are woven between Septimus' hallucinatory insight into life on the one hand and the outer world of the Dalloways on the other. The external time scheme, underlined by the strokes of Big Ben, places both worlds in an identical framework. It matches Septimus' sense of an inner truth (the kind of truth for which Marlow searches in Conrad's *Heart of Darkness*) with the entire social world of the Dalloways' drawing room, Lady Bruton's dining room, indeed even with the streets of London or the gates of the palace or the country house of Clarissa's girlhood. Particular events stress these connections, functioning as conventional narrative aids. The airplane and royal car in the early phases of the book achieve such a result. Peter Walsh, driving to Clarissa's party, meets the ambulance carrying Septimus' body. Finally, particular characters—the psychiatrist Sir William Bradshaw most prominently among them—communicate between the two worlds.

On a lyrical level, narrative motifs produce a design of images. Recurring in the same consciousness at different times, or in different characters at the same time, they weave a pattern whose appropriateness is recognized by the reader; they elaborate one another or act as counterpoints; they broaden the conception of character and the novel's theme through shades of meaning and verbal play peculiar to poetry. For example, when Clarissa withdraws to her attic room after her return from her morning excursion "like a nun withdrawing or a child exploring a tower," she sees before her, as she takes off her things, her own virginal bed. *The sheets were clean, tight stretched in a broad white band from side to side. Narrower and narrower would her bed be.* (D, 45–46) Later, after the surprise meeting with Peter unexpectedly home from India, the motif of the inevitability of death is sounded as the theme of isolation. She had not married him. *It was all over for her. The sheet was stretched and the bed narrow. She had gone up into the tower alone and left them blackberrying in the sun.* (D, 70) The same images are only slightly expanded by *blackberrying,* which recalls the activities of childhood. But the narrow bed, the tower, the cloister, all work not only for Clarissa; they are also thematic images of the novel; they determine the poetic design that immediately reflects its theme: isolation, helplessness before death, the withdrawal from life, and the failure implicit in growing old.

The manner in which the interior monologue is used is an additional source of the lyrical design. Mental associations proceed independently of time or cause and facilitate the interweaving of motifs. But although inner speech was of great importance to her narrative, Virginia Woolf's main object was to use the stream of consciousness poetically and to integrate it into the design as a whole in conjunction with other images. On a lyrical level, therefore, the interior monologue served a peculiar aesthetic end. It converted association into formal soliloquies, imposing controlled imagery on inner speech. The significance of her stream of consciousness is not only that it is logical and planned, as David Daiches has shown, but also that it is used obliquely, transposing each thought into an image that expresses the thought. During the meeting with Peter Walsh, for example, when Clarissa, overcome by emotion, kisses Peter, her feelings are at once translated into images:

> And Clarissa had leant forward, taken his hand, drawn him to her, kissed him—actually had felt his face on hers before she could down the brandishing of silver flashing—plumes like pampas grass in a tropic gale in her breast, which, subsiding, left her holding his hand, patting his knee and, feeling as she sat back extraordinarily at her ease with him and light-hearted, all in a clap it came over her, If I had married him, this gaiety would have been mine all day. (D, 69–70)

"Plumes like pampas grass in a tropic gale" is a brilliant image glossing her emotion, catching in metaphor the substance of what Clarissa might feel; it also objectifies the emotion at the same time that it describes it most succinctly. The author's intrusion—*feeling as she sat back extraordinarily at her ease with him*—is followed by a recognition of what life would be like with Peter, until the entire scene is captured in the vision of this imaginary life as a play. The collapse of the moment becomes the end of the play; it is "now over" and Clarissa is collecting her things. (D, 70–71) The inward drama is formalized, but the formality is not contained in the consciousness itself; it is the imposition of metaphoric imagery on the verbal substance of the mind.

This method also acts as an expansion. It links the image with a narrative scene and finally reconnects it with that scene. For example, one of Clarissa's illuminations occurs when she seeks to define herself in front of her dressing table:

> She pursed her lips when she looked in the glass. It was to give her face point. That was her self—pointed; dartlike; definite. That was her self when some effort, some call on her to be her self, drew the parts together, she alone knew how different, how incompatible and composed so for the

world only into one centre, one diamond, one woman who
sat in her drawing-room and made a meeting-point, a radiancy
no doubt in some dull lives, a refuge for the lonely to come
to, perhaps. . . . (D, 55)

The action centers on a familiar scene: woman and mirror.
The image is that of Clarissa as she would like to be—pointed,
dart-like, definite. Association carries her to the next point which
becomes a pivot for the metaphor. She can be such a self whenever an effort demands it of her (the effort, for example, to
glitter at her party that night). This thought terminates the
direct stream of consciousness and converts it into the poetic
image. For Clarissa now sees herself as a "centre," a thing; she
is depersonalized, the "world" looks at her; she is a diamond
(artificial, impersonal, glittering). The "diamond" at once expands into the figure of the woman. Like a camera closing in
on the significant figure, the passage narrows to the "woman
in the drawing-room" who is crystallized symbolically. She is
seen as an image, still possessed of the impersonal radiance and
attraction of the jewel. But the image also returns us to Clarissa's
personal world. It leads to the kind of attraction she can exert—
once again as a person, becoming the particular woman in the
drawing room, herself; it leads to Lady Bruton's lunch with
her husband and to the dress in the closet.

This manner of transmuting associations or inner speech into
well-organized images affects both the monologues of individual
characters and the vision of the omniscient poet. In Septimus
Smith's inner world, for example, the disconnected associations
of a deranged mind often turn into striking images whose artistic
distortions clarify his mental anguish. "[The] flesh was melted
off the world." "[His body] spread like a veil upon a rock."
(D, 102–103) These images contract Septimus' vision into a
metaphoric statement of his exposed and isolated condition.
Images of this sort also occur in the monologue of the omniscient
poet who establishes by their means a *public self* for Septimus
—the provincial childhood, his love for Shakespeare and Isabel

Pole, Evans and the war, Lucrezia making hats in Milan—which his illness had made inaccessible.

In the lyrical design, as Virginia Woolf conceives it, characters themselves occasionally function as images. An example is that of Miss Kilman, who connects the Dalloways and the Smiths, not on a narrative level as does Sir William Bradshaw, but as a poetic motif. At one end of the scale, this dour woman of God in her shabby raincoat distorts some of Clarissa's own aspirations and foibles. She, too, is a soul struggling to maintain her connection with life, an effort which to her seems possible only through the Church. At the other end of the scale, she becomes, like Septimus, a symbolic figure. In the tea-room scene with Elizabeth, her greed for food is contrary to Septimus' genuine horror of anything physical, but her search for love that cannot hold its object echoes the theme of failure which pervades both worlds of the book. (D, 196–201) Her response to Elizabeth's indifference turns her wholly into an image figure. She kneels to pray in Westminster Abbey, but, unlike the other communicants, who belong in the everyday world, she gives herself to the religious experience. As Mr. Fletcher and Mrs. Gorham saw her, she was "a soul haunting the same territory; a soul out of immaterial substance; not a woman, a soul." (D, 203) If Septimus, at his horrified moment of recognition, becomes identified with his vision just before his death, Miss Kilman, similarly disembodied, becomes an image of the painful way to God. Although she is savagely dissected by the author's scalpel, Miss Kilman, ironically, also expresses man's isolation as part of the novel's theme.[41]

[41] Critics usually identify Miss Kilman (whose very name strikes the death motif) with all that is hateful to Virginia Woolf; she is seen as the counterpart of Bradshaw. Note, for example, R. L. Chambers: "This is why Doris Kilman is hateful and evil,—because, having denied her own personality, she would lay her ugly hands on another's, and swathe it and smother it beneath the drab shapelessness of her green mackintosh coat. . . . So Septimus Smith is not just a case of war-neurosis, mishandled by his doctors, but a cringing, fugitive human soul, escaping from Holmes and Bradshaw, who wish to possess what is not their own to violate the

One of Virginia Woolf's purposes was to distill a symbolic self from its personal involvements. To achieve such an effect, she made her first significant attempt to use *time* not only as an element of the narrative form but also as an image, determining the lyrical design. Seen in this way, time is both an individual component of consciousness and a public form. In its latter function, it unites all aspects of a character—in the present and past—as a single personality, but it works in this way only in the world of the Dalloways. In the universe of Septimus Warren Smith, its *flow* is less significant than its relevance to *eternity*—life or death. It is used more nearly in a symbolic function. Usually unresponsive to others, Septimus is the final symbol of man's failure, contrasting with Clarissa's time-bound world of manners. True, Septimus' past is also explored, but his excursions into the past are few, specific, and selective, as contrasted with the large sweep of explorations conducted by Clarissa or Peter Walsh. His expansive ramblings are in the present. Although they obtain their nourishment from the traumatic moment of guilt (his failure of Evans), they concern only the inner world he has created as a permanent image. This juxtaposition of Septimus as the timeless symbol with the time-bound world of the Dalloways demonstrates metaphorically the contrast and the interrelation between the novel of manners and the tragedy of life.

The opposition between a time-bound plot, which is formed by both inner and outer time, and a timeless symbolic image

one inviolable right." *The Novels of Virginia Woolf* (London: Oliver and Boyd, 1947), p. 4. Most of Miss Kilman's characterization certainly supports this view. But it should also be noted that she is clearly an *outsider,* whose nature allows her to solve the problem of her spiritual isolation without resorting to madness like Septimus. Moreover, Clarissa confronts her as an antagonist for the "soul" of her daughter, and in their great scene they are, briefly, almost equal antagonists. If Miss Kilman is exposed as a drab and single-minded person, committed to a constricting ideal, Clarissa is exposed as a person who shuns commitment, who withdraws. After the tea-room scene with Elizabeth, Miss Kilman is clearly defeated; she is as isolated as Septimus and as impersonal and symbolic.

creates the poetic dimension of the novel. Revealed in individual monologues and scenes, these opposing themes are united in the ending of the book—in Septimus' suicide and Clarissa's party. Both of these passages fuse a keen narrative sense with a vision of figures and objects as images. In Septimus' last hour, the narrative tension is immense. Reader and participants both know that soon Dr. Holmes will knock on the door and Septimus will be taken to the "home." The novelist's skill has made of this scene a time of brief recovery, followed by renewed hallucinations which accentuate the inevitable outcome. Although Septimus shows a faint interest in people—indeed, there are a few moments of unbending—he lapses into his sense of abandonment as soon as he is left alone. The poet's skill is centered on Septimus' visions shortly before his plunge. He perceives things as aspects of the mind, a disordered replica of the artist's insight, confused yet vivified by an internal life:

> He was alone with the side board and the bananas. He was alone, exposed on this bleak eminence, stretched out—but not on a hill-top; not on a crag; on Mrs. Filmer's sitting-room sofa. As for the visions, the faces, the voices of the dead, where were they? There was a screen in front of him, with black bulrushes and blue swallows. Where he had once seen mountains, where he had seen faces, where he had seen beauty, there was a screen. (D, 220)

The insight gone, only things remain. In the actual death scene he experiences just before his leap the violent opposition between life (the hot sun) and humanity. (D, 225–226)

This scene obtains its final meaning in its contrast with Clarissa's party. While Septimus' visions are contained within Septimus, the party is seen from the perspective of the omniscient observer. The ladies walking up and down the stairs, the scene of the steaming kitchen and of the Prime Minister's arrival, the quick sketches drawn by the narrator as she accompanies Clarissa, Richard, or Peter Walsh, all are viewed as parts of a picture. In a sense, this scene is a highly conventional narrative device: the gathering of all the characters illuminated throughout the book in a final review. But it also fills a canvas with people as things, shows the flat surface of life, and proves at last why there can be no real communication between them. As a whole, this highly satiric picture presents the unchanging though glittering surface of men and women as a prelude to the dance of death.

It is in the context of such a juxtaposition between the symbolic image and the time-bound plot that the novel's ending can be understood in its poetic dimension. Being joined momentarily with Septimus in her concluding vision, Clarissa, too, transcends time at last and is defined as an image while simultaneously maintaining her integrity as a credible character of fiction. This junction of an inner world accessible to Clarissa and a symbolic significance beneath even her conscious and unconscious mental experience had been carefully prepared throughout the book by the unexplained contiguities between herself and Septimus. One of the most notable of these connections is a brief sentence which now becomes the familiar *leitmotif* of the conclusion: "She had once thrown a shilling into the Serpentine, never anything more." This line, through which Clarissa compares her own inadequate act of casting away something of herself with the complete abandonment of life by Septimus ("I'll give it you!"), functions as a poetic image. But, as is usual in *Mrs. Dalloway,* it takes its rise from a personal situation.

The vision is constructed in the form of a poem. Rhythmic and repetitive lines reinforce this impression: "What business had the Bradshaws to talk of death at her party? A young man had killed himself. And they talked of it at her party—the Bradshaws talked of death." But as she vividly relives the plunge through the window, Clarissa's lines and images betray a direct and personal involvement. Only the closing "refrain"—"And the Bradshaws talked of it at her party"—maintains a more formal distance. From this physical identification with thud, spikes, and pain, the monologue soon turns from a time-bound involvement to a knowledge of death beyond time. "A thing there was that mattered; a thing, wreathed about with chatter, defaced, obscured in her own life, let drop every day in corruption, lies, chatter. This he had preserved." And later the question: "But this young man who had killed himself—had he plunged holding his treasure?" (D, 280–281)

The primary, personal sensation with which the moment begins gives way to moral recognition (it was "her disaster— her disgrace") and symbolic awareness. The illumination thus transcends Clarissa as the satirically drawn representative of her class. It is completed when she steps to the window and watches the old lady in the house opposite.[42] Her perception through the window reinforces Mrs. Woolf's concept of *window* as a symbolic passage from the inner to the outer; it echoes Jacob's standing before the window in Greece and foreshadows Mrs. Ramsay behind the window in *To the Lighthouse*, but in its most immediate context it also reenacts, through perception, a version of Septimus' suicide which is transcended through her recognition.

This movement, taking place during the closing hour of Clarissa's party, is counterpointed by a further elaboration of the narrative scene. After Clarissa's illumination, but in her absence, we once more meet Peter and Sally, Elizabeth and Richard. The comedy of manners trickles out as the guests say their farewells. The scene serves to illustrate the illumination and to prepare for the concluding line. For meanwhile, like Lily Briscoe in *To the Lighthouse*, Bernard in *The Waves*, or Isa in *Between the Acts*, Clarissa has become an embodiment of *imagination* in which the conflict between mind and "other" is unified at last. This illumination permits the action to rise from private to symbolic experience as a particular self becomes universal and timeless. Momentary, illusory, this brief instance joins the satiric comedy of manners with the tragedy of life in a poetic form.

[42] The "old lady" is a further motif signifying Clarissa's "illumination." She had appeared earlier at the time of her greatest uncertainty, during her conflict with Miss Kilman for Elizabeth; *Mrs. Dalloway*, pp. 191–192.

WINDOW AND LIGHTHOUSE

⌒1

In *Mrs. Dalloway*, the objective vision is still embodied in a
self—the vision is Clarissa's—but in *To the Lighthouse* (1927)
it emerges from a formal drama which underlies and eventually
dominates the plot: the drama of the creative imagination. This
drama, which occurs finally in the mind of the painter, Lily
Briscoe, coincides with the vision of the omniscient author. It
translates her perspective of plot and scene into aesthetic terms.
The poetic quality in *To the Lighthouse* goes hand in hand, not
with a greater emphasis on the self, but with a greater emphasis
on the impersonal vision and the adequate design.

As in *Mrs. Dalloway*, much of the novel is fashioned by a
conventional plot. A conflict is introduced, polarities of characters are exposed, and a resolution is projected. The focal point
of the novel is marriage. Virginia Woolf herself described *To
the Lighthouse* as a personal act of exorcism—an attempt to
place her vision of Leslie Stephen in the center of her "picture"
and to clarify the image of her mother.[43] This fact is as important for the novel as Conrad's experiences as a seaman had
been for *Victory* and *Lord Jim*. It explains not only the conception of the two protagonists but also the almost dialectical
ambivalence in which their relationship is conceived. Mr. Ramsay's academic abstraction is countered by the earthbound solidity
of Mrs. Ramsay; the wife's creative illusions are opposed by the
husband's insistence on facts. Toward the resolution of this
paradox the narrative progress of the novel is directed. It is

---

[43] "I'm now all on the strain with desire to stop journalism and get on
to *To the Lighthouse*. This is going to be fairly short; to have father's
character done complete in it; and mother's; and St. Ives; and childhood;
and all the usual things I try to put in—life, death, etc. But the centre is
father's character, sitting in a boat, reciting 'We perished each alone,'
while he crushes a dying mackerel. . . ." May 14, 1925, *A Writer's Diary*,
pp. 76–77.

caught in the symbol of the lighthouse, which is an illusion never to be attained at the beginning of the novel and a fact reached by lunch at the conclusion. Postponed by poor weather when Mrs. Ramsay was alive, the trip is undertaken in fine weather after her death.

To the Lighthouse—like most novels by Virginia Woolf— is also a novel of manners. Not only the Ramsays and their observer Lily Briscoe but also all of the other figures comprise a picture of middle-class academic society at the beginning of the Georgian era. Characters are treated with the sharp satire and the eye for incongruities within prescribed conventions which is the heritage of Jane Austen. As in its traditional prototypes, the novel is set in a rambling summer house where society can be depicted at leisure with ample opportunity for personal interaction. Charles Tansley, the "atheist," blundering, aggressive, "writing his dissertation," is treated with pitiless satire at one moment and with warm insight at another. The fastidious bachelor-scientist, William Bankes, is shown with his excellent manners and his limited sensibility. On the other hand, old Mr. Carmichael, the social blunderer, emerges as a successful lyrical poet who alone can communicate with Lily Briscoe. This group is carefully devised as a satiric portrait of the times, and of a particular way of life, but it also suggests a pattern of sensibilities illustrating the movement of the narrative. The dinner table, divided between husband and wife, acts as a magnetic field in which the members of his group are in continuous suspension, drawn hither and thither by either pole.[44]

[44] In critical literature, the dinner scene is usually viewed as a representation of the "moment" in which all disparate elements are unified. See for example, Norman Friedman, "The Waters of Annihilation: Double Vision in *To the Lighthouse*," *ELH*, xxii (1955), 61–79. E. K. Brown sensitively compares it to a social communion rendered as poetry and music in which even the most discordant notes (like Charles Tansley) are absorbed; *Rhythm in the Novel* (Toronto: University of Toronto Press, 1950), pp. 66–67. F. L. Overcarsh, whose essay seeks to force *To the Lighthouse* into the symbolic format of the Bible, compares it to the holy meal of communion. "The Lighthouse, Face to Face," *Accent* x (1950), 107–123.

The narrative and the satire of manners are reminiscent of *Mrs. Dalloway,* but in *To the Lighthouse* they are presented with even greater formality. Most obvious is Virginia Woolf's handling of place, which has been moved closer to the formal unity and symbolic concreteness of a poem. The specific landmarks of Virginia Woolf's novels—the streets of London or the Cornish coast—have been replaced by an undefined island in the Hebrides, possibly the Isle of Skye. Anticipating in its symbolic sweep and majestic generality the formal interludes of *The Waves,* this attempt to transpose life to a more universal plane matches a more symbolic reflection of society and human relationships. The characters, though often depicted with sharp realism, are also types—male and female, child and middle-aged adult, scientist and artist—while many of their relationships are almost allegorical. We deal with a typical marriage, a typical friendship, a typical love affair, typical relations among children and between mother and son. Most pronounced is the conscious use of myth. The Ramsays' marriage is enlarged into the archetypal marriage of the sterile, intellectual male and the fecund, sense-ordered female. Mythical motifs, such as lighthouse, skull, or water, are precisely rendered.

The conversion of inner speech into formal monologues, familiar from *Mrs. Dalloway,* is accomplished in an even more stylized fashion. Although sometimes Virginia Woolf achieves her effect through a straight exposition of the stream of consciousness, her significant manner is to translate the substance of inner speech into formal imagery: "The lizard's eye flickered once more. The veins on [Mr. Ramsay's] forehead bulged. The geranium in the urn became startlingly visible and, displayed among its leaves, he could see, without wishing it, that old, that obvious distinction between the two classes of man. . . ." [45] Both

Yet the fact that communion is achieved does not contradict the "magnetic field" within which the characters are distributed and through which they are finally brought together.

[45] *To the Lighthouse* (Modern Library, 1937), pp. 54–55. Hereafter "L" followed by the page number will refer to this edition.

Mr. Ramsay as an object and the world seen by Mr. Ramsay are viewed as things turned into images which become part of the subject's recognition. Similar effects are also produced by the author's statements: "[Mrs. Ramsay] had been admired. She had been loved. She had entered rooms where mourners sat." (L, 65) The image of the last sentence graphically identifies Mrs. Ramsay's qualities as a woman and contrasts effectively with the bland statements preceding the assertion. Images also formalize statements embodied in significant passages. Mr. Ramsay's "Someone had blundered," for example, is accompanied by the image of a beak, and Mrs. Ramsay's response is embodied in the images of the colorful bird and the opening flower. (L, 48–49; 60) Realistic conversation, inner speech and descriptions of characters and events are increasingly absorbed into a pattern of formal monologues which include the perspective of the author.

The distinguishing characteristic of *To the Lighthouse* is its angle of vision. The omniscient poet's view is caught in the act of imagination of which the painter, Lily Briscoe, is the instrument. This act reveals as a formal "drama" of aesthetic relations, the attractions and repulsions suffered by all the characters within the "magnetic field" of the Ramsays. It depersonalizes, and renders symbolic and universal, the varieties of lives, sensibilities, and sufferings which are portrayed in the novel.

—2

The Ramsays' marriage is grounded in fact and expands into imagination. It functions as a key first to society, then to relations among persons, and finally to life itself. This development is also carried out in the symbolic framework of the novel. The marriage is reflected in the opposition between the *window* and the *lighthouse*—two images which likewise expand their meaning from a narrative to a poetic one.[46]

---

[46] An early statement of the relationship between window and lighthouse was made by Charles G. Hoffmann, "Virginia Woolf's *To the Lighthouse*," *Explicator* (Nov. 1951), Item 13. The theme is fully de-

On the level of plot, both window and lighthouse are placed in a narrative world, subject to a narrative use of time. The external time-span is identical in the introductory section, "The Window," and in the concluding section, "The Lighthouse." "The Window" takes place on a September evening from six o'clock until midnight, beginning with Mrs. Ramsay's reading of the bedtime story to young James and ending with the hour of reading alone with her husband before going to bed. In "The Lighthouse," time begins after Lily Briscoe's awakening in the summer house at six and ends with the arrival of Mr. Ramsay and his children at the lighthouse at noon. Moreover, as in *Mrs. Dalloway,* both these envelopes of external time contain internal monologues by individual figures and by the author to create a picture of life connecting present and past. But both external time, rigidly laid out, and internal time, flexible and psychological, are narrative devices, presenting in depth a vivid portrait of society and of human relationships.

Window and *lighthouse,* however, also serve the poetic purpose of presenting with immediacy the point of the novel's vision. In this sense, the *window* can be identified with Mrs. Ramsay. The picture in which she shares the window with young James is the presiding image of the novel. It is this composition which Lily Briscoe tries to paint and which many years later she completes by reinterpreting it in terms of the lighthouse. But the window is also Mrs. Ramsay's organ of perception. Not only is she seen in the window; she also sees through the window, opposing her own place within the citadel of her domestic life to the world outside which includes, among people and things, the lighthouse itself.

Perceiving and being perceived is a basic function of the window as well as a quality of Mrs. Ramsay. On the one hand, she is seen in different perspectives. The book evolves to a great extent from the divergent and complementary visions of her by all the characters. But on the other hand, she is described as a

veloped in Norman Friedman's analysis of the novel's "dialectic," which he sees pervading all of the principal figures of the book. See "The Waters of Annihilation," *ELH* (1955), 61–79 *passim.*

percipient. She gazes out of the window; she surveys the dinner table; she looks out to sea with her near-sighted eyes. Her glance is "full of authority." As the novel progresses, her presence as a percipient and a perceived image becomes symbolic; it is felt especially by Lily Briscoe who sees in Mrs. Ramsay a fixed principle of feminine order.

The window defines Mrs. Ramsay as a percipient and as a setting in which she herself is viewed. Through it she hears the sound of cricket, the men's talk and their fussing with their pipes which arouses her anxiety or puts her at ease. (L, 27–28) The transparency of the window gives the illusion of participation by consciousness in the world of objects; it suggests the momentary union of perception combining self and world. But the window also emphasizes aloofness and isolation. It indicates a barrier of invisible glass—a removed position—behind which the percipient retires. Mrs. Ramsay sits *behind* the window. Encased by its frame—a picture for others—she directs, protects, and organizes, but an invisible wall separates her from her pacing husband and her painting friend. Only young James shares her position—their sensibilities coincide—but James, when he is not listening to fairy tales, is busy cutting out figures from the catalogue of the Army and Navy Stores.

Mrs. Ramsay's view through the window reenacts the illusion attendant upon perception that the self actually creates or determines its world. Both the function and the illusory quality of this vision are elaborated in the first part of the novel. As an occupant of the window, Mrs. Ramsay can believe that she can fashion the world at her will; facts beyond the window are meaningless to her authoritative glance. She can therefore insist, despite all factual evidence to the contrary, that it will be "fine tomorrow," and her protective zeal for James matches the fairy tales she reads to him. For, from her point of view, the lighthouse, too, is a fairy tale. It is not an object in space and time, but an object within: could not imagination make weather fair at will? Mrs. Ramsay's disagreement with her husband is focused on this critical point: from her position in the window she uses the lighthouse to oppose imagination to fact. This symbolic significance of her position is retained even after she leaves the window. Her sweep and capacity are sensorily ordered, while her husband's mind is intellectually controlled. He has to deal with external facts which his wife can ignore.[47]

Several key images and scenes illustrate the identity of perception and imaginative creation exemplified by the "window." For example, the sensually impoverished "sterile" male "bears down" on the "fecund" female who comforts him by creating a colorful world of illusion. With an effort, Mrs. Ramsay collected herself "to pour erect into the air a rain of energy, a column of spray, looking at the same time animated and alive as if all her energies were being fused into force, burning and illuminating . . . , and into this delicious fecundity, this fountain and spray of life, the fatal sterility of the male plunged itself, like a beak of brass, barren and bare." (L, 58) A precise concern for truth, for reaching R from Q in Mr. Ramsay's world, destroys the veneer of color and life that protects sensibilities and feelings and makes civilization possible. (L, 48f.) This quality is also borne out by Mrs. Ramsay's behavior toward her children. When seven-year-old Cam is frightened by the boar's head which James insists on keeping on the wall, Mrs. Ramsay covers the skull with her shawl, telling the girl that it was now transformed and the boy that it was "really still there." (L, 171–173) Such equivocation would have been alien to Mr. Ramsay for whom all illusion is a perversion of facts, but it illustrates Mrs. Ramsay's attitude toward life. It is the view which induces her compulsion to arrange people's affairs. Indeed, her "mania for marriage," which Lily Briscoe deplores, can be partly explained in terms of the window as a symbolic image. It is the window's function to act as the sensuous percipient, variously perceived by others, whose fecund illusions recreate the world of facts.

Outside the window, however, is the *lighthouse*. As Mrs.

[47] James Hafley links the two types of truth with the Bergsonian distinction; *The Glass Roof: Virginia Woolf as Novelist* (Berkeley: Univ. of Calif. Press, 1954), pp. 82ff.

Ramsay views it, the beacon being lit as James is about to be taken to his bath is part of the panorama—an image of her perception. But for Mr. Ramsay, the lighthouse has an external reality. A metaphysician of some note, he had written a book about "subject, object, and the nature of reality." His interest is focused on the relationship between perceptual illusion and the actual nature of things. (L, 38) To be sure, he requires the deceptions practiced by his wife to bolster his self-confidence, but this limitation (which he overcomes occasionally in lucid self-doubting) does not affect his drive for facts. Mr. Ramsay is always "right." But, in seeing matters in their precise factual relations, he loses the accurate insight. His refusal to grant any validity to creative illusion exasperates his wife. It is a sterility from which young James must be protected. (L, 10–11 *et passim*) In the conclusion of the first part, and even more completely by the end of the novel, this opposition between husband and wife is resolved.

On the level of poetry, the Ramsays' marriage is a duel of opposites represented by the contrasting images of window and lighthouse. Through these two motifs, the marriage becomes more than itself. Lily Briscoe perceived it as a unity of opposites —an equivalent in life to the balanced composition she sought to achieve on her canvas. Meeting the Ramsays in the garden at dusk, she felt they were "more than man and wife," that they were a "symbol of marriage" as a whole. (L, 110–111) This view of the marriage as a reconciliation of opposites is elaborated, without Lily as a witness, in the reading scene, in which their idyllic communion displays their most intense divergence. "The Window" ends on a positive note. Mrs. Ramsay "triumphed," because she had refused her husband the verbal assurance of love he required. But she had granted him the outside world; she had acknowledged his greatness. She had recognized the independence of the lighthouse from her imagination: "Yes, you were right. It's going to be wet tomorrow. You won't be able to go." Glancing out of the window in a gesture which completes the image of the opening of the book, she places the lighthouse outside, in the world of facts. (L, 176–186) This gesture establishes both the contrast and the unity of the two partners. A final reconciliation, however, is not achieved until the lighthouse can be defined as an impersonal symbol.

———3

As an image, the lighthouse serves several purposes. In the opening and concluding sections of the novel, it is an opposite of the window and suggests the male as opposed to the female principle. But this relationship is always complex. The two images are conceived in a dual function, constantly alternating with each other. The lighthouse is external to the window's internal vision, but the window is also the recipient of the beam from the lighthouse. Indeed, the lighthouse is shown as revealing, with its rhythmic glare, the disintegration of the window's world. Both images, then, are seen sometimes as perceivers, sometimes as objects of perception. But the difference between them is manifest, and, so it seems, irreconcilable. The concept of the window as passive and sensuous apprehension involves qualities of the fecund and organic, the perceptual and subjective. As an object and an organ of awareness, it reflects the romantic reconciliation of opposites. But the lighthouse is actively engaged in time, movement, and change. It reveals the "moment" in its vivid interaction between consciousness and world.

In "Time Passes"—the interlude termed "lyrical" by the author herself [48]—the lighthouse performs this task without the benefit of human percipients. Anticipating *The Waves,* it depicts the moment through images, transforming it finally into a larger image of time itself. Freed from its dependence on human beings, it renders, in a more abstract form, the interrelation between the inner and outer worlds of protagonists on the one hand and a symbolic world on the other. The night

[48] "The lyric portions of *To the Lighthouse* are collected in the ten-year lapse and don't interfere with the text as much as usual." Sept. 3, 1926, *A Writer's Diary,* p. 100.

which concludes "The Window" becomes the nightmare of war. During the intervening years when many of the participants grow up, or die, only the beam of the lighthouse penetrates the window, fixed and regular. The faults in the house that Mrs. Ramsay had deplored (the creaking doors, the unkempt lawn) now become deteriorating things which take over the house and rub out the traces of people. Sentient life and things are separated, as Jacob had been separated from the things in his room. At the conclusion of this remarkable interlude, they are again reconnected. The Ramsays, whose lives and deaths had been so far only parenthetically mentioned, reappear in the consciousness of the old housekeeper, Mrs. McNabe, as the house is being reopened for the reunion.

As an extended prose poem, "Time Passes" clarifies the epistemological relationships within the novel as a whole. As the glare of the lighthouse penetrates the window and, like Bergson's duration, "gnaws" on the things within, it establishes an active function of the imagination. The dialectic of window and lighthouse has continued even in the absence of people. Seeing their relationship to one another in a purely formal context, the reader has been prepared for the turnabout of the conclusion. He is now ready to move from the passive window to the active journey to the lighthouse.

In the first section—"The Window"—objects are fashioned by an observer. To be sure, even in this part, the female, creative perceiver is matched by her husband's intellect. Nevertheless, Mr. Ramsay is overshadowed by his wife and in most of this section the supposition holds that Mrs. Woolf intended him to be dependent and, to some extent, dominated.[49] We see more of his inability to "reach R from Q" (L, 53–55), than of his actual achievement. But in the third section—"The Lighthouse" —the emphasis is finally placed on a separation of awareness and fact. The journey is described with careful realism. The story of the Fisherman and his Wife read by Mrs. Ramsay in the

[49] See Glenn Pederson, "Vision in *To the Lighthouse*," *PMLA,* LXXIII (1958), 585–600.

window (L, 61; 85–87) is counterpointed by the actual fisher-
men, Macalister and his son. (L, 242–253; 268) The weight
of the narrative shifts toward Mr. Ramsay as the emphasis
changes from creative illusion to a recognition of fact—to movement *in* the world. These transformations had been produced
by the subtle use of the lighthouse. In the "Time Passes" interlude, the lighthouse projects outward and depersonalizes the
dialectic of the Ramsays' marriage. In the final scenes of the
novel, this conflict is ultimately centered in the mind of Lily
Briscoe who restores it to a human consciousness and converts
it into a drama of the aesthetic imagination.

———4

"The Lighthouse" includes both the narrative resolution and
the completion of the novel as a poem. Ten years after the
events of "The Window," Mr. Ramsay insists that the trip to
the lighthouse be completed as a rite in memory of his dead
wife. The reunion is made into a conventional narrative device;
also present at the ritual are the surviving children, the now
famous poet, Mr. Carmichael, and the painter Lily Briscoe.

The conclusion is divided into three parts, two of which serve
chiefly in a narrative function. The first of these is a prologue
comprising Lily's awakening, her reflections, and her encounter
with Mr. Ramsay, in which, by refusing to praise his boots, she
eschews playing Mrs. Ramsay's role. Having ceased to create
him in terms of any image, she has come to see him as separate
and distinct. (L, 229f.) The second part is spliced in with the
third. It describes in various monologues the changes in the
grown children's view of their father as their boat approaches
the lighthouse. It shows how James' hatred for his father, which
had begun in "The Window" at his mother's knee, is exorcised
at last. But this thread of the novel also reveals the essential
nature of the lighthouse. James comes to recognize it as a separate
reality, imposed on the imaginative reality it had assumed in
the window ten years ago. Mr. Ramsay fulfills its original
meaning at last. He travels "out there." As the family reaches
the lighthouse, the cycle is closed.

It is ashore, however, in the mind of Lily Briscoe, who paints the scene, that this reconciliation is matched by poetic imagery. All relations viewed heretofore within individual minds, Lily now seeks to recreate on her canvas. In "The Window," she had tried to paint Mrs. Ramsay and young James—mother and child—in their classical posture. Now she seeks to complete the unfinished picture (as Mr. Ramsay ends the unfinished journey), but in a different form. The picture is turned in the opposite direction—toward the sea, the lighthouse, and Mr. Ramsay. The figures of window and lighthouse are now converted into the more depersonalized vision of "shore" and "sea." Lily's striving for an understanding of the Ramsays is equated with a struggle for self-definition. A reconciliation of opposites in life is equated with a reconciliation of opposites in art.

Four major movements and a brief epilogue dominate the internal drama of Lily Briscoe. The first movement concerns her commitment to the task at hand and to the role of the self as its appropriate instrument. Its beginning coincides with the departure of the boat, followed by the first perception of the scene. As Lily looks out to sea, she also turns symbolically from the window to the sea and the lighthouse, which now become the main focus of her painting. They are brought together by her recognition that as an artist she is a divided self: part of her is "drawn out there" with the Ramsays on the boat, the other part seems doggedly fixed on the lawn in front of her easel. (L, 233) This division perpetuates the conflict between "window" and "lighthouse," that is, between the Ramsays and their different ways of seeing reality. It also indicates her dual commitment to the artistic scene and the human relationship. As the movement progresses, a change in this vision becomes the substance of Lily's imaginative act.

The first commitment to canvas translates a personal and psychological conflict into imagery. Lily first allows the brush to descend, to make a "running mark," then to be fixed by several more purposeful strokes that finally enclose a space. (L, 235–236) The dramatic presentation of this process ("she felt it [the space] looming at her") describes the forming power of the mind confronting recalcitrant blankness: "Down in the hollow of one wave she saw the next wave towering higher and higher above her. For what could be more formidable than that space?" Indicative of Lily's thinking in the passage as a whole is the way the purely aesthetic idea—the struggle for a space—is vivified by sea imagery (the towering wave). (L, 236)

Lily's striving for a definition of herself as an artist comes to be connected with Mrs. Ramsay. Asserting herself, still feebly, against Tansley's deprecating jibe ("women can't write, can't paint"), she still recognizes Mrs. Ramsay as the actual artist. She is, to begin with, the creative viewer, constantly straining in her near-sightedness to discern or reshape the forms she perceives. Lily recalls a scene on the beach in which she and Charles Tansley had been throwing pebbles while Mrs. Ramsay was writing letters. Now and then looking out to sea, she had held the antagonists together through the authority of her presence and vision. This scene acts as an image that defines Mrs. Ramsay and relates her vision to Lily Briscoe's. The near-sighted person's questions about objects dimly perceived on the water—"Is it a lobster pot, an upturned boat"—are repeated with some variations: "Is it a cork or a boat?" or "Is it a cask or a boat?" which also reflect the relationship between the percipient ashore and the boat at sea that is echoed in Lily's vision.

Mrs. Ramsay is also an artist as an intuitive creator of order. Lily exchanges "the fluidity of life" for the "concentration of painting." Mrs. Ramsay, as the ordering spirit of the family, had shown the way. She could make "of the moment something permanent (as in another sphere Lily herself tried to make of the moment something permanent)":

In the midst of chaos there was shape; this eternal passing and flowing (she looked at the clouds going and the leaves shaking) was struck into stability. Life stand still here, Mrs. Ramsay had said. "Mrs. Ramsay! Mrs. Ramsay!" she repeated. She owed it all to her. (L, 241)

But this very cry, unanswered, also requires the boat at sea. Imagination defines the world where Mrs. Ramsay had made a still point from the fluidity of life, but its motion must also be caught by the outer world, "there in that very distant and entirely silent little boat [where] Mr. Ramsay was sitting with Cam and James." (L, 242)

After an interlude in which attention is focused on the party at sea, a second movement begins with Lily's awareness of the boat. (L, 253f.) But at this point, this perception returns her to the remembered scene with Mrs. Ramsay on the beach, which she expands and develops in depth. It seems as if this scene had been set into motion, as if it now paralleled the encompassing waves of space with analogous waves composed of human lives which the vision must transpose into art. Lily moves into recollections of people beyond the scope of Mrs. Ramsay's knowledge. She pursues to their conclusion, beyond her death, the failures of her efforts to make her own image of life "come true" in the outer world. But "the dead"—presenting "an obstacle" to Lily's design—are not that easily discarded. (L, 260) From the features of Paul Rayley, landmark of Mrs. Ramsay's most conspicuous misjudgment, a vision of deep red, or coral and shimmering light spreads over a scene that had heretofore been seen only in tentative browns. (L, 261) Lily begins to master the contiguity of the personal and the aesthetic vision, and, as she does so, Mrs. Ramsay reemerges as the eternally fruitful symbol of life (standing still) to which one turned from one's void ("to want and not to have"). Lily has triumphed, because she paints, has married no one, and is free to place the tree on her canvas where she desires. But this very recognition ties her again to Mrs. Ramsay, who emerges, in opposition to the boat, first as an abstract figure—a symbol of womanhood—finally as herself who had lived, died, and now returned. As Lily emerges from past time and her picture, seeking help and finding none, she once more calls for Mrs. Ramsay.

The cry furnishes the opening of the third movement,

which elaborates the contrasting elements of shore and sea, vision and boat. (L, 269f.) Mrs. Ramsay's near-sighted vision is linked to Lily's present sighting of Mr. Ramsay. But this perception can now be further generalized: Lily can delve not only into past relationships but also into aesthetic *relations*. She can recognize the nature of the moment as a significant awareness, yet always interfered with, requiring fresh creation. This section ends with its emphasis on Mr. Ramsay and his party, a brown point that must now be caught: "But whose boat? Mr. Ramsay's boat, she replied. Mr. Ramsay; the man who had marched past her, with his hand raised, aloof, at the head of the procession, in his beautiful boots, asking her for sympathy which she had refused. The boat was now half way across the bay." And after another, deeper vision of the scene before her: "Where are they now? Lily thought, looking out to sea. . . . The boat was in the middle of the bay." (L, 270–271) The vision has finally prescribed its arc from one pole to the other— the cry for Mrs. Ramsay, who lives only in the mind, has become, in the process of aesthetic recognition, a search for Mr. Ramsay "out there."

The fourth movement deepens and elaborates this recognition as part of the artist's final step. (L, 248f.) Having clarified herself and her personal relationships, Lily must now find the necessary distance and detachment. The moment shapes up as an impersonal, independent, yet manifold entity. As experiences crowd around her, Lily needs "fifty pairs of eyes" to contain them all. (L, 294) Now she can evaluate her love for the Ramsays, their marriage, and the lives of the people who depended on them as further elements of the moment. Distant, no longer wholly involved, Lily's problem as a painter has approached its solution:

What was the problem then? She must try to get hold of something that evaded her. It evaded her when she thought of Mrs. Ramsay; it evaded her now when she thought of her picture. Phrases came. Visions came. Beautiful pictures. Beautiful phrases. But what she wished to get hold of was that very jar on the nerves, the thing itself before it has been made anything. (L, 287)

The shift is noteworthy: at the beginning of her vision, in the first movement, Lily refers to herself before the moment of commitment as being helpless, naked as a babe, "vulnerable, before she had been made anything." Now the same feeling is directed toward the object to be perceived. It would be, like Carmichael's poems, something about life, death, "extremely impersonal." (L, 290–291) Window and lighthouse are brought together at last:

"Mrs. Ramsay! Mrs. Ramsay!" she cried, feeling the old horror come back—to want and want and not to have. Could she inflict that still? And then, quietly, as if she refrained, that too became part of ordinary experience, was on a level with the chair, with the table. Mrs. Ramsay—it was part of her perfect goodness—sat there quite simply, in the chair, flicked her needles to and fro, knitted her reddish-brown stocking, cast her shadow on the step. There she sat.

But the vision is now balanced. Lily also asks: "Where was that boat now? And Mr. Ramsay? She wanted him." (L, 300)

The epilogue ends the movement from window to light-house. It underlines the narrative progression in which the reconciliation of father and children in the boat coincides with their arrival. Ashore, Lily at first infers: " 'He must have reached it [the lighthouse],' . . . feeling suddenly tired out." The distant goal was now "almost invisible, had melted into a blue haze." But in the final effort, the moment returns to the physical act of perception: ". . . the effort of looking [at the lighthouse] and the effort of thinking of him landing there, . . . seemed to be one and the same effort." Strained to the utmost, fatigued, Lily becomes keenly aware of the coincidence between the aesthetic and the spiritual resolution: "Ah, but she was relieved. Whatever she had wanted to give [Mr. Ram-

say], when he left her that morning, she had given him at last."
(L, 308–309) The drama of imagination and the drama of
spiritual exorcism coincide.

This action of imaginative experience through progressive
imagery is also developed in the unspoken communion between
the two artists ashore, between Lily at her easel and old Mr.
Carmichael reading a novel in a chair nearby. Throughout
this difficult morning, they had shared the same post, just as
Mrs. Ramsay and James had shared the place in the window, and
Lily had often tried to break the silence between them. Now the
words could be found: "He has landed. . . . It is finished"
(L, 309), referring to action, picture, and insight with a single
phrase. The two artists view the arrival, two symbolic percipients in their silent communion. The old poet looks "like an old
pagan god, shaggy, with weeds in his hair and the trident (it
was only a French novel) in his hand." He "stood there as if
he were spreading his hands over all the weakness and suffering
of mankind; she thought he was surveying . . . their final
destiny." (L, 309) But as they had shared the same thoughts,
they now share the moment's collapse. Incapable of being
verbalized, it cannot be stated in the present tense. Turning
back to the canvas, Lily sees her picture as a success—"its attempt at something"—yet already a thing apart. Laying aside
her brush with fatigue she separates herself from the vision.
"I've *had* my vision." (L, 310) Her imagination has caught
window and lighthouse, but now the moment, capable of
containing them both, has passed, leaving her again as a person,
separate and spent.

—5

This section has been analyzed in some detail, because its
drama of the imagination defines *To the Lighthouse* as an almost
final step toward the lyrical novel. Lily's vision, combining
symbolic motifs, memories, and aesthetic relations of colors and
shapes, provides a poetic method of presenting the Ramsays'
marriage in its universal significance. This poetic quality does

not depend upon any "dialectic." Any such attempt to place Mrs. Woolf's book in predefined categories would be resisted by a writer whose most scathing criticism had been directed precisely at the absurdities of academic categorizing. The interrelations between window and lighthouse, male and female, exist in very general often even blurred outlines; their reconciliation in the lighthouse, and in the vision of Lily Briscoe, is an imaginative act, reflecting the activity of aesthetic creation.

It is, then, not the dialectic itself that holds our attention but its poetic enactment. Conflicts of personalities within prescribed worlds of conventions and manners are placed in a symbolic framework. The lyrical quality of *To the Lighthouse* lies in its translation of the ordinary methods of fiction—such as character and action—into imagery which derives from the perceptions and memories of the protagonists. Moreover, the notions of *window* and *lighthouse* comprise both content and form; they render the relationships between characters symbolic. But, eschewing a purely narrative use of symbolism, Virginia Woolf employs these two motifs as *images* which absorb time and world in the process of the imagination. The concluding sections show that *To the Lighthouse* has advanced beyond *Mrs. Dalloway* in its poetic refinement. In the earlier novel, the poetic movement consists primarily in the transposition of inner speech into imagery, using time and world within an essentially narrative scheme. In *To the Lighthouse,* time and world actually become images, merging with color and tone as modes of perception. This is evident in Lily's painting, in which an awareness of the vision coincides with its corresponding design. Her enactment of a personal problem through the creative process forces her to take the simultaneously detached and involved attitude toward herself which as an artist she must take toward her material. With this activity of the imaginative act, lyricism in the novel is identified. The picture of life and manners is sensuously apprehended, and then converted into a design. Sensibilities and awareness, as well as men and times, are rendered as components of a *depersonalized* vision.

THE OMNISCIENT PERSPECTIVE

⌐1

"In *The Waves*," David Daiches declared, "Virginia Woolf gives up her attempt to reproduce in fiction directly the inarticulate consciousness of her characters—an attempt so characteristic of British and continental fiction of the period—and turns towards a highly formalized rendition of consciousness." [50] Actually such a transformation had been dominant in Mrs. Woolf's technique since *Jacob's Room*. In *The Waves* (1931), however, formal soliloquies spoken by the characters translate *all* of the usual stage business of the novel into formal prose poetry. Converting both inner and outer worlds into a symbolic design, *The Waves* represents the ultimate step in the development of Mrs. Woolf's lyrical method.

Some of the features familiar from Virginia Woolf's earlier work remain even in this radically lyrical novel. The subject matter is provided by the novel of manners and psychological experience. *The Waves* explores the sensibilities of people of Mrs. Woolf's own time and class and describes the impact of experience upon their individual lives. The *macrocosm* of time and wave, spanning days, seasons, and eons, is matched with the *microcosm* of individual lives in a carefully contrived pattern. The design is that of a long lyrical poem whose images embody but do not directly describe a series of events. Prose poems of varying lengths, which represent the macrocosm through the images of sun, wave, and world, introduce nine segments representing the microcosm given through the lives of particular characters. These two worlds are connected not through narrative methods, like motivation or action, but through a composition of interlacing images. The prose poems are vertically related to the scenes they introduce and are horizontally related to each other by a network of corresponding and contrapuntal motifs. These motifs are siphoned into the main sections of the novel

[50] *Virginia Woolf*, p. 110.

through formal soliloquies spoken by the characters. Poetic descriptions, monologues, and the worlds the monologues are about fashion in their intricate arrangements a formal picture of life.

The prose poems preceding each major section describe simultaneously a cycle from dawn to dusk, from spring to winter, and from the dawn of history to its decline and impending doom. Following the movement of the sun from morning to night, they focus on three presiding images: the waves of the ocean; a garden and its landscape; and a house through whose window can be seen mirror, table, and cutlery. These inanimate objects are transformed according to the time of day or season. The content of the garden changes from blooming flowers to rotting fruit or bare fields of winter over which fly owls and hawks. Sea and rocks likewise change color and form. Indeed, while the arrangement of the scene is maintained throughout the prose poems, these individual elements undergo various expansions as the sun mounts higher. The stage becomes crowded with steamers and passengers; the original Cornwall setting of the garden becomes at one point a landscape in Italy, a scene in the far north at another. The sun passes through all phases in which, for example, the harvest heat of the late summer is identified with the intense heat of the early afternoon. As it descends toward dusk, ripening fullness transforms itself into the beginning decay of early autumn, the darkening evening. Night and winter coincide with the cryptic last line: *The wave broke upon the shore.*

Six characters bear the burden of the soliloquies. Named Bernard, Neville, Louis, Rhoda, Susan, and Jinny, they are known only in their typical features. The reader is told neither their surnames nor details of their occupations, except those aspects of their lives which reflect their symbolic value. We discover from the monologues that the men become a novelist, a poet, and a businessman, and that the women turn into a drifter who ends in suicide, a landowner's wife, and a socialite. These fates and occupations, which the reader follows intermittently from childhood to late middle age, are important only insofar as they signify lives and relationships in a constellation of images.

Macrocosm and microcosm are closely intertwined. Changes depicted by the introductory prose poems are mirrored in corresponding changes of the characters' lives. Dawn coincides with their early childhood, late morning with their adolescence, evening with the closing years of their lives. But, more deeply, their growing maturity and capacity for abstraction are mirrored in the greater scope and more general descriptions of the later prose poems. Most persistent among these is the image of the wave. Constantly in motion, yet timeless and unchanging in its form, the wave expresses the paradox underlying the novel's theme. Changing worlds governed by time and place are rendered as a timeless image by the constantly surviving, rhythmically alternating wave.

In addition to the pattern established by the prose poems, the design of *The Waves* is described by relationships among the characters. In the main sections, various "points" or "moments" depict the protagonists either in combinations of small clusters or as an entire group. In early childhood, at dawn, for example, all six figures are together. Later in the morning, in early adolescence, boys and girls are shown in two groups, each in its appropriate school. In the noon phases, the characters are more or less scattered. Indeed, in adulthood they are brought physically together only on three occasions, reunions which take place in the early noon, late noon, and early evening phases. Together or apart, however, the figures are all connected by an identical memory in which their diverse thoughts and fates are contained.

The essential unity of the six figures is illustrated by two additional devices. The first is the figure of Percival, who is meaningful to all the characters. A heroic man of Empire, he meets an unheroic death by falling off a horse in India. As a symbol of order, an ideal they all fail to meet, he enters their lives at crucial moments. His departure for India is celebrated at a farewell dinner in the early noon phase. His death in the high noon phase is mourned by all the six figures. He is remembered at their gathering in the early evening. His presence, in life and death, casts its shadow upon the human scene; he is the symbolic center around which the characters of *The Waves* are marshaled. The second device is Bernard's soliloquy which takes up the ninth portion of the book. As a novelist, he is the most likely person into whose memory the individual memories of his friends can be projected. Containing all of the figures in series of sharply etched images and scenes, Bernard's summary appears as a poetic version of the conventional device of passing characters in review. The six figures are particular manifestations of a general framework in which individual sensibilities are portrayed as motifs.

—2

Narrative progression is created through images which unify the characters as a chorus—as an image of man in his diverse manifestations—and connect them with the macrocosm of the prose poems. Joan Bennett has likened this movement to that of a formal dance.[51] Comparisons with musical and pictorial compositions would be equally applicable. But its chief characteristics are those of a poem, in which images are related to one another not through cause, space, or time, but through a design viewed from an omniscient perspective.

Seen from the vantage point of writer and reader, the characters are marked by specific motifs. The first main section of the novel opens with a set of formal statements by each of the six protagonists in which they identify themselves:

> "I see a ring," said Bernard, "hanging above me. It quivers and hangs in a loop of light."
> "I see a slab of pale yellow," said Susan, "spreading away until it meets a purple stripe."
> "I hear a sound," said Rhoda, "cheep, chirp; cheep, chirp; going up and down."
> "I see a globe," said Neville, "hanging down in a drop against the enormous flanks of some hill."

[51] *Virginia Woolf. Her Art as a Novelist* (Cambridge, Eng.: Cambridge Univ. Press, 1945), p. 110.

"I see a crimson tassel," said Jinny, "twisted with gold threads."

"I hear something stamping," said Louis, "a great beast's foot is chained. It stamps, and stamps, and stamps." [52]

These sentences foreshadow the characters; they already contain the future. Bernard's quivering loop of light hanging above —in Susan's mind a balloon string mounting through the leaves as it evades her grasp (W, 18)—contrasts with Neville's globe hanging downward, an unmoving form set off against a larger, more sensual backdrop. Susan's own "slab of pale yellow . . . spreading away until it meets a purple stripe" creates a stylized image of grainland and rural sky at dawn through which she is typified. Rhoda's hearing of the bird sounds the warning note of her later anxiety (and eventual suicide): her dread of being pierced by a bird's beak. Jinny's crimson tassel, twisted with gold thread, is variously repeated in sensuous images describing the fire and light of her body "rippling gold." Louis' "chained beast stamping" converts his perception into the dominant image of his fear and strength: the wild impulse held in check by cultures and distilled in civilizations. These motifs, reiterated throughout the novel, not only define characters as such, but also *place* figures in the memories of their friends and function as particular *colors* distributed throughout the novel.

Relationships among characters and scenes are rendered through interlocking motifs. Figures define themselves through images which are also observed by other characters and by the reader to create a network of interrelated qualities. Susan, for example, is revealed not only by her love of grainland and earth but also by her anger. Contemptuous of the shiftless life of the cities, she longs to sink her roots into the soil. This leads her to possessiveness (she wants to own the land, to hold on to her children), as well as to violent hatred and love. In the image of her childhood, she screws "her handkerchief into a ball," a motif

---

[52] *The Waves* (New York: Harcourt Brace, 1931), p. 9. Hereafter, "W" followed by the page number will refer to this edition.

which runs through the novel and is associated with Susan in the minds of several characters.[53] In Louis' description, she pierces those she loves and nails them to the barn door.[54] But this very image also connects Susan and Rhoda; Rhoda fears *being* oppressed, *being* pierced.[55] At the same time, Susan's rootedness also reflects Louis' mystical sense of the "roots of the human race," while it contrasts with Jinny's continuous surrender to the fleeting moment. To compound the human complexity of these interlocking, contradictory qualities, Susan's sense of the body suggests a significant variant of Jinny's. Susan experiences her body as a mother and worker; it is an instrument of labor and a vessel of gathered fruit, while Jinny exults in hers as a lover, an instrument of pleasure and an object for glittering jewels. Yet Susan's maternal possessiveness, her constant concern with the future, and Jinny's abandonment of herself in the present moment, are both negatively echoed in Rhoda, who is obsessed by her dread of being oppressed as a mother and as a lover.[56]

[53] See *The Waves*, pp. 13–15, 33, 40, 53, 143, 240.

[54] "To be loved by Susan would be to be impaled by a bird's sharp beak, to be nailed to a barnyard door." *Ibid.*, p. 120.

[55] Rhoda: "But I am fixed here to listen. An immense pressure is on me. I cannot move without dislodging the weight of centuries. *A million arrows pierce me.* Scorn and ridicule pierce me. I, who could beat my breast against the storm and let the hail choke me joyfully, am pinned down here: am exposed. The tiger leaps. Tongues with their whips are upon me. Mobile, incessant, they flicker over me." *Ibid.*, pp. 105–106. (Italics mine.)

[56] Susan: "I think I am the field, I am the barn, I am the trees. . . ." "I am the seasons . . . , the mud, the dawn"; *ibid.*, pp. 97, 98. "I shall go to bed tired. I shall lie like a field bearing crops in rotation; in the summer heat will dance over me; in the winter I shall be cracked with cold. . . ."; *ibid.*, pp. 131–132. "I am no longer January, May or any other season but am all spun to a fine thread round the cradle, wrapping in a cocoon made of my own blood the delicate limbs of my baby"; *ibid.*, p. 171. "I am sick of the body, I am sick of my own craft, industry and cunning, of the unscrupulous ways of the mother who protects, who collects under her jealous eyes at one long table her own children, always her own"; *ibid.*, p. 191.

Jinny: (as a young girl) "As each thing in the bedroom grows clear,

The men are similarly related to one another through specific motifs. Bernard is a novelist, whose personality and occupation require disguises: he must be capable of identifying himself with many different people and of assuming their masks. He is a *poseur,* enacting the Byronic role in his youth, later that of a literary man. This habit of taking on the colorations of his surroundings is similar to Louis' manner of adopting disguises, although Bernard's habit is caused by a carefree attitude which constantly places him in an imaginary world. Louis' is prompted by anxiety, insecurity about his social position, his Australian accent, and the fact that his father had been a banker in Brisbane. As a novelist, however, Bernard also shares many qualities with Neville, the poet. But Neville is Bernard's opposite: he seeks a classical detachment from personality; he searches for order and coherence. Yet, closing the cycle, Neville's longing for continuity and order corresponds to Louis' desire for rootedness and his withering sarcasm. They are both "outsiders." [57]

These qualities fashion the characters as images at the same

my heart beats quicker. I feel my body harden, and become pink, yellow, brown. My hands pass over my legs and body. It feel its slope, its thinness"; *ibid.,* p. 55. (Later in a train as a man watches her:) . . . "We are out of the tunnel. He reads his paper. But we have exchanged the approval of our bodies. There is then a great society of bodies and mine is introduced; mine has come into the room where the gilt chairs are"; *ibid.,* p. 63. Also: "My body goes before me, like a lantern down a dark lane, bringing one thing after another out of darkness into a ring of light"; *ibid.,* p. 129. See also *ibid.,* pp. 42, 54, 102–103, 104–105, 176–177; 193, 220–222.

Rhoda: "Now I spread my body on this frail mattress and hang suspended. I am above the earth now. I am no longer upright, to be knocked against and damaged. All is soft and bending. . . . Out of me now my mind can pour. . . . I am relieved of hard contacts and collisions"; *ibid.,* p. 27. Her body is also an outside being that causes pain: "There is some check in the flow of my being; a deep stream presses on some obstacle; it jerks; it tugs; some knot in the centre resists"; *ibid.,* p. 57. See also *ibid.,* p. 40, 105–106, 107, *et al.*

[57] Bernard: *ibid.,* pp. 67–78, 78–80. Neville: *ibid.,* pp. 31–32, 35, 180. For their clash, *ibid.,* pp. 85–88. For Neville and Louis, *ibid.,* p. 47.

time that they develop the implicit plot. Rhoda and Louis become lovers, drawn to each other by mutual fear, but soon Rhoda flees in horror, while Louis, rooted to his place, makes do with a down-at-heels actress. Rhoda has flights of the imagination like Bernard's and anxieties like Louis'.[58] Neville, as insecure as Rhoda or Louis, shares Susan's desire for order but hates her because in seeking it, they go in opposite ways: Neville withdraws from "shop girls" to seek the love of men; Susan withdraws from London to seek fulfillment as a mother.[59] Similarly, Bernard is linked with Susan because they both manage to establish a conventional family life in very different worlds in which they both feel unhappy. But as a novelist, seeing himself pursued by the "invisible biographer," he also echoes Jinny's habit of seeing herself in the mirror.[60] Bernard waits for a self, a "call," his inspiration; Jinny waits for a call from another person, a man. As Jinny says "Come" and is "rippling gold," Bernard beckons his muse.[61] Yet the image of the evanescent fire is common to

[58] *Ibid.*, pp. 169–170, 200–205. Note Rhoda's imagination which converts petals into a fleet of ships (*ibid.*, pp. 18–19, 44, *et al.*). Her sense of "order" in comparison to Louis, e.g.: Rhoda: *ibid.*, p. 40; Louis: *ibid.*, p. 47.

[59] Neville (his sense of order, his appeal to the Romans, his intellectual concentration): *ibid.*, pp. 31–32. Susan's sense of the order of nature: *ibid.*, pp. 98–100. Note also Neville: "But by some inscrutible law of my being sovereignty and the possession of power will not be enough; I shall always push through curtains, to privacy, and want some whispered words alone"; *ibid.*, p. 60. See also *ibid.*, pp. 180; 215. Susan about Neville: *ibid.*, p. 215. Neville: *ibid.*, pp. 86, 88, 90, *et al.* Susan: *ibid.*, pp. 61–62, 100, *et al.*

[60] For Bernard, *ibid.*, pp. 9, 18, 36–37, 49, 50–51, 76–77, 84, 189, 215. For Jinny's looking-glass, *ibid.*, pp. 41, 63, 193, 221. For "simple relationships" Bernard hails a cab and goes to Jinny; *ibid.*, p. 158.

[61] Bernard: "But *you* understand, *you*, my self, who always comes at a call (that would be a harrowing experience to call and for no one to come; that would make the midnight hollow, and explains the expression of old men in clubs—they have given up calling for a self who does not come.)" *Ibid.*, p. 77.

Jinny: "Only when I have lain alone on the hard ground, watching you play your game, I begin to feel the wish to be singled out; to be summoned, to be called away by one person who comes to find me . . . , who cannot keep himself from me, but comes to where I sit on my gilt chair,

them both, to Bernard as an artist and to Jinny as a magician of the body. Virginia Woolf speaks of a society of bodies and their communication, then of a dance of bodies, finally of bodies as sources of light, capable of imagination, of seeing things in outline.[62] But it is part of her artistry that the motif which unites Jinny and Bernard as artists is also the point of meeting and contrast with Susan and Rhoda. Through such a network of interlocking qualities, which branch out into the minutest details, a picture is created that portrays these six figures not as a social group but as a single organism—one symbol of a common humanity.[63]

————3

The combining qualities we have noted not only achieve transitions in the ordinary sense but also constitute significant "windows" by which characters are connected. Figures appear to be distinct from each other—each ensconced in its own impenetrable world—except for combining images or scenes, which briefly achieve moments of contiguity.

Frequently, the figures are brought together by a shared memory which each of the individuals recalls with significantly different implications. Examples of such scenes include the kiss Jinny bestows on Louis when they are small children or the bath they are given by old Mrs. Constable.[64] Since each character

with my frock billowing round me like a flower"; *ibid.*, p. 46. Also: "There will be parties in brilliant rooms; and one man will single me out and will tell me what he has told no other person. . . ."; *ibid.*, p. 55.

[62] *Ibid.*, pp. 63, 102–103, 129, 176, 220.

[63] Bennett, *Virginia Woolf*, pp. 108–110. John Graham refers to *The Waves* as the representation of a "human communion." A combining figure represented by the symbolic Percival in their youth and by Bernard in middle and old age (whose summing up joins all the characters), *creates* this moment. The movement from Percival (the man of Empire) to the perceptive novelist Bernard also indicates a progression from action to understanding with the decline of the active power. "Time in the Novels of Virginia Woolf," *Univ. of Toronto Quarterly*, XVIII (1949), 193–194.

[64] The event of the kiss is described from the several points of view in

witnesses at least two such scenes, memories overlap until a net-work, sometimes expressed as a composition of alternating soliloquies, emerges like the inner life of a single person.

The most important use of imagery to sustain the flow of the novel is found in the placement of specific motifs at those points of intersection when the monologue moves from one figure to the next.[65] In one childhood scene, for example, Susan and Rhoda are combined by a petal:

> "Here is the garden [said Susan]. Here is the hedge, Here is Rhoda on the path rocking petals to and fro in her brown basin."
>
> "All my ships are white," said Rhoda. "I do not want red

The Waves, pp. 12–16; it is then repeated in crucial memories throughout the novel. Susan, who had been most strongly affected, links this scene frequently to her memory of Jinny. See, for example, *ibid.,* p. 100. Similarly, compare the following memories of their childhood bath by Bernard: "Water pours down the runnel of my spine. Bright arrows of sensation shoot on either side. I am covered with warm flesh. . . . Water descends and sheets me like an eel. . . . Rich and heavy sensations form the roof of my mind; down showers the day—. . . ." *Ibid.,* p. 26. And later: "Old Mrs. Constable lifted her sponge and warmth poured over us," said Bernard. "We became clothed in this changing, this feeling garment of flesh"; *ibid.,* p. 124. See also Neville's boys "squirting water" as a variant of this motif; *ibid.,* pp. 35, 180–181, 196. See also *ibid.,* pp. 239, 289. A similar childhood theme proliferated throughout the novel is a vision by Neville. He recalls overhearing a conversation in which servants describe a man whose throat had been cut. He hears these remarks while walking up a flight of stairs and at once visualizes the man, his throat cut, while an apple tree stands under the moon; *ibid.,* p. 24. Later, all these events are brought into a single image; *ibid.,* p. 124. Susan's trauma had been her observation of the boot-boy trying to make love to the maid among fluttering washings on the line; *ibid.,* pp. 25, 124. As the above page numbers show, these motifs are interwoven with one another as the soliloquies alternate.

[65] One such transition would be the use of a concept like the passage of time. For example, Louis' "time passing" is his schedule: ". . . Mr. Prentice at four; Mr. Eyres at four-thirty. . . ." Susan picks up this motif in terms of "seasons": "Summer comes and winter . . . the seasons pass"; *ibid.,* p. 171.

petals of hollyhocks or geraniums. I want white petals that float when I tip the basin up." (W, 18)

Susan perceives the petal, which to her has no particular significance but which is enormously important to Rhoda. As Rhoda seems to continue Susan's statement, she endows it with a personal meaning which she later amplifies—the petals must be *white;* they are her *ships.*

Connections also occur in an opposite direction. A phrase with a personal meaning is brought out by one of the characters and taken up only on its surface by another. Thus, as the monologue shifts from Susan to Bernard:

"I see the beetle," said Susan. "It is black, I see; it is green, I see; I am tied down with single words. But you wander off; you slip away; you rise up higher with words and words in phrases."

"Now," said Bernard, "let us explore. . . ." (W, 16)

A remembered event can also provide a moment of communication for wholly separated characters. For example, Susan recalls on her lonely farm the childhood scene in which Jinny had kissed Louis. Her memory provides a transition to Jinny riding to a crowded London party:

"I hear the traffic roaring in the evening wind [said Susan]. I look at the quivering leaves in the dark garden and think, 'They dance in London. Jinny kisses Louis.'"

"How strange," said Jinny, "that people should sleep. . . ." (W, 100)

A similar typical event can combine two characters and relate them to one another in their opposite attitudes. The party, for example, provides a further transition from Jinny to Rhoda:

"Oh, come [said Jinny], I say to this one, rippling gold from head to heels. 'Come,' and he comes towards me."

"I shall edge behind them," said Rhoda, "as if I saw someone I know. But I know no one . . ." (W, 104–105)

The contrast between Jinny and Rhoda extends through the entire section, transforming Jinny's joy in the body, the golden "come," into Rhoda's agony. At last Rhoda veers off and takes up the childhood image: "Alone, I rock my basins; I am the mistress of my fleet of ships." (W, 105–106) Yet their moment of contact is defined by the common situation from which both their reactions are derived.

Such areas of contact between characters may sometimes comprise entire scenes. For example, Louis, uncomfortably seated in a London lunchroom, contemplates his insecurity while Susan sits stitching in the window of her farm. A connection is established when the swinging doors opened with some gusto by the waitress cause a wind, duplicated in the wind-blown curtains of Susan's window. The connection is underlined by the fact that Louis had compared Susan's security ("Susan gives us safety") with his own insecure self. (W, 94–97) This type of communication serves to identify the lyrical pattern with the narrative situation. The subtle communication achieved through interlocking qualities or combined images can express conversations or interactions among characters directly and metaphorically. The subtlest type of communication occurs when the characters' memories and thoughts are "pooled" in one consciousness on the occasion of a specific event which they share, such as Percival's death. (W, 151–164) Another way of pooling the figures is that of the summary, such as Bernard's, which acts as a moment in which the six figures are unified in a mind.[66] As we shall see, these

[66] See three of Bernard's identifications of his friends in the final summary. Note how he not only sums up their characterizations but also utilizes each of their significant motifs: "Rhoda came wandering vaguely. She would take advantage of any scholar in a blowing gown, or donkey rolling the turf with slippered feet to hide behind. What fear wavered and hid itself and blew to a flame in the depths of her grey, her startled, her dreaming eyes? . . . The willow as she saw it grew on the verge of a grey desert where no bird sang. The leaves shrivelled as she looked at them,

methods are closely linked with the technique of the soliloquy and its use both in the lyrical pattern and in the narrative movement of the novel.

———4

The composition of images indicates a semblance of communication among the figures, because it is based upon metaphoric inferences from a narrative which is suppressed. The means whereby this is accomplished is the novel's most distinctive feature: a system of formal soliloquies into which the images are built. They never approach the directness of fiction, but function, instead, like stanzas of different lengths in verse poetry. Virginia Woolf's only concession to the conventional form of the novel is her way of introducing each of these set speeches with the traditional clauses "he said" and "she said." Otherwise, all description, action, even conversation and inner speech are portrayed exclusively through their lyrical imagery and language.

These soliloquies are Virginia Woolf's unique invention. In prose poetry transfiguring the subject matter of the novel, the speakers picture themselves, each other, and the progress of time and life. Their speeches and interpolations are not surface renderings even of the stream of consciousness. Nor are they

tossed in agony as she passed them. The trams and omnibuses roared hoarse in the street, ran over rocks and sped foaming away. Perhaps one pillar, sunlit, stood in her desert by a pool where wild beasts come down stealthily to drink.

"Then Jinny came. She flashed her fire over the tree. She was like a crinkled poppy, febrile, thirsty with the desire to drink dry dust. Darting, angular, not in the least impulsive, she came prepared. So little flames zigzag over the cracks in the dry earth. She made the willows dance, but not with illusion; for she saw nothing that was not there. It was a tree; there was the river; it was afternoon; here we were; I in my serge suit; she in green. There was no past, no future; merely the moment in its ring of light, and our bodies; and the inevitable climax, the ecstasy.

"Louis, when he let himself down on the grass, cautiously spreading (I do not exaggerate) a mackintosh square, made one acknowledge his presence." *Ibid.*, pp. 252–253.

actually spoken. Rather, they are poetic constructions of the subjects to which they refer. Suppressing all experience, they exist only as inferences. All speech, internal as well as external, is displaced by these artificially "silent" monologues which present the sounds and actions of life by implication.[67]

The idea of the monologue is based on Mrs. Woolf's conception of the moment. It arises from an awareness of one's relationship with oneself, with others and with things, finally with life as a whole, occasioned by one's meeting with the objects of immediate experience. The following soliloquy, spoken by Jinny in middle age, shows how in *The Waves* such moments are converted into prose poetry. In a busy London underground station, for a moment the hub of her universe, Jinny meets up with herself:

"Here I stand," said Jinny, "in the Tube station where everything that is desirable meets—Piccadilly South Side, Piccadilly North Side, Regent Street and the Haymarket. I stand for a moment under the pavement in the heart of London. Innumerable wheels rush and feet press just over my head. The great avenues of civilisation meet here and strike this way and that. I am in the heart of life. But look—there is my body in that looking glass. How solitary, how shrunk, how aged! I am no longer young. I am no longer part of the procession. Millions descend those stairs in a terrible descent. Great wheels churn inexorably urging them downwards. Millions have died. Percival died. I still move. I still live. But who will come if I signal? (W, 193)

This speech presents narrative clues about the person, her appearance and mannerisms, her "moment of illumination" in a lyrical movement and form. Jinny is placed underground in the center of London. We witness her self-encounter in the mirror— at the midpoint between upper and lower worlds—and share her awareness of aging, of what aging and impending death

---

[67] Cf. Blackstone, *Virginia Woolf*, pp. 168f.

might mean to a person dedicated to the physical life. But these narrative touches are not only generalized, as they are often in prose fiction, but also translated into formal imagery from which Jinny's inner speech is inferred.

When the passage opens, Jinny stands in an actual station of an actual city: the hub of life as she knows it. The enumeration of street names adds factual concreteness. A vivid picture is created, reinforced by descriptive words like "rushing wheels" and "pressing feet." But by the time Jinny is aware of her reflection in the mirror, these images have become generalized: the heart of London has turned into the heart of life and the different underground lines into avenues of civilization. The movement from the particular to the general has been completed. Each term that follows this recognition—"wheels" or "procession" or "descent"—must be taken figuratively as well as literally. The soliloquy combines the motif of the procession—the throng of life Jinny longs to join—and the motif of death. In the mirror she meets herself, marked an outsider, while above her life goes on and below her wheels "urge inexorably." The procession of men and women from the street into the station and down the escalators toward the trains becomes a movement from a world above to an underworld of death. As Jinny, standing between both levels, contemplates her aging image, the wheels above and below become wheels of life and time. Pressed from above, facing a vortex below, an image of dread is created in almost Dantean proportions. But, characteristically, Virginia Woolf at once withdraws this vast symbolic suggestion and narrows her passage to the peculiarities of her heroine. The death of millions, the death of the self as the death of man symbolized by Percival, becomes Jinny's preoccupation with herself. "But who will come if I signal?" Tragedy is replaced by pathos. Jinny's awareness of her own image in the mirror metaphorically compresses both an awareness of her life and of her dying and death in a single moment of consciousness.

Poetic soliloquies in *The Waves* turn objects into general images symbolizing experience and into motifs weaving the pattern of the novel. The following monologue, spoken by Susan as a young girl, defines her present and future as she meets the familiar objects of her world. Walking on her farm, Susan says:

"For soon in the hot midday when the bees hum round the hollyhocks my lover will come. He will stand under the cedar tree. To his one word I shall answer my one word. What has formed in me I shall give him. I shall have children; I shall have maids in aprons; men with pitchforks; a kitchen where they bring the ailing lambs to warm in baskets, where the hams hang and the onions glisten. I shall be like my mother, silent in a blue apron locking up the cupboards." (W, 98–99)

Jinny's soliloquy looks from life to death, but Susan's speech contrasts the present and the future. The passage begins with a poetic image presented in a carefully contrived movement of rhythm and sound (including assonance and rhyme). It then turns to enumerations of specific reveries, portraying concretely what this future life will be like, until the reader is left not only with the complete image of what Susan wishes to happen but also of her qualities as a person and of her place in the novel.

In the monologues, structures of imagery and poetic diction recreate inner speech as poetry. At the same time, they also produce a narrative progression. Occasionally, entire narrative scenes are produced within a design of images, rendered with the same detached formality as private sensibilities or thoughts. The following scene between the novelist Bernard and the poet Neville takes place in the former's room at college. Its setting is a cluttered table and spilled tea sopped up by a greasy handkerchief:

"But I am too nervous [said Neville] to end my sentence properly. I speak quickly, as I pace up and down, to conceal my agitation. I hate your greasy handkerchiefs—you will stain your copy of *Don Juan*. You are not listening to me. You are making phrases about Byron. And while you gesticulate, with your cloak, your cane, I am trying to expose a secret told to nobody yet; I am asking you (as I stand with my back to you) to take my life in your hands and tell me whether I am doomed always to cause repulsion in those I love?

"I stand with my back to you fidgeting. No, my hands are now perfectly still. Precisely, opening a space in the bookcase, I insert *Don Juan;* there. I would rather be loved, I would rather be famous than follow perfection through the sand. But am I doomed to cause disgust? Am I a poet? Take it. The desire which is loaded behind my lips, cold as lead, fell as a bullet, the thing I am at shop-girls, women, the pretence, the vulgarity of life (because I love it) shoots at you as I throw —catch it—my poem."

"He has shot like an arrow from the room," said Bernard. "He has left me his poem. . . ." (W, 88)

Here both the poetic and the narrative currents are fused. The very ingredients of the narrative—Neville's movements back and forth in the room, his reference to greasy handkerchiefs, Bernard's refusal to listen to him as he goes on spinning phrases —contract into a poem about the feelings suggested by the action. Neville's sense of order, his fear of relationships are played against Bernard's disorder, his many disguises and his strong sense of relationships. In Bernard's soliloquy, which follows Neville's, similar images—including the allusion to perfection and sand—are turned into their opposite meaning. (W, 88–92)

Narrative can also be implied from various responses to a common situation, signified by an image. For example, at one of their reunions, Bernard announces his engagement. The announcement is built into his formal statement; the responses of his friends express their common shock. The unifying motifs are the "chain" and the "circle." Neville indicates their limitless opportunity before the announcement. Susan, who has loved Bernard since childhood, is the first to "speak" afterwards, registering her shock by introducing the motif of the confining chain.

"With infinite time before us," said Neville, "we ask what shall we do? . . . . All is to come."

"For you," said Bernard, "but yesterday I walked bang into a pillar-box. Yesterday I became engaged."

"How strange," said Susan, "the little heaps of sugar look by the side of our plates. Also the mottled pealings of pears, and the plush rims to the looking-glasses. I had not seen them before. Everything is now set; everything is fixed. Bernard is engaged. Something irrevocable has happened. A circle has been cast on the waters; a chain is imposed. We shall never flow freely again." (W, 141–142)

The images describing Susan's reaction move from her familiar preoccupation with food and fruit to the motif identifying the limits drawn by social commitments: "a chain has been imposed. We shall never flow freely again." The circle of their hitherto limitless lives is now closed.

Louis and Rhoda, by contrast, take up the same motif with an opposite meaning. Louis uses the "chain" with connotations typical of his person and of his constant motif of the "chained beast stamping." He sees action, jealousy, passion released by Bernard's revelation:

"For one moment only," said Louis. "Before the chain breaks, before disorder returns, see us fixed, see us displayed, see us held in a vice.

"But now the circle breaks. Now the current flows. Now we rush faster than before. Now passions that lay in wait down there in the dark weeds which grow at the bottom rise and pound us with their waves. Pain and jealousy, envy and desire, and something deeper than they are, stronger than love and more subterranean. The voice of action speaks. Listen, Rhoda (for we are conspirators, with our hands on the cold urn), to the casual, quick, exciting voice of action, of hounds running on the scent. . . . Susan screws her pocket-handkerchief. Jinny's eyes dance with fire." (W, 142–143)

The key image of this passage, which expands the motifs of chain and circle, is that of the *cold urn*. Only Louis and Rhoda

understand the "stamping beast" which can be checked by utmost rigidity alone. As the chain breaks, they can stand aside
with their hands on the cold urn. But Rhoda does not really share
Louis' rigidity. Her response expresses anxiety:

> "They are immune," said Rhoda, "from picking fingers and
> searching eyes. How easily they turn and glance; what poses
> they take of energy and pride! What life shines in Jinny's
> eyes; how fell, how entire Susan's glance is, searching for
> insects at the roots! Their hair shines lustrous. Their eyes burn
> like the eyes of animals brushing through the leaves on the
> scent of the prey. The circle is destroyed. We are thrown
> asunder." (W, 143)

Rhoda omits the motif of the urn but takes up that of the hunt—
of beasts of prey pursuing the scent. Moreover, the image of the
circle is expanded by an allusion to their dispersed group: "We
are thrown asunder." In this way, different personal reactions,
which would ordinarily be described in conversations or inner
speech, are depicted through an interplay of images. In the first
three "speeches"—of Susan, Louis, and Rhoda—the motifs of
the chain and the circle convey their reactions: a check placed
upon their infinite lives in the first instance, and the destruction
of the checks on passion and disunity in the second.[68] As characters continue to respond to the announcement, these images
vary to render a narrative event without the use of plot, overt
speech, or direct statement. This method transforms the narrative scene into a formal world, in which even private sensibility
is converted into objective metaphor.

---

[68] Note the circle motif early in the novel. Louis says: "Now grass and
trees . . . and our ring here, sitting, with our arms binding our knees,
hint at some other order, and better, which makes a reason everlastingly.
This I see for a second and shall try tonight to fix in words, to forge a
ring of steel. . . ." *The Waves,* p. 40. Note that *ring* is used in both meanings: their circle or ring as a communion and the ring which confines
them, individually and as a group, to impose order.

The network of images within the monologues is echoed in the prose poems. Indeed, the novel's structure on the level of the macrocosm preenacts the more complex structure on the level of the microcosm. Similarly, the method of progression through expanding images which establishes the quality of the monologues is reflected in the expansions of the prose poems.

The design of *The Waves* as a whole is shaped by the macrocosm. In the prose poems, apprehension is likened to the sun's illumination of the world of objects, broadening and deepening as time goes on. The first section of the novel demonstrates this analogy between the action of the sun and the process of awareness. It concerns itself with *creation,* both in a cosmological and in an epistemological sense. The rising sun differentiates and ultimately creates the forms it illuminates:

> *Gradually as the sky whitened a dark line lay on the horizon dividing the sea from the sky and the grey cloth became barred with thick strokes moving, one after another, beneath the surface, following each other, pursuing each other, perpetually.* (W, 7)

The motif of separation of the individual form from the mass is also suggested by the sediment in an old wine bottle. As the sun rises higher, it is joined with the motif of creation through the image of a woman concealed behind the horizon, raising her lamp:

> *Gradually the dark bar on the horizon became clear as if the sediment in an old wine-bottle had sunk and left the glass green. Behind it, too, the sky cleared as if the white sediment there had sunk, or as if the arm of a woman couched beneath the horizon had raised a lamp and flat bars of white, green and yellow, spread across the sky like the blades of a fan.* (W, 7)

A third image, that of the bonfire, is then added to describe the first erratic spread of light and creation:

Gradually the fibres of the burning bonfire were fused into one haze, one incandescence which lifted the weight of the swollen grey sky on top of it and turned it to a million atoms of soft blue. (W, 7)

In the end, sediment, woman, and bonfire are combined in a single image to complete the transformation from predawn to morning:

The surface of the sea slowly became transparent and lay rippling and sparkling until the dark stripes were almost rubbed out. Slowly the arm that held the lamp raised it higher and then higher until a broad flame became visible; an arc of fire burnt on the rim of the horizon, and all round it the sea blazed gold. (W, 7–8)

As the sun turns toward the house, awakening the garden and the birds, it also expresses the "productive" nature of illumination:

The sun sharpened the walls of the house, and rested like the tip of a fan upon a white blind and made a blue fingerprint of shadow under the leaf by the bedroom window. (W, 8)

The idea of creation through growing light, which defines the passage, is translated in the main sections of the novel into an idea of creation by apprehension. The movement of sun and waves parallels the protagonists' growing awareness of themselves, of each other, and of their world. The problem of succession is solved by Virginia Woolf's manner of picturing changes in time symbolically. Accordingly, identical motifs are repeated with accrued connotations. For example, the woman holding the lamp in the first prose poem reappears in various forms. An image for the sun, she holds the lamp higher and higher until an arc of fire is created. Later, the image is repeated through the face of a girl refracted in the water: "The girl who had shaken her head and made all the jewels, the topaz, the acquamarine, the water-coloured jewels with sparks of fire in them dance, now bared her brows and with wide-opened eyes drove a straight pathway over the waves." (W, 73) Nearer noontime, the couched woman and the mid-morning jewels are brought together; the risen sun "no longer couched on a green mattress darting a fitful glance through watery jewels" now "bared its face and looked straight over the waves." (W, 108) But at high noon all these motifs are joined to picture a further passing of time:

> *The sun had risen to its full height. It was no longer half seen and guessed at, from hints and gleams, as if a girl couched on her green-sea mattress tired her brows with water-globed jewels that sent lances of opal-tinted light falling and flashing in the uncertain air like the flanks of a dolphin leaping, or the flash of a falling blade.* (W, 148)

A similar expansion occurs through the wave image, which supplies the element of aggression ("lances" and "blade") included in the last passage. In the first prose poem the wave had been seen as a single unit likened to a sleeping person; it "paused, and then drew out again, sighing like a sleeper whose breath comes and goes unconsciously." (W, 7) But in the noon passage the same rhythmic movement is performed by many waves, which now resemble "the muscularity of an engine which sweeps its force out and in again." (W, 108) At the same time, different images for the waves supplement and expand the image of the engine. In a forenoon passage, the waves are also likened to riders on horseback. They drum on the shore "like turbaned warriors, like turbaned men with poisoned assegais, who, whirling their arms on high, advance upon the feeding flocks, the white sheep." (W, 75) In the high noon passage the same image is repeated in a changed atmosphere of color and tone. Now the waves' "spray rose like the tossing of lances and assegais over the riders' heads." And, returning to the jewel image: "They [the riders] swept the beach with steel blue and diamond-tipped water." (W, 108). Finally, in the early afternoon, the lances of the waves, already suggested at noon, are decisively connected with the bejeweled girl; the passage refers to the girl's "water-globed jewels that sent lances." (W, 148)

Just as these compositions of images connect the introductory prose poems with one another, so they also establish links with the monologues of the characters. In the opening passages of the novel, chirping birds, transparent leaves, and loops of light, occurring in the prose poems, are incorporated into the statements of the six figures. The observation of light floating upon objects in the house is used in one of Rhoda's childhood monologues in which she declares: "Walls and cupboards whiten and bend their yellow squares on top of which a pale glass gleams." (W, 27) Similarly, in her ensuing dream, Rhoda says:

> "Oh, to awake from dreaming! Look, there is the chest of drawers. Let me pull myself out of these waters. But they heap themselves on me; they sweep me between their great shoulders; I am turned; I am tumbled; I am stretched, among these long lights, these long waves, these endless paths, with people pursuing, pursuing." (W, 28)

This passage is followed by the next prose poem which starts: "Blue waves, green waves swept a quick fan over the beach." (W, 29) It also echoes all the other attributes of the wave image, its aggression and the turbaned warriors' pursuit. Similarly, Bernard's growing awareness of the complexity of things, his readiness to face life as "horde" and "chaos," is reflected in the image of the horsemen. Later he refers to time as "drops of water" so that the imagery of his consciousness is brought into accord with the basic images of the prose poems. Other connections arise from the activity of birds—their building of nests and their pecking in rotten undergrowths—or from images of dazzling light, described in the prose poems, which often suggest Susan's lines about soil and hard labor, or Jinny's about her presence, "rippling gold." In this way, the contiguity between the two interlaced parts of the novel extends from general periods of life, day, and season to individual motifs and particular characters, relating all the participants to the timeless images of the sun and the wave.

The complex relationship between prose poems and monologues indicates a common development of point of view. The "sun" of the prose poems, illuminating the objects of the world within the alternating, yet eternal rhythm of the waves, becomes, in the body of the novel, the poet's omniscient perspective whose light reveals the characters' lives within the constant rhythm of life. This analogy explains the nature of Virginia Woolf's objectivity—her depersonalized vision. In *Mrs. Dalloway* and *To the Lighthouse,* she had perfected a method whereby characters were linked with one another through shared experiences or scenes. In *The Waves,* this method is wholly absorbed into imagery perceived by the poet and reader. The translation of fortuitous connections of life into contiguous images echoes Mrs. Woolf's distrust of the possibility of ordinary communication, her belief that states of mind alone can become true points of contact among human beings. Her characters in *The Waves* are hermetically sealed off from one another, except for their particular *images* or *motifs* through which they are joined. Although each figure is both a subject and an object of consciousness—and although they are all included in the poet's vision— their relationships exist only within a design, composed of their thematic "colors" or shapes. They are like Leibnitz's monads, whose pattern is regulated by a kind of "preestablished harmony" —the poet's point of view. The arrangement of these "atoms" as the landscape of life viewed by an omniscient poet lends them their unified stature as a composite figure of man. It is also typical of a novel whose first working title had been *The Moths*.

———— 6

The Waves is not a prose poem, nor is it a surrealistic novel. Rather, it fulfills our expectations for the novel as a picture of lives, things, and relationships, but within a detached vision and a design rendered as formal poetry. This formality—and concomittant *stasis*—leads to a suppression of the usual land-marks of the novel, such as evident characterization or overt action. But within its dense and seemingly immobile structure, a narrative movement and a fictional world are retained, acting through the set monologues spoken by the cast of figures. The images in *The Waves* are neither narrative symbols nor decorations of feelings; rather, they form part of an abstract design which creates the novel as a poem. This pattern is fashioned by the concealed author, whose "higher" vision is most appropriately embodied in the image of the sun radiating from the prose poems to the novel itself. In this way, the poet's "moment" embodies all the complex elements of the book as a vision combining awareness and fact into a universal image of man's relations with life.

AWARENESS AND FORM

Virginia Woolf's life and work reflect her development toward a successful rendition of consciousness in forms of poetry. She sought to translate facts and scenes into song, to reflect individual time and inner lives within a framework of public time and public life, and ultimately to recreate the world as an image which would be immediately accessible to the apprehending mind. These, in any event, were her intentions: to portray through her themes and images the modes of thought and action which she encountered in her world.

The Waves is the only novel in which Mrs. Woolf found a complete expression of her aims. Restless as any writer must be who searches for perfection, she turned to a relatively more conventional form in *The Years* (1937), in which time is both more loosely rendered and more externally perceived. Only in *Between the Acts,* posthumously published in 1941, might a reconciliation have been found had she lived to complete it. *The Waves* was bound to remain unique and isolated. Although Leonard Woolf's judgment that it was her greatest work is undoubtedly justified, the obstacles to sustained reading are immense. The method of inferring action from prose poems and monologues makes reading a difficult, though a rewarding, task. But the notion of presenting time and life as a symbolic image impressed itself on Virginia Woolf with obsessive urgency. In *Between the Acts,* the problems of *The Waves* approach their solution. The moment of illumination in life is juxtaposed with an archetypal image of time; the social world is transfixed by a mythical world through the intervention of art. Both levels are brought together by the performance of a play which acts simultaneously as the content of the novel and as a symbolic motif.

Nevertheless, a study of the lyrical novel finds its climax in *The Waves.* In this work Mrs. Woolf expressed most fully her dual vision as a novelist and a poet. At the same time it also defines her place as a writer; it distinguishes her from her contemporaries and predecessors. The prevailing view in romantic and symbolist traditions usually presupposed that experience is primarily a mental quality and that the mind reflects a "reality" which is obscured by the physical world. In many important ways, Virginia Woolf shared this attitude. But it is one of her paradoxes that, despite all her indebtedness to this tradition and despite her concern with the conditions of consciousness, her poetic imagery was focused on the *process* of awareness, the analysis of its inherent relations involving both self and world.

This attitude toward mind and life, elusive and subject to many fluctuations, has resulted in Virginia Woolf's growing refinement of poetic forms and her particular interpretations of time and experience. For her, time remained a symbol of the "moment," including both the external framework of consecutive time and the individual's internal journeys into past, present, and future. In her novels, inner time is always as deeply involved with the external world as is external or physical time. Both are parts of the narrative. They are joined in a unified experience in those isolated moments, sustained in art, in which their relations are most fully revealed.

This concept of time—obviously related, despite subtle differences, to Bergson's formulations and Proust's practice in the

novel—underlies Virginia Woolf's use of the internal monologue and the stream of consciousness. Both, as we have seen,
can be narrative forms, defining each self through the exploration of inner worlds and their interrelation with outer events.
They emphasize a direction in her work toward variations of the
novel of manners in which the self is continuously measured
against the worlds of others, their conventions and things. But
neither the interior monologue nor the novel of manners is in
itself symptomatic of her poetry. Beginning in *Jacob's Room* and
culminating in *The Waves,* Virginia Woolf created poetry
through a progressive depersonalization, a *formal* rendering of
consciousness. Paradoxically, the more fully she perfected that
conventional device of fiction, the omniscient point of view, the
more closely she approached a perfection of poetic form that finds
its apex in *The Waves.* The poet, distilling himself from his
world, separating his work from the source of his imagination,
becomes the novelist who creates his figures from behind the
scenes and manipulates their feelings and thoughts.

One of Virginia Woolf's most important aims had been to
revive the novelist's craft. As a novelist she continued to be concerned with lives and relationships; she focused on people and
things, on people in contact with one another, on people's final
connection with the human condition, the inexorable impact on
life by time and death. As a poet, however, she also wished to
convey this vision with an impersonal formality, sustaining the
"moment" in forms which act with the incisiveness and simultaneity of lyrical poetry.

THE LYRICAL NOVEL
Retrospect and Prognosis

THE TYPES of lyrical fiction we have examined share a similar approach to the novel's traditional confrontation between self and world. The "I" of the lyric becomes the protagonist, who refashions the world through his perceptions and renders it as a form of the imagination. The poetic imagination of the lyrical novelist, however, functions differently from that of his conventional *confrère*. The world he creates from the materials given to him in experience becomes a "picture"—a disposition of images and motifs—of relations which in the ordinary novel are produced by social circumstance, cause and effect, the schemes fashioned by chronology. At the same time, lyricism in the novel assumes a significance which it does not possess in verse. Whether he addresses an audience, a beloved, or himself, the lyric poet, too, speaks on the occasion of a situation or an object: Laura's hair, a Grecian Urn, a Golden Bird. But in the novel, as, surely, in epic poetry, the extended narrative introduces a further dimension. The lyrical process expands because the lyrical "I" is also an experiencing protagonist. The poet's stance is turned into an epistemological act.

The exploitation of awareness as such is, of course, no prerogative of lyrical fiction. Self-conscious narrators, who modify or deform the worlds they observe, have populated novels from Richardson and Sterne to Conrad and Henry James. Some of their novels appear to be lyrical; others do not. The selective mind of the narrator or hero may deform its world to achieve a greater penetration of society or a more pervasive analysis of character, or, like Moréas' clown, it may draw a mask that bears the features of a suffering humanity. We observed in the lyrical novel how the protagonists rearranged their perceptions, how they dissolved outward forms or reproduced them in various arrangements that created the effect of poems. These transmutations of perceptions into images of "artifice" can be pictorial; as in many romantic novels, the protagonists' knowledge may be caught in sequences of pictures or encounters "mirroring" an ideal. But they can also reproduce the unconscious impulse or a deliberately shaped interior monologue, as in many novels since the eighteen-eighties. They can depict figures and objects within the texture of prose poetry, or they can constitute intellectually contrived metaphors. In such novels communication is sometimes difficult, especially when the forms are too private or too strained in their meanings—Djuna Barnes' *Nightwood* might be an example. But occasionally the shifts in perspective induced by the lyrical mode can make communication easier. The metaphor on which the narrative is constructed may be readily understood by the audience and hence the peculiar slant given to observed reality may seem welcome and familiar as, for instance, in poetic folk tales or in novels like Hesse's *Demian*.

The contribution of lyrical fiction has been this peculiar way of looking at perception. Narrative by definition deals with man and world; it has done so since Odysseus' epic encounters. Leaving aside the drama, which must cope with this problem in a different way (involved as it is with visual effects, staging, incidents, audience response, etc.), the engagements of a knowing self in the world are the novel's mark of distinction. But the novelist has many different ways at his disposal to express this relationship. He can ask how a hero relates to the historical process, to environment and ideas; he can inquire into the reciprocal relations of man and society, man and man. But novels can also ask these questions differently: how does the mind know its world? what is the functional relationship between the inner and the outer? what is the relationship of awareness or knowledge to human conduct and choice? This is how Stendhal, Flaubert, and, above all, Henry James, addressed themselves to their craft. And this is also the dominant mood in the lyrical novel.

Lyrical fiction, then, is a special instance of the novel of awareness. Yet the lyrical novel has also remained a distinct genre. In Germany, as we have had occasion to notice, it has remained to this day a potent survivor of romanticism; in France, it produced that fruitful fusion of the psychological investigation of consciousness with the aesthetic purposes of *poésie pure,* which has had a crucial effect on the novel of the mind. If it is more useful to describe the engagement of lyrical fiction in epistemological rather than in psychological terms, its distinctive quality lies nonetheless elsewhere. It must be found, not in the modes of apprehension, but in the way images are formed. The characteristic differentiating lyrical from nonlyrical fiction is portraiture, the halting of the flow of time within constellations of images or figures. In this fashion, the lyrical novel has continued to project a unique quality and has been a most influential genre, at least up to the present.

—2

The lyrical novel, then, is closely related to the evolution of the narrative genre as a whole. In its range from narrative to poetry, it has utilized compounds of both its elements, although, as they endure the stresses and strains between types of narration and designs of imagery, lyrical novels preserve a poetic approach. But the questions remain why so early in the evolution of a genre this type of aboriginal "anti-novel" should have developed and why its peculiar way of illuminating human awareness should have shown such persistence.

In the eighteenth century, the "poetic" manner of *Werther* and *A Sentimental Journey* had been prompted by a desire to penetrate to the substance of emotion underlying the behavior of characters. The form most suitable for achieving this purpose seemed to be the sentimental novel, which had been invigorated by the work of Richardson. In *Tristram Shandy,* the emphasis on sensibility was combined with a bizarre displacement of reality, a disruption of logical continuity, a creation of unexpected effects. It is easy to see why this work should have transcended its immediate context and should have become significant for the poetic inspirations of lyrical novelists. The romance and the Gothic tale, too, introduced a realm of fantasy which came to nourish the romantic strand of the lyrical novel. But the romance, as it was understood in the eighteenth century, was ill suited for the purpose of catching the essence of feeling. Rather, in novels such as Beckford's *Vathek* or Walpole's *Castle of Otranto,* it caught a weird rearrangement of the world. It took a nineteenth-century sensibility to see such shifts in the normal expectations of the real as forms of the poetic imagination, to experience man's pilgrimage through the world as Coleridge viewed his Mariner's symbolic quest.

The rationale for turning toward lyrical fiction was generally different among German romantic writers from that of their predecessors in England and elsewhere. Although these novelists were still concerned with rendering feelings, their main interest was the role of the hero as the poet's ideal image. In novels like *Hyperion* and *Heinrich von Ofterdingen,* the hero actually functions as the poet's "I." Many of these writers were indeed also poets, but they often believed that the novel was a superior form, a *Gesamtkunstwerk,* in which they most completely fulfilled their poetic function. The impetus toward the form came from a feeling of dissatisfaction with the supposed realism of the classical novels of the eighteenth century. The medieval romance and *Don Quixote,* or Sterne's novels of sensibility, appealed to them as more meaningful. Of course, not all German romantic fiction was lyrical, but the ideal of the novel coincided with that of lyrical prose narrative. The poet's *persona* was to approach the transcendental seer; time-bound reality was accordingly deformed into poetic imagery.

The French symbolists came to the same conclusions from a similar sense of dissatisfaction. But the naïve reaction against the "mercantilistic spirit" of most eighteenth-century English fiction, as it had been expressed by the German romantics, was no longer possible following a century that had seen the development of the novel from Balzac and Flaubert to the Goncourts and Zola. Here the break became most decisive for world literature, for it is mostly through symbolist efforts in the novel— Villiers de l'Isle Adam, Rémy de Gourmont, Édouard Dujardin, Huysmans, and especially Maeterlinck—that the impulse of romantic aestheticism was spread throughout the literary world. Schopenhauer's aesthetics and philosophy, the practice of Novalis and E. T. A. Hoffmann, had helped mold a new "romantic" novel which now appeared in a rather different guise. If the German romantics had thought of the novel as a comprehensive genre, a "super-poetry," the French symbolists believed that poetry was the more satisfactory form and sought to adapt the methods of poetry to prose narrative. The romantic emphasis on the mind (as a way of knowing and allegorizing reality) was now more closely connected with consciousness, and the rendering of the unconscious became an important means of portrayal. Other methods, as we have seen, are concerned with the more violent distortions of life to suit the poetic emotion, the rendering, however bizarre, of a situation, a theme, a perception or inner life as a concrete image from which the self is ultimately withdrawn.

Both the German romantic and the French symbolist conceptions of the lyrical novel, then, had been conditioned by dissatisfactions with conventions that seemed inadequate: the realism of the eighteenth century and nineteenth-century naturalism. Similarly, in the twentieth century the lyrical novel emerged as a reaction against a prevailing mood. Apparent in both poetry and prose, this reaction was produced by the writer's awareness of his role as an heir of the romantic exile. Modern writing has perpetuated the nineteenth-century ambivalence between hero and world and its emphasis on the self's isolation. At the same time, the novel has expanded its scope, especially in view of the increasingly restricted audience of poetry, and has approached, in its comprehensiveness of content and its variety of techniques, an almost romantic breadth. Poetic sensibilities, sharpened by methods inherited from romantic and symbolist writers, could legitimately choose the novel as a form in which man's awareness is mirrored as poetry.

Although lyrical writing is a rather specialized genre, it bears deep implications for modern writing as a whole. But if, beneath its enormous variety of individual forms, we notice a certain uniformity of purpose, the peculiarities of literary as well as historical traditions in each country produced considerable variations in the critical acceptance of the genre. In some national literatures a lyrical form appears to be more welcome than in others; a fashion which is conventional in one country may be *outré* in another. We have seen that there has been a secure place for romantic lyrical fiction in German literature. The reasons for the relative prominence of lyrical novels in Germany and in German-speaking countries are complex, but are partly discerned in the national history of the novel. For if we exempt the rather halting beginnings of the eighteenth century, German prose narrative owes its chief impetus to romanticism and to the model of Goethe's *Wilhelm Meister,* which, though not itself lyrical, is a rather "un-novelistic" kind of novel that easily lent itself to allegorical distortions.

Lyrical fiction is not pervasive in the French novel, but, from Chateaubriand and Nerval to the twentieth century, it has always been a viable alternative. We may recall that the prose poem had developed since the early nineteenth century into an embryonic lyrical novel which stressed at first, not the hallucinations or vagaries of the unconscious, but the precise dispositions of images related to the poet or to his *persona*. Indeed, whatever its hesitant public may have thought of this hybrid form, the prose poem is a uniquely French contribution. But even in full-length fiction, Rivière's impassioned, if one-sided, debate with symbolism in his "Roman d'aventure" attests to the importance of the lyrical genre for French writers. Aestheticism in the novel—its original connection with "pure poetry"—has reinforced the exploration of awareness which has so often characterized French fiction. Nor is the hospitality to lyricism confined to the early interest in consciousness, an interest which has been much commented upon in discussions of Dujardin, Valéry Larbaud, and, of course, Proust. From Gide to Maurice Blanchot's *L'Arrêt de mort* we encounter various efforts to recast imaginatively a world of perception into poetic forms. For all these tendencies, however, French lyrical fiction has still been a far less oppressive heritage than a corresponding tradition has been for German writers.

Perhaps because of the accident of Bloomsbury, surely because of the stature of Virginia Woolf and the importance of Joyce, there has been a recent flowering of lyrical fiction in England, despite a notorious inhospitality to the genre in the English literary tradition. None of the traditional romantic forms of the novel (early or late) had been taken seriously as valid lyrical modes. For reasons connected with the unique role played by the English novel as middle class entertainment, an aestheticist or poetic approach to a form held to be reserved for a portrait of society was frowned upon by influential arbiters of literary taste. If not poetry, at least the novel seemed inviolably English, whose norms had been set by Fielding, Thackeray, and Trollope. To be sure, even George Eliot, certainly Meredith, Hardy, and Conrad, had in some ways strayed from the narrow path of this tradition, but none so much as to question its basic outlines. Despite poetic rebels like Emily Brontë or D. H. Lawrence, there remained a formidable barrier to lyricism in fiction. New vistas were opened only when experimentations with language were identified with a new psychology of the novel.

The stream of consciousness, nourished partly by the backwash of symbolism of the early nineteen-hundreds and partly by the rise of psychoanalysis as an exciting new discipline, offered possibilities for poetic fiction which were whole-heartedly exploited by several experimental writers in English. But it seems pertinent to observe that this way of looking at reality (unlike, for example, that of the romantic picaresque or the aestheticist prose poem) was still rooted in a native tradition: the associationist doctrines of the seventeenth- and eighteenth-

century British empiricists which had found their most sublime
literary echo in Laurence Sterne. For Dorothy Richardson, the
stream of consciousness was not yet a lyrical mode; for Joyce it
had become more than lyricism. Perhaps Virginia Woolf was one
of the few typical poetic novelists in England to find a wide audience, because, far-fetched as her poetry was for the uninitiated
reader, she was so deeply steeped in her national tradition, in the
literary history of her country, and especially in the basic purpose
of the novel that she combined lyricism with a type of narrative
that still revealed the qualities of traditional English fiction. It
is one of her greatest triumphs and paradoxes that in *The Waves*
she achieved her purest lyricism precisely as she accomplished
her most objective novel of manners.

This paradox has remained a legacy of the lyrical novel in England which has communicated itself to our day. Beyond Virginia
Woolf, Joyce's *Finnegan's Wake* had reached perhaps the apex
of the "novel as poem"—without a commitment to traditional
forms of narrative—but, like most of Joyce's seminal work, its
quality as a lyrical novel in our sense is open to question. Perhaps the most uniquely lyrical novel to come from this ferment
of the nineteen-twenties and thirties has been Djuna Barnes'
Nightwood. Obviously owing a great deal to Joyce, this novel
tries to maintain the form and even the plot of narrative but to
convert them into poetic imagery. Extravagantly praised by
T. S. Eliot as a novel which appeals to the reader as a poem, this
book seems to avoid both the pitfall of pure poetry and that of
plain psychologizing. The world is transformed into the soliloquists' images (including those of the author) from which
character and action are made to emerge. Yet Djuna Barnes was
never fully accepted in spite of her esoteric emulators. To be
successful in English, a lyrical novel must be capable of maintaining itself as a "novel of fact." With the demise of Bloomsbury, lyrical fiction has entered upon a new phase.

⟶ 3

At present we confront a paradox in the fortunes of the lyrical novel. At a time when narrative has evolved toward a greater penetration of the self, the lyrical novel, which has fostered this condition, has undergone a decline. This is not to say that the lyrical novel is finished. It is merely to suggest that following its great importance in the first half of this century as a response to the naturalistic novel, a hiatus in its influence has occurred. Nevertheless, its methods have had a lasting effect. Whatever its difficulties, the lyrical novel developed a new orientation toward experience: internal without being necessarily subjective; reflective without being essayistic; pictorial or musical without abandoning the narrative framework of the novel. All these qualities have entered current fiction, but they have nourished a different, if related strand in prose narrative.

The new concern with awareness implies a different sort of involvement from that of the lyrical novelists we have so far considered. Awareness is neither the idealistic portrait of the world within the mind nor the act of consciousness as such. "I" and "other" are opposed; by measuring itself against that which is "other," the self obtains its identity. A famous novel of awareness and action—Malraux's *La Condition humaine*—dramatizes this relationship. It is illuminated by the opening scene in which Ch'en faces the sleeping body of his intended victim. Self confronts "other"; in a foreknowledge of the murder, the assassin is intensely aware of the noises in the street; at the same time he already senses the yielding flesh against the point of his dagger. There is nothing lyrical in this confrontation. The knife has replaced the eye, the contact of blade and flesh the pictorial *blason* embodied by a mind. Yet the situation defines the man, the victim, the place, and the human condition as surely as would have a poetic image. Although in its date of composition, *La Condition humaine* is closer to *Les Faux-Monnayeurs* and *The Waves* than to contemporary fiction, it suggests a technique which so-called "existentialist" novels—

like Sartre's *La Nausée*—have refined. Rather than blending self and world into imagery, it renders them in a narrative contest.

Albert Camus was similarly involved with the self and its appropriate stance toward an independent world; his techniques, more than Malraux's or Sartre's, approach those of the lyrical novel. His evocative fiction is connected with imagistic portraits of life. This is especially true of *L'Étranger,* in which, as in a lyric, sensuous imagery depicts a moral point. Yet even here the hero's awareness continuously dissociates, separates itself from its objects. The alienation of the theme is also revealed in the form. It would stretch the point to suggest that *La Peste* and *La Chute* are lyrical novels. But the fact remains that, especially in his earlier work, Camus' sensibility draws men and objects into patterns of imagery, whereas Sartre, even in his experimental *Le Sursis,* relies largely on the design of the realistic novel.

More recently, the novel of awareness has gone an even more diversified way. Nathalie Sarraute (like Blanchot) seems close to a lyrical genre, but the work of a writer such as Alain Robbe-Grillet typifies a new spirit, which, however, would have been unthinkable without the "lyrical" generation before him. In *Le Voyeur,* he uses precisely the epistemological situation favored by the lyrical novelist, but, instead of deforming the image aesthetically, he turns the method in on itself. Outward appearances are not illuminated by apprehension; rather, a distinct world of objects gradually reveals a character, a situation, an act. This type of novel has been made possible by the fiction of "abstract lyricism" Gide had perfected, which is based on a sensitive denuding of external life.

In England, as we noted earlier, lyricism has again reverted to a minor role, yet Virginia Woolf had a lasting effect even on those who most strongly rejected her. For she achieved what Jane Austen could not: an exploration of the quality of experience which required a concept of the imagination that had been nurtured by the nineteenth century. Her technical achievement left its mark on the new partially "symbolic," partially "episte-mological" novel—that of Iris Murdoch, for example, and of William Golding. Golding especially reflects an awareness of a lyrical mode which occasionally he even approached. His *Pincher Martin* dramatizes in a gigantic concluding image the struggle between the "inner" and the "outer" which had concerned Virginia Woolf. In this momentary vision of a dying sailor, the "mouth" and the "center"—consciousness and its awareness—are engaged in a terrifying dialogue which culminates in the vision of God as a Mariner in his Sea Boots. Naturally, Golding does not epitomize English fiction which is also prominently represented by Joyce Cary and C. P. Snow (who have hewn a path back to the tradition of Trollope and Thackeray); nor is his work comparable to that of Graham Greene, who has called upon different conventions altogether. Recently, we have even witnessed in the fiction of Lawrence Durrell a return to the lyrical novel in larger dimensions. The success of Durrell's *Alexandria Quartet* (more even than his accomplishment as a writer) has shown that lyricism in the novel is by no means dead. But Golding has revealed most clearly what lyrical fiction can, at its best, contribute to a contemporary writer even as he rejects its conventions and its indrawn concern with sensibility.

Even in German-speaking countries a turn away from the lyricism of the romantic novel has materialized. Not that Germany has lacked naturalistic novels, didactic novels, novels of political tracts, and realistic novels of education, but its fiction has been somehow infected by the virus of romanticism which few novels have escaped. Such different writers of the first half of the century as Heinrich Mann, Stefan Zweig, Alfred Döblin, Klabund, Rudolf Binding, and even Franz Kafka and Robert Musil, have been beset in some fashion by a romantic form such as the legend, the episodic quest, or the imagistic portrait of the self. Thomas Mann seemed sometimes oppressed by this heritage as by a burden, although often (as, for example in

Doktor Faustus, which occasionally even borders on lyrical fiction) it forced him to create with great intensity and depth. Kafka's work, too, employs many conventions of romantic lineage, but his philosophical rationale moved him in an opposite direction. The Kafkaesque nightmare is based on an interaction of self and world similar to Dostoyevsky's. He emphasized relations between man and the furnishings of a distorted physical world. Yet there remains an intimate kinship between Kafka's "engagement" of mind and "other" and a lyrical mode based on their union in imagery. Significantly, Kafka admired the Swiss writer Robert Walser, who was a lyricist *par excellence,* delicate in the imagery and poetic movements of his narratives, yet who also produced bizarre reconstructions of every day reality with which Kafka felt an immediate kinship.

The situation confronting the German novelist is somewhat different from that faced by his fellow writers in England or France. Since lyricism has always been an accepted tradition in the German novel, it has been part of the "establishment." The writer searching for new forms of expression is not likely to find it exciting or fresh; he is more disposed than others, perhaps, to expunge traces of its influence rather than to absorb them. This attitude, directed particularly at the "transcendental" lyricism of the German novel, was summarily expressed by a Swiss writer of the new generation, Friedrich Duerrenmatt, when he began in his introduction to *Die Panne:*

Are real stories still possible, stories for writers? If the writer does not want to tell about himself, romanticize, poeticize, universalize his ego; if he feels no inclination to talk about his hopes and failures, no matter how truthfully, or of the ways he sleeps with women . . . ; if he does not want this, but prefers to decently keep personal matters to himself, to work the material before him like a sculptor his stone, shaping and developing it, and hoping thereby to gain something of the classicist's faculty of not falling too readily into despair, . . .—if this is his endeavor, then writing becomes a far more difficult and lonely as well as a more senseless occupation.[1]

In its many different forms, from the poetic image of the ego to the enactment of consciousness, the lyrical novel emerges as a genre to be overcome as well as to be used. It has been an immensely fertile corrective for the conventional novel, and yet, compared to more concrete explorations of life such as *Le Rouge et le noir* or *The Brothers Karamazov*, it has always suffered from a certain anemia. But no detailed examinations of conscience, no discussions of motives, sensibilities, or realistic portraits of manners can make up for the intensely inward projection of experience in which the lyrical novel excels. Few other forms allow the author, or his *persona*, to penetrate so directly into the very act of knowledge and to represent it in immediately accessible portraiture. The limitations of this approach are obvious enough: an underemphasis on character and an overemphasis on image, dream-like encounter, or allegory. The excitement created by the plot is largely absent and the excitement instilled by the expectations of the lyrical process does not usually make up for it. Nevertheless, at its best the lyrical novel can be a voyage of discovery onto a strange subterranean sea in which the lyrical mood—abbreviated, even truncated in verse—is acted out in worlds of fiction populated by an imagery of figures, emblazoned by an imagery of scenes.

[1] Friedrich Duerrenmatt, *Traps,* tr. Richard and Clara Winston (New York, Knopf, 1960), pp. 3–4. Original edition, *Die Panne* in *Die Arche* (Zürich: Peter Schifferli, 1956).

INDEX